Robert Lewis
DABNEY
A Southern Presbyterian Life

AMERICAN REFORMED BIOGRAPHIES
A Series

D. G. HART AND SEAN MICHAEL LUCAS
Series Editors

Robert Lewis
DABNEY

A Southern Presbyterian Life

SEAN MICHAEL LUCAS

P U B L I S H I N G
P.O. BOX 817 • PHILLIPSBURG • NEW JERSEY 08865-0817

Scripture quotations are from The Holy Bible, English Standard Version, copyright © 2001 by Crossway Bibles, a division of Good News Publishers. Used by permission. All rights reserved.

Page design and typesetting by Lakeside Design Plus

Printed in the United States of America

Library of Congress Cataloging-in-Publication Data

Lucas, Sean Michael, 1970–
    Robert Lewis Dabney : a Southern Presbyterian life / Sean Michael Lucas.
       p. cm. — (American Reformed biographies ; 1)
    Includes bibliographical references and index.
    ISBN 0-87552-663-2 (cloth)
    1. Dabney, Robert Lewis, 1820–1898. 2. Presbyterian Church—United States—Clergy—Biography. 1. Title. II. Series.

BX9225.D2L83 2005
230'.51'092—dc22
[B]
                                           2004063194

For my parents,
Steve and Susan Lucas

"The glory of children is their fathers."
—Proverbs 17:6

"Her children rise up and call her blessed."
—Proverbs 31:28

Contents

Acknowledgments

A large portion of this biography had its first life as a dissertation on Dabney's public theology. Credit for whatever merit that first foray into Dabney's thought and life possessed belonged, at least in part, to D. G. Hart, who was my mentor at Westminster Seminary (Philadelphia) and continues as my friend and co-editor in this series, and to Clair Davis and Carl Trueman, who served as my faculty readers at Westminster. Thanks also go to Donald Mathews and Eugene Genovese, who wrote some stimulating (and widely divergent) notes on that first work and encouraged me to rework the material. I am very grateful to Richard Bailey, Tim Harrelson, Sara Lucas, Jack Maddex, Wayne Sparkman, and Nick Willborn, who read the entire manuscript and offered numerous insightful comments and corrections. I received feedback regarding some of this material at venues as disparate as church meetings, seminary lectures, and academic conferences. But I especially thank Beth Barton Schweiger, Mitchell Snay, Robert Calhoon, D. G. Hart, and Jim Farmer for serving as commentators on ideas found mainly in chapter 6, and Bert Wyatt-Brown and Christine Hyerman for reflections on parts of chapter 4.

Work of this kind must enjoy institutional support. I received a great deal from the Southern Baptist Theological Seminary, where I worked as the archives and special collections librarian while this manuscript took shape. In particular, I thank Bruce Keisling, associate vice president for academic resources and seminary librarian, for his strong encouragement of my work, and Daniel Akin, former senior vice president of academic administration, for supporting two conference presentations of this material through the Dean's Council. Working as a librarian at Southern offered me the added benefits of using the excellent collections housed in the Boyce Centennial Library and having the valuable assistance of the interlibrary loan department. I am grateful also for the support and friendship that I have received at Covenant Seminary, where I have served since June 2004.

A different kind of institutional support is found in the various archives where Dabney materials are housed. I am pleased to acknowledge the Presbyterian Historical Society, Montreat, North Carolina, particularly Bill Bynum; the William Morton Library at Union Theological Seminary, Richmond, Virginia, particularly Paula Skreslet; and the Alderman Library at the University of Virginia. I also acknowledge the permission that I have received from these institutions to quote from collections in their care. I am grateful to David Coffin for allowing me to use his index of the Dabney Papers at Union Seminary. That this work is appearing in this series is due to the vision of Al Fisher at P&R Publishing. His support of the biography series, reviving an idea first proposed in 1997, was unexpected and indispensable. My friend from seminary days, Steve Nichols, has followed this work throughout its stages with constant encouragement. Finally, though not least, while I was in Louisville, Kentucky, my brothers and sisters at Community Presbyterian Church (PCA) provided support and opportunity to minister. David Dively, our pastor, was both encourager and friend.

Portions of chapter 6 appeared in a different form in " 'Old Times There Are Not Forgotten': Robert Lewis Dabney's Public Theology for a Reconstructed South," *Journal of Presbyterian History* 81 (2003): 149–63. Part of chapter 8 is revised from "Southern-Fried Kuyper? Robert Lewis Dabney, Abraham Kuyper, and the Limitations of Public Theology," *Westminster Theological Journal* 66 (2004): 179–201. I acknowledge the kindness of the editors for publishing my work and for extending me permission to reuse it here.

Though my family is acknowledged last, their place in my heart is first. My wife, Sara, demonstrates her love in innumerable ways, but especially in her faith in me. Her love, expressed in all her daily kindness, as well as in her perseverance in reading Dabney, makes all of this worthwhile. Our children—Samuel, Elizabeth, Andrew, and Benjamin—have made forgetting about this project once I leave work and come home very easy and enjoyable. While we lived in Kentucky, my parents-in-law, Ron and Phyllis Young, provided free babysitting, a refuge when the cupboards got a little empty, and free rounds of golf; they also gave us their love and support throughout. This book is dedicated to my parents, Steve and Susan Lucas. There are not many great men and women in this world who stand on principle in the face of adversity and yet who recognize that they are sinners saved by grace, who believe in themselves and others while at the same time believing overwhelmingly in God, who hold others to a high standard but hold themselves to a much higher standard. Most who appear to be great all too often disappoint in the end. Yet I can honestly say that, by God's grace, my father is a great man and my mother is a great woman. And that is why the dedication is true and appropriate.

We shall be wise, therefore,
if we harken to the striking instruction of these instances,
and make it our method to submit with modesty
to the sober teachings of the past in all our legislation for the future.
—Robert Lewis Dabney

Introduction

A few months before Robert Lewis Dabney died, he made a final grand tour of the eastern seaboard from his exilic location in Victoria, Texas. One of his stops was the General Assembly of his beloved Presbyterian Church in the United States, meeting in Charlotte, North Carolina. There to represent the Synod of Texas as well as to present a paper for the 250th anniversary of the Westminster Confession of Faith, Dabney was received with great feeling and acclaim. One observer held that Dabney was "the Moses who had been the leader in 'times that tried men's souls.' " Throughout the Assembly, "his every utterance was heard with profoundest interest, and his counsels received with the utmost deference and respect. He took an active part in the deliberations of that great Assembly, and served with his accustomed diligence as chairman of one of the leading committees." At the end of one session, Dabney, who had been blind since 1890, was led to the moderator's table to close in prayer. His searching prayer "seemed almost gifted with the seer's sagacity." After serving as both a Southern Presbyterian Elijah and Moses one final time, Dabney retired to Asheville, North Carolina, to spend the summer away from the Texas heat.[1]

Undoubtedly those who knew Robert Lewis Dabney, both as friends and as enemies, felt him to be larger than life, closer to a biblical prophet than a theological professor. Even as a young man, Dabney's gaze bored through others; his scowl suggested a thunderstorm; and his speech could be furious. As an older man, with the chin beard draping down like a vestment, he was most often viewed by observers as a prophet or an apostle. One student, upon hearing falsely of Dabney's death, claimed to be in the position of Elisha, who had lost his Elijah in Dabney's demise. Another former student claimed that "his students in his old age at Austin, were wont to speak of him as St. John." A ministerial colleague also viewed Dabney like the apostle John, "who denounced heresy and falsehood like a very Boanerges, as he was." Others accounted him to be like one of the Reformers. "Had he occupied Calvin's position he might have done Calvin's work," S. Taylor Martin claimed. "Had he been substituted for John Knox he could have performed the part of Knox." Like a mythic figure from a long-ago time, Dabney seemed to stand for principle and truth in an age gone mad.[2]

Not only was he akin to a character from Bible times or church history, his contemporaries held Dabney to be among the most important men of their generation. Moses D. Hoge, Dabney's lifelong friend, placed Dabney in a Southern Presbyterian triumvirate: "No church on this continent has been more favored of heaven in having at its very organization three such men as Thornwell, Palmer, and Dabney—each fitted by splendid genius, profound scholarship and consecration to the noblest ends, to give direction to its future life and to enrich it for all time by their published contributions to theological science." Another admirer placed Dabney in the pantheon of Southern heroes: "No bad cause ever had men like Lee and Jackson to fight its battles, nor intellects like Calhoun, Thornwell, Hammond, Bledsoe, Dabney, and Laws to settle its problems." His biographer, Thomas Cary Johnson, stated quite firmly, "Dr. Dabney was a great man. We cannot tell just how great yet. One cannot see how great Mt. Blanc is while standing at its foot. One hundred years from now men will be able to see him better."[3]

After Dabney died in 1898, however, his reputation suffered precipitous decline. While James Henley Thornwell's name bore great cultural weight in the Southern Presbyterian church, Dabney appeared to embarrass New South Presbyterians. Although his systematic theology textbook was used at Union Theological Seminary in Virginia until 1940, and the seminary had endowed the Robert Lewis Dabney chair of systematic theology, the New South Presbyterians who used the seminary as a base for their progressive program did not know what to make of Dabney. For example, Union Seminary church historians Ernest Trice Thompson and Frank Bell Lewis were fascinated by Dabney's intellectual power and foresight, but they were repulsed by his rigid adherence to the Westminster Standards, his criticism of higher-critical scholarship, and his virulent racial prejudice. Further, Dabney's bitterness toward the North in general and Northern Presbyterians in particular made him less than useful for Southern progressives who sought organic union with the Northern church, and economic and social integration with Northern society.[4]

Most recent historians have not been friendly toward Dabney either. For example, historian Charles Reagan Wilson observed that Dabney was "a racist, a strident reactionary, and an embittered man," an essentially unattractive historical figure. Likewise, Donald Mathews excoriated Dabney as "a Presbyterian theologian who mistook his own punitive Calvinism as gospel, railed against the barbarian hordes of Northern abolitionists for despoiling his homeland, and screamed at his Presbyterian colleagues for daring to consider the training and ordination of African-American presbyters." In addition, Mathews faulted Dabney's formulation of the penal substitutionary theory of the atonement for providing the cultural justification for lynching. Even Dabney's contemporary friends often view him in a limiting way. Those who show an interest in him do so for his staunch Southern nationalism, social conservatism, or unapologetic Calvinistic theology; typical is the praise of one Dabney admirer: "How many of you have heard of Generals Lee and Jackson? Of course, all of you. Well this man [Dabney] ranks with those generals as one of the greatest Americans that ever lived." Others uphold Dabney for his prophetic insight and patriarchal sensibilities. One contemporary writer praised Dabney's writings for their "virility," claiming that "one must not forget that Dabney wrote in the last great period of American history in which men were proud to be men, and to call someone a 'patriarch' was to pay him a compliment." This same writer claimed that Dabney was "the quintessential prophet" who accurately pointed out the evil potentialities of the modern worldview.[5]

But Dabney was far more complex than either historians or admirers concede. More than a "Lost Cause" defender and a spokesman for "racial orthodoxy" and rigid Calvinism, Dabney was in many ways a representative man, one who embodied the passions and contradictions of nineteenth-century Southerners. In fact, his contemporaries understood these contradictions better than modern-day commentators. Johnson admitted that Dabney "was not a sinless man. His massive nature was qualified all through his long and vexed life with sin; but grace dominated." Others sought to distance Dabney from his caustic reputation, emphasizing his compassion toward students, his undying devotion toward his friends, and even the respect he demonstrated to his enemies. S. F. Tenney claimed that Dabney was "misunderstood because of the vehemence of many of his expressions." This misunderstanding was due to the fact that "readers could not see the kindly expression of his face which ever accompanied this vehemence of utterance." While admitting Dabney's notoriety as a "Christian Warrior," B. M. Palmer pointed to Dabney's "gentler traits" and "amiable virtues which endeared him to his pupils and to his friends of every degree." Thornton Sampson also distanced Dabney from his intransigent partisanship by accentuating the fact that Dabney "was a kind neighbor, a tender and most affectionate husband, an over-indulgent parent, and a most faithful friend." The chief evidence of Dabney's tenderness was his lifelong devotion to the memory of Sampson's father, Francis Sampson, who had been Dabney's teacher and later colleague at Union Seminary. "Nothing could have been more beautiful than this love of a strong man, for one whose gifts, whatever they were, excited no sentiment but admiration in him," Sampson testified.[6]

These reminiscences of Dabney's contemporaries complicate the conventional wisdom that he was merely an implacable warhorse of the Old South. Doubtless Dabney was a defender of the South, but he was particularly worried that the New South after the war was forsaking the classical republicanism of the American founders. Dabney was a public intellectual, respected throughout the country for his theological moderation and his political conservatism, but he was also a

be inconsequential. Similarly, Dabney affirmed the "five points of Calvinism" in a winsome fashion—for example, admitting that Christ's death had great benefit for all humankind even though its intent was to secure the salvation of the elect, and attempting to hold together boundless divine love with vindicatory divine wrath. The basis for Dabney's theological moderation was his close adherence to the Westminster Standards. Because the Westminster Confession did not employ "extra-scriptural distinctions," Dabney held that religious teachers should conserve the truths summarized in the confession rather than seek to innovate by adapting to contemporary intellectual trends.[8]

The "comprehensive ideal" for nineteenth-century theologians also meant that Dabney's intellectual reach extended to moral, mental, and natural philosophy. Dabney demonstrated a lifelong interest in "natural philosophy," as physical science was called in his day. He left Hampden-Sydney College to go to the University of Virginia so that he might master "the principles of science." He had felt that the natural science course at Hampden-Sydney was poorly done. The entire subject was covered in one year, three lectures a week, a scant amount of time when compared to how diligently the study of languages was pursued. In Dabney's view, however, "the natural sciences are worth all the others put together, and yet not a sixth of the whole time is devoted to them." Dabney apparently excelled at chemistry and physics, sustaining examinations on the subjects at the University of Virginia on short notice. He later claimed that he spent much of his adult life reading the leading scientific writings and pondering them. Toward the end of his life, Dabney had a paper read at the Victoria Institute in London, on the teleological argument as proved by the "final cause" of creation, demonstrating his continuing interest in scientific issues. His grasp of "natural philosophy" led him to assail Edward Hitchcock's attempt to reconcile science and religion, and produced a lengthy debate with Columbia Seminary professor and professional scientist James Woodrow.[9]

More important, perhaps, was Dabney's long-standing interest in moral and mental philosophy. In the eighteenth and nineteenth centuries, moral philosophy was the capstone of the college educational course, encompassing modern-day psychology, sociology, political science, and economics. Generally, the focus of moral philosophy was what could be called natural theology—those areas of thought revealed by God to all humankind through nature and conscience. Yet it was also considered a science—the offspring of Enlightenment rationalism that focused on the duties of humankind in their social relations. Moral philosophy in America was particularly associated with the Scottish schools of philosophy, hailing from Thomas Reid, Dugald Stewart, and Adam Smith. The Scottish moral philosophers held that truth was one, whether the truth was gained from the observation of physical phenomena or the investigation of human consciousness. The way to discover the truth was to apply the laws of logical "induction" as taught by Francis Bacon. Such Baconianism, when applied to human consciousness, taught certain intuitive or primary truths that served as the basis of all other thought and activity. Hence, moral philosophy was both philosophical—dealing with metaphysical moral issues—and scientific—using "scientific" methods of induction to discover truth. Dabney was intimately familiar with moral and mental philosophy as taught by the Scottish school, and it was part of the furniture for his theological understanding and development. His familiarity came through regular teaching of Scottish philosophy in moral philosophy courses. In 1857, Dabney taught moral philosophy at Hampden-Sydney College as part of his duties as interim president; and in 1883, he accepted the position of professor of moral and mental philosophy at the brand-new University of Texas at Austin. In addition, one of his final books was a compilation of his notes from his moral philosophy classes, revised thoroughly upon delivery of a condensed version of the course at Louisville Presbyterian Theological Seminary in 1894.

The importance of the Scottish version of moral philosophy was demonstrated by the way it informed every part of Dabney's work. In his lectures on systematic theology, Dabney included a lengthy section on the "sources of our thinking" that spelled out the basics of his Scottish philosophy. He also offered a defense of the Scottish philosophy in his *Sensualistic Philosophy of the Nineteenth Century*, in which he took positivist and radical empiricist thought to task for its materialism. The commonsense assumptions of this school played into his defenses of the inspiration of Scripture and the penal substitutionary theory of the atonement. In addition, Dabney penned a lengthy defense of induction and the laws of causation for the *Southern Presbyterian Review* and defended the teleological argument, based on the inductive method, in his 1881 Victoria Institute paper. He even worked Scottish philosophy into his biography of Stonewall Jackson, in which he claimed that Jackson believed that the "mind has its natural laws as well as matter, to be learned in the same way, by correct induction from our observations; and they are just as regular in their operation as those of the stars, the waters, or the vegetable world." Clearly, not only did Dabney imbibe the Scottish philosophy; it was the glue that held much of his thought together.[10]

Not only then as a Southerner, but also as a Presbyterian theologian, Dabney was representative of postbellum Southern conservatism. Committed to preserving modes of thought and action associated with the antebellum intellectual world, Dabney frequently appeared to be an "apostle of the Old South." But even in this appearance, Dabney confounds and complicates historical pigeonholes. For while he defended the old paths, he often admitted that the new generation would have to make its own intellectual choices. What Dabney desired above all else was that the past be remembered and given its due weight in contemporary discussions. "Prove all things; hold fast that which is good" not only was the biblical motto placed on Dabney's tombstone in the Union Seminary cemetery in Farmville, Virginia, but also was Dabney's policy for New South Presbyterians. What was necessary, Dabney claimed, was for the rising generation to "learn the history of the past truly." The organic connection of new institutions to those that had gone before was undeniable; hence, if Southerners properly learned the "principles of 1861," the immutable nature of "honor, justice, and right," and the abiding truths of the Westminster Standards, then the New South would "be safe from any base decadence." In short, in order for one to act rightly in the present day, attention must be paid to the concrete past, not to the unseen future.[11]

And that is what is most compelling about Dabney. While many of his positions and pronouncements may produce intense disagreement or even disgust, Dabney's historical significance as a voice for postbellum Southern religious and political conservatism stems from his understanding that, as John C. Calhoun also held, "the past is the parent of the present." As a representative figure, Dabney and his life and work can help illuminate not only the vagaries of the Southern Presbyterian mind, but also the importance of nineteenth-century theology and witness for contemporary issues and debates. After all, the distance between this present day and the past is not nearly as vast as moderns like to believe.[12]

1

Preparation

In a eulogy written after Robert Lewis Dabney died in 1898, James Henry Rice Jr. praised Dabney as a "lover of the South." Though "modern teaching would have us believe it; modern turncoats are ready to criticize and bow to a new order, raised to nobility by dollars got God knows where," Dabney knew that "the old South cannot die." This passionate love for the South, and particularly for his native Virginia, was perhaps the most important factor in his intellectual vision, superseded only by his intense devotion to God. Dabney's commitment to the South was molded and shaped by his upbringing and his education, by his influences and career decisions, by sheer geography and travel plans. Raised as the son of middling gentry in a central Virginia county that had rung with the words of Patrick Henry forty years before he was born, Dabney took great pride in his family's mainly honorable history and connections. Trained at Virginia field schools and later at a Virginia college, university, and seminary, Dabney came to believe in the superiority of Southern education for Southern people. During these years in Farmville and Charlottesville, Virginia, Dabney came to embrace the Old Republican tradition associated with the Virginian John Randolph of Roanoke and later with the South Carolinian John C. Calhoun. After receiving his seminary certificate, Dabney served as a missionary in Louisa County,

Virginia, before moving to his first pastorate in Tinkling Spring (near present-day Fishersville), Virginia. He moved from the pastorate to Union Seminary, where he served for thirty years, and to the University of Texas at Austin, where he served until 1894. When entreated by Charles Hodge to come to Princeton Seminary in 1860, Dabney firmly rejected the offer. In fact, unlike other prominent Southerners who spent time in the North, Dabney crossed the Mason-Dixon line only three times—each time to go to New York City, twice on Presbyterian business before the Civil War, the other in 1880 when he went to Europe. Otherwise, Dabney spent every day of his entire life within the bounds of the old Confederacy, if one included Kentucky and Missouri in that reckoning. And of course, Dabney fought for the Confederacy with his sword and his pen, both during and after the Civil War. Unlike others who turned their backs on the South or Southern principles, throughout his seventy-seven years on earth Dabney remained a "lover of the South."[1]

It is not surprising, then, that Dabney's devotion to the South shaped and colored his entire worldview. He wholeheartedly embraced the Southern ideal of gentility, the "Virginia gentleman," which prodded him toward sociability, learning, and piety as the chief marks of the upper class. Moreover, Dabney's identification with the South was exemplified by his acceptance and promotion of mastery and slavery. While Dabney held that his belief in hierarchy, patriarchy, and household relations was drawn from Scripture, his anti-egalitarianism was deeply influenced by his unbiblical antipathy toward African Americans. Dabney also saw himself as a man of honor, but he baptized the Southern ethic of honor with Christian meaning. The result was a merger of honor and grace: for Dabney, the truly honorable man was the one who embraced the Christian faith. True honor did not belong to the duelist or the warrior actuated by pagan fury; rather, it belonged to men such as Thomas "Stonewall" Jackson, who derived his courage from Jesus Christ, "the divine pattern and fountain of heroism." The merger of honor and grace was not unique with Dabney, but it was pronounced and undeniably Southern.[2]

By imbibing and later defending this Southern ethic, Dabney became a conservator of what has become known as the "Southern tradition." The Southern conservative tradition was a strong belief that civilization required a religiously grounded society that sanctified social distinctions (class, gender, and, especially for Dabney, race distinctions); exalted local agriculturally based societies; stood for a limited, representative, republican form of government; and cherished Southern ideals of civility, gentility, and honor. This vision of the Southern tradition stretched back to Randolph and Calhoun and forward through the Vanderbilt Agrarians to Richard M. Weaver and M. E. Bradford. By any comparative measure, Dabney belonged to this Southern tradition, staking out positions remarkably similar to those of later proponents. Coupled together with his Old School Presbyterianism, Dabney's Southern tradition forged a distinctively Southern Presbyterian worldview.[3]

These early years—from Dabney's birth on March 5, 1820, until he took his first pastorate at Tinkling Spring in 1847—provided the foundation for all that followed in his life. He would not forsake either his Southern partisanship or the religious convictions to which he came during these years. Many of his closest friendships, particularly with Moses D. Hoge and C. R. Vaughan, were made in this period. Indeed, Dabney would pine for those college times at Hampden-Sydney, writing to Hoge in 1841, "Of all the friends from whom I parted when I left Hampden-Sydney, how few are there now with whom I have any intercourse whereas I once thought that we were linked together by ties never to be broken." Still, Dabney was able to keep up with a few; Hoge and Vaughan continued as friends till the end of Dabney's life, though Hoge and Dabney would oppose each other in the 1870s over ecumenical relations with Northern Presbyterians. In order to understand how such close friends for nearly fifty years could divide over seemingly minor issues, it is vital to grasp Dabney's actions and character as revealed through these early years of preparation.[4]

Southern Gentleman

That Dabney viewed himself as a member of the old Virginia gentry was due largely to his ancestry. His great-uncle, Colonel Charles Dabney, was the epitome of a Virginia gentleman, setting the standard for all his nephews. The colonel, a Revolutionary War veteran who was promoted for bravery, was remembered as one who "was never known to seek advancement, and scrupulously shunned the broils, the intrigues, and the debasing scenes which disgraced our popular elections." As a man of honor, "he disdained to court public favor, either for the gratification of personal vanity or the promotion of his private interests." The colonel's "moral excellencies" were summarized in his generosity, frugality, and liberality. He saved not to hoard for himself, but so that "he might have wherewithal to give." In addition, Colonel Dabney was a pious man, who "embraced in the circle of brotherly love every denomination of sincere Christians." In short, the colonel was a gentleman who had the freedom to give to the lower classes as well as freedom to serve his peers, a man whose liberality and sociability merged with his piety.[5]

Likewise, Dabney's grandfather, Samuel Dabney, also exemplified the character of Virginia gentry, although in a different way. Married into the Meriwether family, which would produce the famous Meriwether Lewis, Samuel was viewed as "an honorable and upright man, but too fond of hunting and sports, and of the court-house company." He was also "a poor man of business." Samuel died and orphaned his thirteen children, but these children were shepherded by their mother, Jane Meriwether, and Samuel's brother, the colonel. Samuel and Jane's third son was Charles, Robert Lewis's father, who assisted the colonel in the management of his lands. Charles eventually took over his father's lands in Louisa County, Virginia, and, at a farm that he styled Walnut Grove, lived "the usual life of a Virginia planter of moderate means, superintending in person the usual operations of the farm, and when necessary putting his hand to manual labor." Charles Dabney served in the War of 1812, was chosen colonel of the county militia, and was elected to the state legislature, an unremunerated position of honor. He also served as a ruling elder in his local Presbyterian church and as a commissioner to the 1832 General Assembly. Family legend claimed that he was "one of the first, if not the first man, in his county in his day."[6]

Such was the stock from which Robert Lewis Dabney came. Not only was his great-uncle a man of great dignity, but also his grandfather and father were honorable men, pledged to ideals of gentility and honor. Dabney's later concern with pure bloodlines is understandable in that his heritage placed upon him the responsibility to be a gentleman, to live up to his ancestry. Moreover, Dabney's first biographer claimed that the society of Louisa County, where Dabney was born and grew up, was "the best Virginia society," characterized by tight kin-relations, a paternalistic care for poor whites and African-American slaves, a "truly aristocratic type of representative government," and a commitment to principles of honor. The Virginia gentry of Louisa County were not rich, but ran households of moderate means, which meant that they had to be frugal in many areas in order to be generous in others. The gentry reprobated universal male suffrage and secret ballots; all the property holders would declare their votes out loud—direct representation at its most basic.[7]

Dabney appropriated the ideal of gentility, which he believed to be the glory of the Old South, and the peculiar characteristic of Virginia gentlemen. By all accounts, he extended himself in social kindness toward his friends and social betters. While a student at Hampden-Sydney College and Union Seminary, he shunned the attention of the young ladies to strike up a relationship with Mrs. John Holt Rice, the widow of the esteemed Virginia Presbyterian leader. Eventually becoming one of her boarders, he maintained a lengthy correspondence with Mrs. Rice that lasted until her death. That was not unusual, however, because Dabney was an inveterate correspondent. Not only did he ply his family with letters, searching for the latest family news, but he also exasperated his friends with his prolixity. Moses Hoge teased him, "It seems to me that your pen is always rampant—curling its very feathers with impatience to entertain some far-away acquaintance. Wonder not if you excel your friends in the possession of such a ready servant, as in other things." Dabney's two most important correspondents throughout his life, aside from his immediate family, were Hoge and Vaughan. But Dabney would later engage in a widespread correspondence, writing numerous letters to university leaders (such as John B. Minor of the University of Virginia), fellow Southern Presbyterians (particularly William S. White and G. B. Strickler, as well as B. M. Palmer and Stuart Robinson), and even Baptist leaders (such as

John A. Broadus). Dabney's sociability in correspondence was one mark of his gentility; he was a Southern gentleman who welcomed contact from far-flung acquaintances as well as his kinfolk.[8]

Dabney's sociability extended beyond correspondence to social visits as well. His first biographer claimed that Dabney "craved society, the society of refined, elegant and interesting people." He played his role as a sociable gentleman, engaging in "a good deal of social visiting in the families" of Hampden-Sydney. He also believed that "improvement in manners" was "very important in the minister, and that it was a part of his preparation to acquire agreeable manners." Thus, Dabney worked very hard to improve his manners, having "access to almost every family in the immediate neighborhood." It was also during his time at Union Seminary that Dabney took an excursion to visit the house of John Randolph of Roanoke, who had recently died. Though Dabney never actually met Randolph, he cherished stories of the great man—at the end of his life, he wrote all the various stories that he had collected of Randolph in a reminiscence for the *Union Seminary Magazine*. Sociability through visits and letters marked Dabney as a gentleman.[9]

He was also committed to learning. Trained in one of the better field schools of the day, Dabney took a curriculum that leaned heavily toward the classics and a mastery of Latin and Greek. When he was sixteen, he matriculated in the Presbyterian college, Hampden-Sydney in Farmville, Virginia. There his education once again followed the classical path, emphasizing Greek and Latin as well as mathematics and physics. His ambition throughout his early education was to become learned, and he was anxious not to fail and so besmirch the family's honor. Dabney wrote his mother in 1836, "It is said that a student is almost certain to stand throughout his whole course just as he stands in the first session, and if he gets a bad name at first, it requires the greatest exertions to get rid of it." Dabney did well, but was forced to leave the college early in order to attend to his mother's financial affairs after his father died. When he was ready to return to his education, he decided to go to the University of Virginia. While he complained of his classmates' "low standard of honor" and dissipated ways, he sought to make a name for himself academically. Determined to take the master of arts degree, he graduated in physics and chemistry shortly after he matriculated at the university. He later graduated in mathematics, Latin, philosophy, political economy, Greek, French, and Italian. Dabney received the best education that his state could provide and obtained his degree two and a half years after he matriculated. Two years later, after seeing to his mother's financial matters again, he went back to Farmville to attend Union Theological Seminary in a day when theological education was still a novelty. He completed the three-year course in two years, received the seminary's certificate (the equivalent of the modern-day master of divinity), and prepared to take his first pastorate. By any reckoning, his education and later endeavors as an educator demonstrated his love of learning.[10]

While Dabney's commitment to learning was an important mark of his quest for gentility, the ideas that Dabney embraced in this period were even more crucial. During his time at the University of Virginia, he sat under the teaching of George Tucker, professor of moral philosophy and political economy, who used Jean-Baptiste Say's *A Treatise on Political Economy* as his main textbook. Say's popularity in Southern schools such as Virginia was, in part, the result of his application of Scottish commonsense realism and its inductive approach to political economy. Further, Say was deeply committed to free trade, deploring tariffs as an unwarranted interference with market mechanisms, a position welcomed in the anti-tariff South. Also from Tucker, Dabney imbibed the Old Republican doctrines represented by John Randolph and later by John C. Calhoun. As Thomas Cary Johnson noted, Calhoun was Dabney's *beau ideal* of a statesman: "Of all the representatives of Jeffersonian Democracy, he had the greatest respect for Mr. John C. Calhoun, a good engraving of whose face he kept on his study walls. He read and studied Calhoun as one of the great masters on constitutional government." From Randolph and Calhoun, Dabney learned that, while God himself had ordained human government, human sinfulness also made government a necessity. Dabney also followed the Old Republicans in believing that any government tended toward tyranny unless restrained by constitutional checks to extremely limited powers. The need for constitutional barriers did not derive from a "social contract," the Old Republicans argued, nor did the Declaration of Independence serve as the foundational American document. Rather, governments derived their authority primarily from God and secondarily from the people. Dabney's embrace of what came to be known as the Calhoun doctrines was so thorough that upon graduation from the University of Virginia, he was offered the editorship of a Calhoun newspaper in Petersburg, Virginia, an opportunity he rejected. Another indication of the importance of these ideas for Dabney was that when he taught moral and mental philosophy in Texas in the 1880s and 1890s, he was still using Say's textbook on political economy and holding Calhoun forward to his students as the preeminent constitutional theorist. These ideas, gained during these years of preparation, shaped Dabney's approach to public issues for the rest of his life.[11]

Dabney's piety, another mark of his gentleman status, was unquestioned. He credited his profession of faith to a "powerful and genuine awakening" at Hampden-Sydney in 1837. This profession, made when he was seventeen, occurred four years after his father's death and may have served as a rite of passage wherein he assumed his father's patriarchal responsibility. Afterward, Dabney was fully committed to Christian piety and particularly to the Old School Presbyterian heritage. Though Dabney was often viewed as an embittered man, his later students and friends claimed that he was "meek and humble," compassionate to the weak, and imbued with "a large generosity in judging of the characters of his fellow-men." Though he stood firm for what he viewed as the right, Dabney was accounted a pious man who was "remarkably free from base affections" and who despised slander and falsehood. Dabney was many things, but he was not a hypocrite. One observer wrote, "Religion was never a sham with him. It was the business of his life."[12]

This combination of sociability, learning, and piety signaled Dabney's embrace of the Southern ideal of gentility. Though Dabney claimed this ideal as his own, he believed that not everyone could be a gentleman. In every society there had to be a laboring class, "a social sub-soil to the top soil," that would work and not read. Rather than adopt the leveling doctrines of the free-soil North, Southerners urged one another to accept the providential order—an elite, educated, gen-teel class ruling and influencing the lower classes. This structured society did not mean that the truly noble man who happened to be poor would be kept down. Dabney firmly believed that "men of innate nobility born in the lower classes will raise themselves by an invincible energy to the grade they deserve." Such a view was consonant with Dabney's considered prejudice in favor of the ideals of gentility associated with gentleman status in the South.[13]

Mastery and Honor

Dabney's commitment to an ordered society naturally displayed itself in a defense of mastery and hierarchy. With his father's death when Dabney was thirteen, and with his older brother already established on his own farm in Hanover County, Dabney assumed mastery of the family. Constant responsibility for his mother's financial affairs devolved to him; twice, Dabney interrupted his education in order to straighten out his mother's precarious financial condition. Not the least of these responsibilities was managing the twenty to thirty slaves who assisted in running his mother's farms. At one point, in 1840, Dabney appeared weary of the challenge of mastery. "Whatever may be the influence of slavery on the happiness of the negroes, it would most effectually destroy that of the master, if they were all like me," Dabney complained. Yet he got used to dealing with African-American slaves. Later, during his pastoral ministry at Tinkling Spring, he "hired" two African Americans from their owners to serve him and his family, and he owned at least one slave (given to his wife by his mother-in-law). When the Emancipation Proclamation was issued in 1863, Dabney lost mastery of thirty-three slaves—twenty-seven that belonged to his mother and six of his own. By the time he wrote *Defence of Virginia* in 1863, Dabney claimed that the master–slave relationship, while not an inherent positive good to either party, was the best possible social relation between white and black Americans, an opinion formed, he claimed, from his personal experience as a master.[14]

31

As Dabney knew from firsthand experience, the place where slavery occurred and where hierarchy was learned was the household. He held that the household was the basic integer of society and stood prior to both the church and the state. In the household the principles of government by divine ordinance, universal subordination, and caste distinctions were learned and reinforced. Likewise, in the household, slaves took their place alongside children and wives under the rule of the master, the white male head. As Dabney would later observe, the household made up a little commonwealth where slaves, wives, and children were viewed by the state as minors "under the master's tutelage." The master acted as "magistrate and legislator" for all the minors in his household—transacting business, performing slave marriages, writing letters, going to court in slaves' behalf—and represented the household in the body politic through the exercise of his franchise. Likewise, the master was solely responsible for the education of his children and slaves. The master alone had the native affection and authority to provide properly for the education of his children. In addition, the master had the right to either encourage or deny the education of his slaves. All was under the master's control as he stood under the government of God. Such was Dabney's heady position at the mere age of thirteen—master of the household upon the death of his father.[15]

Not only was Dabney committed to gentility and mastery, he also upheld the Southern ideal of honor. Dabney later claimed that "I am not one of those who hold that these sentiments [of honor] are the birth of only pagan ferocity or unholy pride." The Stoic ideal, however, perverted honor "into a code of wickedness and bloody retaliation," particularly in its exaltation of the duel. Dabney firmly believed that the *code duello* was not "a proper remedy" for affronted honor. Dueling emphasized revenge, which was forbidden by God in every case; it failed to prove that the duelist was truly courageous or honorable; it did not settle the question of the truth or falsehood of the affront; the duel was manifestly unfair by placing both honest man and scoundrel on the same level; and it was "monstrous" because the duel made the wronged individual "accuser, judge and executioner in his own cause," a violation of the most basic principles of law and order. Societal honor could be regained only through the proper administration of the law, not by taking the law into one's own hands in a duel.[16]

One notorious scene of dishonor and violence for Dabney occurred during his student years at the University of Virginia. On November 12, 1840, law professor John Davis was murdered by one of the students in the midst of a student riot. Several students in masks had fired blank charges at the doors of the professors in commemoration of the infamous student "Rebellion of 1834." Upon hearing that Davis was on the watch, one of the students loaded a bullet with the powder and shot Davis. The student fled, but the university community was in such an uproar that a committee of students determined to apprehend the criminal and placed Dabney at the head of their search. Dabney found the student, named Joseph Semmes, interrogated him, but was forced to release him because of the posse's unofficial nature. Based on testimony that Dabney then gave the police, a warrant was issued for this student's arrest, but he escaped the law due in part to the influence of the dead man's wife, who urged forgiveness. Dabney's honor was unsatisfied: "I must confess that it would have been more proper for a well-balanced mind to have admitted the importance of the claims of the law, and, while she disclaimed everything like revenge, to have permitted the paramount interests of society to be vindicated by the punishment of the lawbreaker." When society experienced a violent dishonor, punishment and vindication through the application of law was required to restore honor. While Charlottesville society thought that the new widow's actions were Christian, Dabney believed that neither she nor the student's murderous intent betrayed any understanding of genuine honor. This situation's dishonorable tinge was increased when Semmes's defense lawyers succeeded in delaying the trial and apparently convincing key witnesses to withdraw from the case. In the end, honor was not restored to Charlottesville, for Semmes was allowed to go free.[17]

As Dabney would later observe, true honor did not belong either to those who celebrated the Stoic, martial ideal typified by the duel or to those who failed to seek punishment, repentance, and restitution. Instead, true honor, "which cometh from God and not from man," belonged to the man "who from pure motives braves the direst evils and pays the costliest sacrifice for the noblest object." For Dabney, the most obvious exemplar of honor was Jesus Christ, who was "the divine pattern and fountain of heroism." Jesus' entire mission was "a divine exemplification of courage" and, thus, of honor. "What was it," Dabney asked, "save the unselfish sentiment of duty, overruling the anticipations of evil . . . [that] caused him to press forward with eager, hungering haste, through the toils and obloquy of his persecuted life, to that baptism of blood which awaited him in Jerusalem?" When Jesus was on the cross, he refused to give "one word of disclaimer [that] might have rescued him" from all his enemies. Just as Jesus exemplified honor perfectly, Dabney believed that human beings could follow in Jesus' steps. "He is the bravest man who is the best Christian," Dabney claimed. "It is he who truly fears God, who is entitled to fear nothing else." Those who trusted in God's special providence and in Jesus' atonement for sinners were able to conquer all fears and to sacrifice themselves for others, thus winning true honor for themselves and their progeny. Christian honor, then, did not belong exclusively to the soldier or duelist; rather, it belonged to all those who sacrificed themselves for a noble cause, fearing Jesus Christ alone and no other human being. Dabney longed to be an honorable man and felt keenly any slight to his sense of honor.[18]

Dabney's quest for honor was challenged by his disadvantaged circumstance of losing his father. It is interesting to speculate on the effect that the death of Dabney's father had on the thirteen-year-old. On the one hand, Dabney appeared to deny that his father's death affected him much, writing to Moses Hoge in 1841, "What the loss of a parent is, I have experienced, though not to its full extent, for I was too young to appreciate fully his worth, or to estimate my misfortune." But it is hard to believe that Dabney was unaffected. He took his responsibilities of mastery with the utmost seriousness, making him old before his time, so much so that his family named him "the old gentleman." Further, one does not need to be a psychologist to see that his later hatred for ambiguity and his quest for certainty were fueled by a fatherless upbringing during his key intellectual years. Likewise, Dabney's penchant for order could be attributed at least partly to the family disorder that his father's death caused. Longings for certainty and order often led to overheated and hypercertain public rhetoric in

Dabney's later years, so much so that people were often surprised by his personal kindness and affection.[19]

His father's death also meant that Dabney as master had to maintain the family honor, particularly in sorting out his father's confused financial dealings. Chief among them was maintaining Walnut Grove, the family's 550-acre farm in Louisa County. The plantation's chief cash crop was tobacco, but it also produced timber, wool, and cotton. With his father's death, and his older brother's general inability to help, Dabney ran the farm with assistance from his mother, her hired overseer, and their slaves. Unfortunately, before his death, Dabney's father had followed the typical Virginian land-lust, and became entangled in numerous financial difficulties from land speculation and merchandising schemes. Save for the fourteen months he attended Hampden-Sydney, Dabney did the best he could during the 1830s to manage his mother's affairs, restore the property (which had experienced extreme neglect and careless use), and oversee the education of his two younger siblings, Frank and Betty. Part of restoring his mother's financial stability meant that Dabney had to teach in a field school from 1837 to 1839. The first year, he taught school in a cabin that he had built on the family property; later, he took Frank and Betty to a field school four miles away from Walnut Grove, where he pounded academic "rudiments into heads as hard as stones for seven long hours." Dabney ended up teaching about seventeen students and earning almost six hundred dollars for the family. Again, after graduating from the University of Virginia in 1842, he was forced to open a classical school on his mother's farm in order to recoup his mother's losses. At the end of his second two-year stint as manager of his mother's financial affairs, Dabney had once again rescued his mother from debt and returned Walnut Grove to respectability. In doing so, he maintained his family's honorable name by discharging their debts promptly. It was all part of exercising mastery over his clan as a man of honor.[20]

Presbyterian

It was also during these years that Dabney committed himself whole-heartedly to the Presbyterian church and to the Christian ministry. While he credited his profession of faith in Christ to a "power-ful and genuine awakening" that occurred at Hampden-Sydney when he was there in 1837, it does appear that his circumstances of life, par-ticularly leaving college to assume mastery once again of his mother's affairs, had as much to do with his conversion as the "great deal of feeling in the college" that resulted in "about twelve of the students [becoming] religious," including himself. When Dabney joined Prov-idence Presbyterian Church upon returning from college in Septem-ber 1837, he took his first communion in the same church where his father had served as ruling elder, and came to community leadership by assuming his father's place in the church.[21]

However, Dabney was not content with assuming his father's mas-tery in every area. Rather than be a Virginia planter, Dabney deter-mined to serve as a Presbyterian minister. He revealed his plans to Moses Hoge in 1841: "To give you some idea of my future movements in life, I will state that my mind is, I believe, fully made up for the min-istry, but that I do not expect to go to the seminary for about three years to come . . . This delay is according to my sense of duty, rendered absolutely necessary by the claims of my family." Though he was will-ing to take time off to prepare for seminary, Dabney was concerned about the seminary course. He asked Hoge:

> Do they make you study hard at the seminary and are the studies interesting, or not . . . ? I suppose you have to dig into the old Latin Commentators pretty extensively. They are the chief bug bear to me, but I reckon like every other bug bear I ever feared they diminish and lose their formidable appearance, as you approach them. Still, I should think it a great waste of time and labor to read divinity in Latin if it can be gotten in English.

Though his opinion would change about Latin divinity, Dabney fol-lowed this plan to pursue still nascent theological education.[22]

After graduating from the University of Virginia and spending two years working on his mother's behalf, Dabney went to Union Theol-ogical Seminary in Virginia. Situated on the backside of the Hamp-den-Sydney campus, the seminary building was one long, low-slung building. In 1844, the seminary faculty was made up of three men: Samuel Wilson in theology, Samuel Graham in church history and polity, and Francis Sampson in Old Testament and Hebrew. The relationships that Dabney forged with the faculty during this time would lead to closer ties. In his future work at Union Seminary, he would serve as Wilson's adjunct in theology for ten years until Wilson's death in 1869; as well, Dabney was a close friend of Sampson, writing his memoirs and editing his commentary on Hebrews after Sampson's premature death. Only eighteen students attended the seminary in 1844; Dabney characterized his class by telling his brother Charles William:

> There are a few of them of good families, and of pretty high character, as to acquirement and manners. The rest seem to be just what Aunt Coles would call "good creatures," very kind and quiet and very uninteresting. All of them, I believe, are young men in limited circumstances. Not many of the rich of this world cast in their lot among us. Some of them are sons of mechanics, and are supported partly by charity, or by school teaching, and so forth.

Dabney's evaluation of his peers was fairly shrewd. Of his own class, only Dabney and Vaughan would make major marks on the church; in the classes before and after Dabney's, William Henry Ruffner, Virginia's first superintendent of public instruction, and J. Henry Smith, longtime pastor of the Presbyterian church in Greensboro, North Carolina, were the most prominent.[23]

Ultimately, Dabney was at the seminary in order to gain the professional knowledge that he would need in order to be a successful minister. In 1844, seminary education was still a novelty, barely a generation old—Union Seminary was founded in 1807, Andover Seminary in 1808, and Princeton Seminary in 1812. Most potential Presbyterian pastors were still trained in the older way, apprenticing to some well-respected pastor and reading theology with him for several years before sustaining the licensure and ordination exams. Theological seminaries were part of the denomination-building that was going on throughout American religion and particularly in the South. As American Christianity became more institutionalized during the nineteenth century, increasing emphasis came to be placed on denominational activities. This new emphasis on the denomination was near the heart of the Old School–New School division of the Presbyterian church in 1837. While the New School ministers were quite active in interdenominational religious activities that centered in New York City—the American Bible Society, the American Education Society, the American Board of Commissioners for Foreign Missions, the American Home Missionary Society, the American Sunday School Union, and the American Tract Society—Old School Presbyterians increasingly demanded that the church support denominational boards that promoted a distinctively Presbyterian approach to these church functions. By excising four recalcitrant Northern New School synods, Old School Presbyterians were able to consolidate church support for the denominational boards. In the same way, Presbyterians increasingly came to put a heavy emphasis on their theological seminaries as the approved way of training ministers. While most of the church's financial resources were funneled to Princeton Seminary as the "national" Presbyterian seminary, the synods of Virginia and North Carolina sponsored Union Seminary at Hampden-Sydney College as their regional training center for prospective ministers.

Presbyterian seminaries were expected to train their ministers with professional knowledge of theology and biblical studies so that their ministers would be able to reach the upper classes. The professional knowledge that theological education had to impart included, at the minimum, a thorough knowledge of "the body of divinity." Dabney would later affirm the historical Presbyterian ordination standards: ministers were expected to have "the interpretation of the Word, and the preaching of the body of divinity" as "their great, their main, their every day work." Thus, while other seminaries and divinity schools focused on "literary novelties," Presbyterian theological education emphasized "a thorough and regular course of instruction in the body of divinity." In addition, Presbyterian ministers needed to demonstrate a mastery of the original languages of the Bible: Greek and Hebrew. English translations were helpful, but in a theological controversy, the "question is not fully settled until the original is examined." Dabney believed that it was "the duty of the pastor to go himself to the fountain head of the exposition." The only way to refute opponents of the gospel was to have a thorough knowledge of the biblical text, which meant a working knowledge of Hebrew and especially New Testament Greek.[24]

Dabney gained all of this knowledge, and by all accounts was the leading student of his class. But during his time in seminary, he was plagued by digestive problems, which were common for the day, as well as weak eyesight. There was so much concern about his health that he feared that he would go blind at a young age; and upon receiving his seminary certificate, his presbytery later assigned him to a missionary field close to his home, allegedly because of concerns about his health. Still, Dabney was able to complete the three-year course in two years' time, to preach regularly in the country churches surrounding Hampden-Sydney, and to write his first series of articles for the Virginia Presbyterian newspaper. At the end of his seminary course, Dabney appeared before West Hanover Presbytery and was licensed to preach the gospel on May 4, 1846. He was dispatched immediately to his home area to be the stated supply for several churches, including his home church. Though he would remain in this missionary labor for only a year, this time provided Dabney with an opportunity to minister in surroundings that were familiar and to continue to oversee his mother's affairs. His labors were certainly approved by his home church; Providence Church attempted to secure his services as its permanent pastor.[25]

Yet Dabney's ministry in his home area was still overshadowed by his father's reputation. Launcelot Minor wrote to Dabney in May 1847, ostensibly to encourage him: "What I mean is this, that as the son of Col. Charles Dabney, and being what you are in qualifications, with an humble dependence on God for his blessing, no other man could do in Louisa what you could." For over a decade, Dabney had attempted to fill his father's shoes and to exert mastery within his household and his native county. But the continued communal memory of his father was oppressing; Dabney needed to strike out for his own place where he could make his own reputation. As it so happened, Dabney had been in conversation with a church in the Shenandoah Valley, Tinkling Spring Presbyterian Church. A former classmate from the seminary, William Richardson, had mentioned Dabney's name to the church in February 1847.[26] After preaching for the church in April, to that point the largest congregation to which he had preached, Dabney was extended "an almost unanimous call" to the pastorate. Though he hesitated to accept the call because of the duties he continued to feel he owed his mother, the need to strike out on his own and out from the shadow of his father, as well as the flattering letter sent by the pastoral search committee, swayed his mind toward acceptance. As he would do throughout his life, Dabney would later use the excuse of his health as the prime reason for accepting the call to the valley. Yet the fact was that he had spent much of his life preparing to leave Louisa County, to experience the type of social mobility that ministers of evangelical denominations often experienced in the mid-nineteenth century. Dabney did not labor to become one of the best-educated Presbyterian ministers of his day in order to serve a forty-mile circuit of small country churches. During these years of preparation, as he became a "gentleman theologian," Dabney had learned to love Virginia and to embrace the Presbyterian and Reformed faith. This preparation would serve him well during the next fifty years of life and ministry.[27]

2

Pastor

*T*he six years and two months that Dabney spent as pastor of Tinkling Spring Presbyterian Church were among the most important of his life. When he arrived, Dabney was a young minister, aspiring to professionalism and successful church-building. When he left, he was going on to what had probably been his ultimate goal all along, a position on the faculty of Union Theological Seminary in Virginia. In between, Dabney found his lifelong and only love, owned two houses, had two sons, and established himself in his own household. Above all, Dabney demonstrated to himself and to others that he was a professional minister, one able to preach regularly and rule authoritatively in the councils of the church, to build church buildings, and to preside over revivals. These years were full and fast-paced for Dabney. He embraced his opportunity at Tinkling Spring, "receiving the greatest kindness," though he spent nearly half his years there "on a salary of $600 [a year], no manse." In the end, Dabney was able to look back on these years as ones in which he "labored hard and successfully" in the work of the ministry.[1]

Dabney as Pastor

Dabney arrived to his charge at Tinkling Spring in Augusta County, Virginia, in mid-July 1847. His eagerly awaited debut in the pulpit was delayed by "a slight attack of colic," which was just as well as far as Dabney was concerned: "I think it was very fortunate that I was prevented from preaching, for it is next to impossible for a man to satisfy expectations on such an occasion; and the people were not met in a temper of mind which promised any profit." Aside from that initial inconvenience, Dabney was well satisfied with his arrangements. He was boarding with a bachelor in his congregation, Hugh Guthrie, who had a large farmhouse in a central location. "I believe, on the whole, the place suits me better than any other where I could be taken in," Dabney confided to his mother. "Here the table is generally good, and the house comfortable. I can be more unconstrained and can have a better command of my time. And the neighborhood is so thick that 15 minutes walk will bring me into company at any time. I have a large room with four windows on the second floor, and with a porch in the front of it."[2]

Though he appeared to be enjoying the bachelor's life, being settled with Guthrie in a snug house, Dabney turned his attentions almost immediately to gaining a wife. Perhaps fellow minister B. M. Smith mentioned his sister-in-law, Lavinia Morrison, to Dabney during their first shared communion season in July 1847. Regardless, by the time presbytery met the following month, Dabney made sure that he accepted the invitation of Lavinia's father, James Morrison, minister of New Providence Church in Rockbridge, to stay with his family on the way to the presbytery meeting. Though he barely mentioned the visit to the Morrisons in his letter to his mother, that visit was fateful. Dabney had imagined that Lavinia was "one of your pattern young ladies of Partier manufacture. So I shall find her a tall angular person with sandy hair and bland complexion, sharp Roman nose and gold rimmed spectacles and very primpy manners, and talk of *Missionary Herald* and theology." Instead, when he first saw her, Dabney admired "a young looking girl, I thought about 18, [who] crossed the hall and tripped up the stairway, her hair and eyes brown, her cheeks rosy, very slender in figure, was dressed in a blue gingham, [with] a white housekeeping apron on." He fell in "love at first sight."[3]

Dabney pressed his suit with full vigor. Apparently, the couple became engaged shortly after their first meeting, and Dabney urged a quick wedding. But events appeared to be conspiring against him. Though he was able to dissolve Lavinia's commitment to teach at a school north of Staunton, the death of one of her younger brothers almost led to an interminable postponement. Dabney was determined not to allow a lengthy delay, observing that Lavinia's father "will have to be a more obstinate man than I think, if I do not persuade him out of this." Another apparent difficulty was that Dabney's own kinfolk were unhappy with the match and with the rate at which he pursued it. Dabney's brother Charles William seemingly accused him of having blindly chosen Lavinia, claiming that Dabney knew little about women and their entangling ways. Further, Charles William intimated that Dabney was "nervous in meeting the folks at home" because of his engagement. Dabney was forced to defend his choice of Lavinia to his kinfolk, praising her character and beauty and claiming that "I think if you will judge by the results you should rather give me credit for a good deal of acumen."[4] Eventually, he successfully convinced all the parties involved to agree to a wedding date of March 28, 1848, at the Morrisons' home.[5]

The new couple set up housekeeping at Hugh Guthrie's house, now using two rooms rather than the one that Dabney had previously occupied. But almost immediately, Dabney was involved in a measure of conflict with his new relations. His new brother-in-law, B. M. Smith, made "the modest request that I and Lavinia would leave home, and abide three weeks at his house, to take care of his affairs, in order that Mrs. Smith may go with him to General Assembly." Dabney's annoyance with the request spiked his sarcasm: "[Mrs. Smith] has only some six boarders, and three small children; so that, of course, it is very reasonable that a person so little encumbered should avail themselves of the occasion to cajonick about." He was determined to put his foot down, for he was convinced that "Lavinia has been so completely the drudge of the connexion formerly, that it never seemed to enter her head that she could, or ought, to demur." A few months later, when Dabney and his wife were expecting their first child, his attitude toward the Smiths was so poisoned that he decided that if Lavinia was determined to stay with her sister, she would stay as a boarder, paying her own way: "Although she has been little else than a handmaid to his wife and his children often staying with them two months at a time, and sitting up every night, and nursing, I know brother Benny well enough to be sure of my ground here." Though his relationship with the Smiths would gradually improve, these first interactions characterized Dabney's generally negative feelings toward his brother-in-law and potential rival.[6]

Once his marital state was satisfactorily established, Dabney turned his attention to his ministerial affairs. One of the first major projects that he tackled was building a new church structure. The old stone church building was in very bad repair, and Dabney convinced the congregation to tear down the old building and build a new brick edifice. From the very beginning, he grumbled that the building project was a major headache and hassle. Early on, he observed that "the congregation generally have wrong ideas as to the cost of building; and expect to get the job done too cheaply. They have raised us about $3100, and want to build a house some 62 feet long with it. I fear they will find their expectations unwarranted." In addition, the congregation wanted to keep the business in Staunton, which Dabney believed would run up the cost. "As is usually the case in a little hole of this sort," he claimed, "they are all banded and cohogling together, architects and builders, and I believe are fully determined to keep the game in their own hands and fleece us to the tune of a thousand dollars or so." Though Dabney tried to encourage outside competition, eventually he took matters into his own hands, designing the church building himself as the chairman of the building committee.[7]

Almost immediately, Dabney began to complain about the people's reluctance about raising the money for the building. He complained to his mother, "The people grunt and groan very much about raising the money, but very unreasonably. They are well able to build such a house, or a much finer one. The sheriff of the county told me that the people who attend regularly at our church own about $800,000 worth of property." Likewise, Dabney was frustrated by the congregation's constant fussing and fickleness. In April, he told his brother Charles William, "I find it almost impossible to quiet the various discontents, desires for alterations, suggestions that are perpetually thrown out. I have told them that I am convinced the plan will never be settled till the mortar sets; perhaps not then." Revealingly, Dabney claimed that his expertise as a "professional man" was superior to the knowledge that the "ploughman and cow grazer" in his congregation had on architectural matters. But he said, "I have long ago learned to hold on . . . [to] my way, unmoved by unreasonable people; for the world is so thick with them that if a man should be so foolishly tender in his hind, as to let them prick him, his fate would be equal that of a naked man in a den of porcupines." Later, in July 1849, Dabney feared "that by the time the house is finished, there will be no congregation to worship in it. They seem to be, a part of them, possessed with the desire to quarrel about every trifle in the arrangement of the matter." Though he wanted to put these malcontents in their place, Dabney reported that "by an exertion of great forbearance, I steer clear of both, and try to keep the peace between them, but in vain."[8]

Finally, toward the end of the year, the building began to take shape. Dabney bragged to his brother, "Our church is now almost done and promises to be a perfect gem, plain, chaste and propitious and convenient. Some say, that although it cannot compare in the costliness of ornaments and in size with many others, it will be one of the most tasteful churches in Virginia. It is withal a very cheap house. Our church will cost about 3400. Seats about 500 people commonly, 700 by cramming aisles and pews." Eventually, the church building was completed in February 1850.[9]

While Dabney was busy building a new church structure, he was also building up his household. On February 19, 1849, his firstborn son, Robert Jr., or Bob as the family called him, was born. The next day, Dabney teased his brother: "I remember you told me once, in 1841, that you claimed some sort of precedence and superiority over me, in virtue of your fraternal honors. My wife has, in good time, rolled away this reproach; and since 9 o'clock last night, I can count equally with you, in number, sex, etc., excepting the 'personal pulchritude.' " The new father later reflected that "I have never yet attained to the parental achievement thought so essential by old women, to the character of an affectionate husband and father, of seeing beauty in a new born infant. I suppose he has as much as usual;

that is, as much as can be found in a little red face, pug nose, short chin, carp mouth, and bald pate." Dabney was confident that Bob would "make a noble fellow in the end." Later Dabney told his mother that "the grandson is a week old tonight, and, we flatter ourselves, is nearly ready to go to plough. He is the strongest, biggest, healthiest, and greediest dog of his years (or rather days) that ever was seen." The child's red hair led Dabney to observe that his firstborn was "destined, if he lives, to be a red-haired, white eyebrowed, freckled face, Scotch Irish giant."[10]

Shortly after the church building was finished, Dabney added a second child to his growing household—James, named after Lavinia's father, was born on April 1, 1850. Dabney wrote his mother about the "April fool" born a few days prior, "a black haired, long legged Dabney boy." The doctor did not arrive in time to deliver Jimmy, as the family called him, so Lavinia instead had "a very kind and experienced old neighbor woman, a member of our church, and a professional lady of color, old Aunt Dinah, who did as well as a whole faculty of physicians and a jury of grandmothers could have done." Even so, the child was almost born before anyone could arrive; Dabney told his mother that if he were the doctor, he would "beg my patients not to serve me the same trick which Lavinia served her respected mother, and very nearly served the old colored practitioner, the same impolite trick for which a similar class of functionaries in Pharaoh's time, reproached the Israelitish women."[11]

Eventually, Dabney decided to find a place to call his own, moving out of the comfortable quarters at Hugh Guthrie's. He purchased a little piece of property called "Sleepy Hollow." While at this property, Dabney wrestled with the intractable problem of hiring good help. He tried to rent African-American slaves from their owners or hire free blacks and lower-class whites to assist his wife in running the household or to work in his fields. But he constantly complained about his help. Dabney admitted to his brother that he had been forewarned "that I would find the business of hiring negroes a disagreeable one; and your information has been fully verified in one or two respects. One is that they leave you Christmas day, just in the most inclement season of the year; and the new hirelings do not come in till new year's day." Later, Dabney related to his sister Betty that "we are all very well here now except the negro man I hired. He has most inopportunely taken a fit of cholera morbus in the midst of harvest and when I was hiring him out at a dollar a day in the hope of making a little part of the exorbitant hire I have to pay for servants." While this slave was "reasonably good," his wife "is a free negro and the most intolerably worthless creature in this country of worthless negresses . . . She is lazy, excessively vain, and impertinent. The only virtues she has are two that are more in this filthy community, cleanliness and freedom from pilfering." A couple of years later, Dabney related to his brother that "I have hired a man and a woman for this year, both rather more juvenile, and happily, therefore more whip-able than those we had last."[12]

This struggle with the hired help led Dabney to desire to purchase his own slaves. He already had two slaves from his mother to help Lavinia in doing the household work, one of whom was "of a breed which has a natural turn for cooking." But by 1851, Dabney confessed that he was tired of hireling help, which led him "into the notion of buying me a negro man." Slaves were now affordable because of the fall in cotton prices, he observed. As a result, Dabney told his brother that "I would greatly prefer a negro of good character raised in east Virginia . . . I should prefer to buy from some estate of respectable negroes who are sold not for bad conduct." A few months later, Dabney continued to ask his brother to be on the lookout for a male slave whom he could purchase from an eastern Virginia estate. Part of the reason, he maintained, that he preferred a bought slave from the east was that "if I got hold of a bought servant and he became spoiled, I should feel less regret at selling him." In the end, it does not appear at this point that Dabney was able to purchase a male slave as he had planned, so he was resigned to being a "negro-hirer."[13]

When he was not wrestling with his household affairs, Dabney continued to pursue his ministerial work. His labors were rewarded in the summer of 1850 with a revival that significantly increased the church's membership and confirmed his pastoral gifts. Throughout 1849, Dabney had been despondent that his preaching produced little effect. He reported to his mother that "my preaching seems to human eyes to be utterly without effect; bad for me, and bad for them." The result was that he claimed to have "experienced more depression of spirits the last few weeks than for many a month before" because of "the apparent fruitlessness of my ministry." A few months later, Dabney complained that "there is a dreadful lukewarmness and I frequently come from church, after preaching to a drowsy congregation, half fit to hang myself. But I ought not to complain for too large a share of this lukewarmness is in my own heart." But during the summer of 1850, shortly after the completion of the new church building, Dabney finally experienced revival at his church. Spurred by the spiritual interest of his parishioners, he held protracted meetings to supplement his other preaching services, which were twice on Sunday and once on Wednesday evening. About six weeks after the revival began, he reported that the spiritual "interest in my church has rather declined. We have no inquiry meetings now . . . but one thing very gratifying to me was that almost all who ever attended inquiry meetings made a profession of religion, and the most of them a highly credible profession." Dabney received twenty-nine new members into his church as a result of the brief revival. Of those, though, only five were men, indicating that while the revival was "successful," he experienced difficulty in reaching the men of his area and projecting a masculine faith. Still, it was the largest number of new members to be added in any single year in over twenty years, and the revival validated his professional gifts.[14]

At the end of 1850, Dabney meditated on the significance of that year in the life of the congregation. Preaching from Psalm 116:12, he proclaimed, "This year has been a year of peculiar blessings to us, as a Church. God has given us, what I am sure you all appreciate as no small blessing to yourselves, and no small advantage to the interests of religion, this 'holy and beautiful house' of worship." Even more important than the new building was the way in which "this has been to us a year of the right hand of the most high: a year which will be eternally memorable to us for the glorious and manifest answer of prayer, for the pouring out of his grace, and the revival of his work among us." Shortly after the consecration of the new building, Dabney observed that "these walls were made solemn and awful and blessed by the glory of the Holy Ghost even as the gate of heaven. They received a baptism from on high, which, we trust will make them ever a sacred and awe-inspiring place to us and to our children. Precious souls, we believe were this year born into life and immortality and glory; and love and peace and spiritual joy were poured like holy oil on many hearts." Both church construction and revival made 1850 an important year in the life of the people of Tinkling Spring. Even more, they were also vital for validating the work of Dabney as a professional minister, as one skilled in the ways of church growth and management and one aspiring to places of higher usefulness.[15]

Unfortunately, the work of the ministry did not constitute merely the spiritual heights of revival or the details of church construction. Dabney also led as a professional minister in matters of church discipline. As the minister, Dabney presided as moderator at all church session meetings and led the session in interviewing new members and investigating church discipline cases. In order to maintain the respect of his lay leaders, Dabney had to conduct these meetings with the requisite balance of authority and compassion. When church discipline cases came before the session, he would lead his session in the trial of unrepentant church members. One particularly difficult case was that of William Cullen. In October 1851, Cullen was charged with fighting with George Antrium of Fishersville, near Gibb's Hotel. The session ordered Cullen to appear in order to explain this breach of Christian conduct; and though Cullen was acquitted by the church session after he explained his "great provocation," the rumors concerning Cullen's behavior were not quieted. In April 1852, the session discovered that Cullen was guilty of greater sins: he had committed fornication with Diana Smith, apparently causing her to become pregnant, and he had unlawfully butchered a beef without the consent of its owner. Both of these sins landed Cullen in the county's poor court as well as the church's court. When Cullen failed to appear before his church's session to answer for these sins, the church excommunicated him in June 1852. Throughout the lengthy process of investigation and discipline, Dabney led his session in a professional manner, validating that he was a minister "approved by God."[16]

As if these aspects of ministry were not enough, Dabney consented to start a school. Growing increasingly concerned by the shortage of ministers for the Shenandoah Valley, he encouraged his people to consider starting a school under private oversight. Finally, in September 1852, Dabney started the school in the church's session room and soon had twenty boys enrolled. Eventually, a building was built in Barterbrook, an area near the church, and the school continued to grow, netting Dabney an additional seven hundred fifty dollars in income. Dabney's teaching methods were typical for the day, including a heavy dose of discipline. Students were regularly whipped if they failed to meet his standards of deportment. Dabney told his sister Betty about one case in which a boy sought to withstand a whipping: "I told him that we must settle the question of supremacy at once; and while I was gone to get some switches, he might make up his mind either 'to cut dirt' or take a thrashing again. He elected the former." On another occasion, a group of the boys sought to band together to flog Dabney in retribution for a particularly harsh round of discipline. At recess time, he collected "an extra handful of stout switches, and also a stout hickory cane, with which he could have felled an ox." When Dabney returned, he did not need to use them, for the boys recognized who was the master. It was not his intention, though, to manage the school full-time. After the first year, he hired J. M. Craig as his assistant "to do the work of the school" while Dabney taught "one or two of the advanced classes" and "retain[ed] the supervision."[17]

Dabney as Preacher

Above all, the most important work that Dabney did as a minister aspiring to professionalism was to preach to his congregation week by week. And apparently, if later testimonials are any indication, Dabney's preaching was memorable. One reminiscence observed that while Dabney was not "the polished orator that Moses Hoge, or Thornwell, or B. M. Palmer was," he was more like "the Prophet Elijah, rugged, but at times sublimely eloquent." Another pointed out the relentlessly "didactic" purpose of his preaching: "The great impression he made was of didactic power. He seemed to be clearing with huge instruments the highway of truth for men to walk in, with a threat of awful consequences if they did not walk in it, and a promise of glory if they should walk in it." Others defended the dogmatism that came through in Dabney's preaching, claiming that "as a teacher, in the pulpit and in the classroom, he was a dogmatist. So ought every teacher to be. Away with that namby pamby courtesy and politeness that smirks and bows and extends its mantle of charity to falsehood and sin, and concedes to heresy equal rights and standing with truth under deceitful plea of honest conviction and the right of private judgment." One final appraiser was quoted as evaluating prominent Presbyterian preachers by saying, "[One] is perhaps the best furnished of the three; [another] is the most eloquent and attractive in the pulpit; but for blasting rocks, I would take Dr. Dabney."[18]

The common threads in all of these contemporary appraisals of Dabney's preaching were his pulpit intensity, his lack of polished oratory, and his didacticism. And an examination of the extant sermons demonstrates that these appraisals were fair and accurate.[19] These sermons indicate that the majority of Dabney's preaching generally shifted back and forth between passionate and direct evangelistic appeals to unrepentant sinners to come to Christ, and doctrinal sermons on points related to soteriology. In addition, an examination of the sermons reveals that, as Dabney's confidence as a sermonizer grew through the years, what he took into the pulpit diminished. While Dabney started his ministerial career by often manuscripting his sermons nearly in full, by the 1880s he generally took only short outlines or briefs into the pulpit. The only times he varied from this pattern in his later years was for major events, such as baccalaureate sermons or sermons preached before gatherings of ministerial peers. However, the extent and quality of Dabney's preaching was generally unknown because so few of his sermons were published. Unlike the sermons of his contemporary B. M. Palmer, who published his works in serial form for over two years, Dabney's sermons rarely found newsprint. In fact, in the 1880s, when compiling his collected writings with the assistance of C. R. Vaughan, Dabney struggled to think of sermons that would work for the volumes. As a result, his preaching has been generally ignored.[20] Closely tied with this observation, however, is the way Dabney preached his sermons over and over again. While only around four hundred sermons are extant, they may well represent over a thousand different preachments. Hence, the sermons that Dabney preached repeatedly were probably ones that he believed to be particularly effective or meaningful.[21] Finally, in keeping with the logic of the spiritual nature of the church, Dabney's preaching stuck fairly close to "spiritual" as opposed to "secular" matters. That being said, several times Dabney preached sermons that echoed the public theology that he would later work out in published essays for theological journals and Presbyterian papers—focusing on parents' role in education or temperance or religion's role in promoting public morality. The nonsecular nature of the church did not prevent Dabney from having a public voice on social issues, but it did seemingly convince him not to preach on the duties of masters and slaves: only a few sermons were apparently preached to separate black congregations, and none on texts that would lend themselves to addressing the issue of slavery.[22]

One of Dabney's first sermons, written in 1841, was a sermon "skeleton" that highlighted the nature of sin and the need for the new birth, and provided a paradigm for the type of preaching that Dabney engaged in throughout his ministry. Taking Genesis 6:5 as his text, Dabney opened by observing that "convictions of sin [are] usually progressive." At first, sinners would admit only to sinning occasionally. But under the conviction of the Holy Spirit, some men and women "remember many more sinful acts." And then, the Spirit would teach human beings that "there are sinful feelings as well as acts and that their hearts are wicked as well as their lives." When conviction was complete, sinners would "learn that all their acts and thoughts are evil." In order for conviction to be saving, Dabney argued, it "must be thus extensive . . . All short of this 'heals the hurt of the people slightly.' " This Holy Spirit–wrought conviction, Dabney pointed out, agreed with the doctrine of Scripture, which taught that "all the acts and thoughts of the unconverted man are sinful. The indifferent acts, the acts externally right, the best religious exercises and emotions [are] all sinful." The Bible doctrine of human depravity was that "all acts not done from regard to God's will are acts of disobedience, whether formally right or not. For the intention gives moral character to the act." After driving his congregation to this conclusion, Dabney asked finally, "When sin [is] thus habitual, what chance of reformation? Your only hope is in a new birth." Regeneration was the only hope for the depths of depravity in which humankind found itself.[23]

This sermon was paradigmatic for Dabney as he sought to accomplish a basic twofold goal—to drive sinners from their self-confidence by showing them the depths of their depravity, and to point them to the salvation provided in Jesus Christ. Another example of this approach was a sermon that Dabney preached early in his ministry at Tinkling Spring on Romans 5:6 and John 6:44. In this sermon, Dabney demonstrated that human beings did not have the innate ability to save themselves. He opened the sermon by observing that "most heretics have repudiated the doctrine of inability. Pelagians, Socinians, Arminians, and the semi-Pelagians of our day and nation. Arminians in part, by doctrine of common grace, etc. The reason is, it is the last stronghold of human pride." Human pride must be humbled, Dabney claimed, because a sinner would "not let Christ do for him, till taught that he cannot do for himself." God most often humbled men and women through their progressive experience of their inability. This inability "is not his infirmity, but his sin; not natural but moral; not involuntary or regretted but voluntary . . . His inability is in his depravity," which affected the sinner's understanding, disposition, and will. That did not mean that sinners would not try to save themselves by law-keeping or by attempting to receive the gospel when they chose. Such attempts, though, would end in failure. Even "persuasions," eloquence, and reason have been tried on sinners, but have failed to exact repentance. Why have all these things failed? Dabney asked. "Because you can't come [to Christ], without divine aid." God must grant sinners a new heart before they will be saved. That does not mean, however, that sinners should wait for God to work. Rather, until God does this work, sinners should "do their part in the use of all means, godly living, and meanwhile, consent for Christ to do the work." Dabney promised that "as soon as you are willing for him to do for you, he will do it."[24]

During the revival that Tinkling Spring experienced in 1850, Dabney preached a sermon on Genesis 27:38 that sought to continue the revival by using the dialectic between human depravity and divine grace. Drawing on the differences between the biblical characters Jacob and Esau, Dabney accused some of his congregation of being like Esau:

> How blessed these Jacobs, compared with you Esaus? Sins gone; storm weathered, they safe in port while you exposed. Painful question settled. Strife decided. True, they still have Christian warfare to finish. But God is underneath them. Their everlasting friend, your enemy. No more guilty conscience (only soft repentance); no more despair; no more wrath. You still tossed and buffeted. In them sweet peace, calm, heavenly quiet. In you a restless spirit, full of hesitations, guilt and strife.

God had held out the spiritual birthright to these modern-day Esaus— salvation during the revival season—but they had rejected God's offer of salvation for a "mess of pottage," represented by the present cares of the world. But the problem was not "irreparable," Dabney encouraged. "There is, then, this happy difference between Esau's cause and yours . . . To you, the blessing is still offered, if you will repent of your choice and accept it. God still stands with generous arm extended, holding out the gift, in spite of your rejection, in spite of your late slight, as ready and willing as ever." And because God was still willing that sinners might come, they should act today: "Remember!" Dabney exclaimed, "God's offer and promise are not that you may come tomorrow, this evening and obtain, but now . . . If you delay from now, [there is] no assurance that you may not pass" to the same final condition as Esau.[25]

One of Dabney's favorite sermons was from 1 Kings 18:21, which he first preached at Tinkling Spring in October 1852, but repreached at least nineteen times, including six times during the Civil War. In the sermon, Dabney cast himself as Elijah remonstrating with the Israelites, arguing with those who were delaying a commitment to Christ. Castigating his hearers for their indecision, Dabney proclaimed:

> A halting service between the world and God is useless and foolish . . . We say: Why halt ye, vacillate ye, between the world and God? If the world is not sufficient for your God then this halting is absurd

because God accepts no divided service. Your partial labor is thrown away and goes for nothing. Of course, such a strife, warfare, wrestling, race, cannot be effected by the halting man.

Dabney upbraided those who play at religion:

> If you intend to make the world your God, then why trouble yourselves with a partial halting religion? Hinders your enjoyment of the world. Troubles you with importunate thoughts of future. Restrains indulgences. You lose full enjoyment of world here, and lose heaven, too! Therefore, settle the matter, at once, and give up this futile hope of heaven. Embrace world; enjoy to full [and] make up your minds deliberately to go to hell.

Instead of bold action one way or the other, Dabney accused his auditors of painful hesitation "as dangerous and as much to be dreaded as an act, which would irretrievably close the bargain with Satan." He urged them to give up this indecision and to close with Christ, charging them, "I want every man to take this as a question and when he has found an answer which commends itself to his own good sense, come and tell me." Such evangelistic preaching was a major part of Dabney's ministerial work.[26]

Dabney, of course, preached on topics other than salvation. For example, he twice addressed issues related to money early in his ministry at Tinkling Spring. In December 1847, he preached a sermon from Matthew 6:25, urging his congregation to find "the golden mean of gospel contentment . . . which arises from true humility and moderation, and from a sincere preference for other and best objects of pursuit!" Dabney held that Christians "should be contented thus with our lot because undue anxiety about the world is necessarily attended with an indifference to God which is sinful and offensive to him." Further, Christians must seek contentment because "our anxiousness is impotent." In fact, Dabney taught that "an undue anxiety about worldly good indicates a sinful distrust of God's providential protection." Moreover, Christians were better off not caring for great wealth because of "the responsibility attached to riches" and "their unsatisfying nature." Instead of focusing on wealth and riches, Christians should be content with their lot here on earth and strive after "heaven," which "is the only right object" of human affections. A few months later, Dabney preached on Matthew 16:26, comparing "the everlasting salvation of the soul" with "the possession of all the natural indulgences and gratifications which the whole world could give if owned by one man." This comparison highlighted the great importance of the soul; Dabney's object in the sermon was to make his congregation "feel (and feel in such sense as to act) that the salvation of your souls is a thing of more importance, not only than the little pursuits which are postponing it, but than the greatest scheme of worldly ambition." For members of a congregation that Dabney deemed to be quite wealthy in worldly goods, these sermons were meant to strike at the core of their beings.[27]

Dabney also preached on standard themes of the Christian life. In January 1849, he preached a sermon on "bearing the cross," from Luke 9:23. Christians were to take up their cross daily, which he understood to refer to "any or every thing grievous to the natural inclinations, borne for Christ. It may be explained by 'deny thyself.' This cross is to be taken up when the path of duty leads us up to it, not invented or sought out." Cross-bearing was not something that Christians could avoid. "No man is a follower of Christ," Dabney averred, "who is not . . . daily and actually bearing something grievous for Christ. No man is a Christian who is not willing to bear anything rather than offend Christ and who does not find himself habitually crossing his natural dispositions to please Christ."[28]

The following month, Dabney took up the issue of prayer. Unanswered prayer, he observed, produced different effects in different sorts of people: "In some, a delay produces increase of pious desire and of fervency in petition. In others, a gradual relaxation of the pious desire and omission of the request. The one betokens an approaching reward; the other gives promise of final failure." The key for Christians, Dabney claimed, was to learn the secret of "prevalent prayer." For prayer to succeed with God, "it is not requisite that it be formal, well-expressed, or long." Rather, what was required was "a most sincere and a truly fervent desire for the thing asked," "a distinct, rational apprehension of Jesus Christ, as the one appointed mediator and approach to him as such with true faith on him," "a most hearty humility and sense of unworthiness," and "a perseverance in spite of delays of an answer." Dabney applied this sermon to those parents who had children who were "grievously vexed with sensual and devilish lusts." He urged them to continue to pray to God for the desired benefit:

> Go to him. Say, have mercy on me, O Lord, thou Son of David. Does he answer you not a word? "Cry after him." Does he seem to neglect you? Fall at his feet and worship him and cry, "Lord help me." Does he tell you, "It is not meet to take the children's bread, and to cast it to dogs"? Does he say you are unworthy? "Truth, Lord." You have set this child so bad an example that you have no right to expect anything but its ruin? "Truth, Lord." Your prayers are unworthy in motive and kind? "Truth, Lord." Your faith is weak and wavering? "Truth, Lord." Admit all, and tell that such is the glory of the Savior's righteousness, the vilest are so suitable objects of the mercy it purchase as any. "I am a dog, but it was just for dogs, that the crumbs of pardoning mercy are made." Therefore, I ask as a dog. [29]

In June 1852, Dabney took up the topic of assurance of faith. Preaching from Romans 8:16, he sought to debunk "the fanatical and arrogant notion of those who believe that on hearing the 'experience' of another they can pronounce on his new birth." Dabney urged against such fanaticism that "we may not know with absolute certainty, but may have reasonable assurance concerning piety of others. What the meaning then of the examination before church sessions?" Still, it was the Christian's duty to gain a genuine assurance of faith or the "witness of the Spirit." Dabney first argued that the witness of the Spirit did "not consist in a revelation directly from God to the soul," nor was it "immediate power communicated to a young convert of recognizing his own feelings as certainly regenerate feelings." Instead, the witness of the Spirit, according to Dabney, was a combination of evidences: Christian conduct coupled together with "the comparison of the feelings of our hearts with those imputed to the saints in Sacred Scripture." Indeed, he stated that "we are to lay the Bible character and conduct along side of our own and seek the Holy Ghost to shine on them, to enable us to conclude aright." Necessarily, then, assurance took some length of time to gain. Dabney believed that "the young convert has no right to certainty in first moments" of salvation. "Hope may be his; and this hope, the trembling, full of glory."[30]

Dabney's preaching also focused on contemporary issues and ecclesiastical problems. For example, he preached two different sermons on temperance from Genesis 4:9. In the sermon that he first preached at Tinkling Spring in 1852, Dabney argued that Christians had an "obligation on us to promote and protect the virtue and moral character of our brother." This was proved from a variety of sources, particularly from the nature of virtue itself, "a disinterested and spontaneous love of the good or the hatred for the evil for their own intrinsic qualities." Because Christians had a responsibility to seek the salvation of their neighbors, they ought to be involved in temperance reform in order to stamp out the "giant mischief" of drunkenness. Dabney held that drunkenness was a "heinous sin" that led one to "indulgence" and led others to sin by an unholy example. Likewise, manufacturing intoxicating drink was "unscriptural." And because drunkenness was such a plague in local society, temperance associations were worthy vehicles, having "done great good and are to be approved under safe limits."[31]

Moreover, Dabney focused his auditors on the biblical perspective on human governments in a sermon he preached on Independence Day 1852. While human beings must live under some orderly government by divine appointment, Dabney held, no particular form of government or manner of selecting leaders was established by divine law. Still, Christians had to act their part as faithful citizens in whatever society in which they lived. In nineteenth-century America, Christians had a responsibility given them by God to "choose able men, not only men of mental ability; it means men of stability." And in order to have stability of character, elected leaders "must be such as fear God." That did not mean that American Christians should pay heed to denominational adherence in electing their political candidates; to do so would be "hateful." Rather, it was merely required "that rulers shall be men believing in God and future rewards, responsibilities, etc., and sincere friends to social institutions of Christianity." These beliefs were vital, for "religion [is the] only secure foundation for morals." Christians had to elect religious men, not only to protect the society's morals, but also to ensure that the church's work would not be violated or overthrown. Dabney urged his congregation, "Vote for no man, for any place, who is not the friend of religion[; this] should be [an] absolute rule." If a candidate was a friend of religion, then he would be a man "of moral honesty, integrity, and truth." Strict integrity must be required in politicians "because there is an almost universal looseness of conscience about public money and public interests." Again, the importance of public example was key: "High station gives to example whether good or bad, double power. Seen further, afterward to be imitated, when seen. These public vices corrupt morals of the whole community. Fountains of corrupt principles, which send down poisonous streams." Such a view was consonant with Dabney's firm conviction, expressed later, that "influence descends" and that "God has made a social sub-soil to the topsoil." Since politicians and ministers were at the top of God's social order, it was imperative to have honest men in those positions.[32]

Dabney also preached sermons that sought to promote education within Presbyterian circles. Early in 1851, the Synod of Virginia urged the churches to set aside a day for prayer for Presbyterian colleges, and Dabney took a Thursday to preach to his congregation about the need to provide for the education of their children in order to raise up ministers. Dabney held up the pressing need for ministers within the synod and the neighboring North Carolina Synod. The only solution to this problem was through education, revival, and prayer. But "Christian mothers can do much" as well. Dabney urged them to "teach the child to look upon itself as consecrated to God . . . In childhood instructing him; in youth wrestling for his conversion; then toiling to pay expenses for education; then in gray hairs hearing him preach; then in heaven, beholding him receiving his crown with many jewels." Toward the end of 1851, the synod appointed another day for prayer and fasting in order to ask God for more ministers. Preaching from 1 Samuel 1:27–28, Dabney urged his congregation to consecrate their male children to the ministry. Dabney claimed that in order to produce young men who desired to enter the ministry, parents should have "a distinct, practical purpose . . . to rear each child, not to be a respectable and pious citizen merely (after the world's pattern); not to make a fortune in the destined profession; but to rear each one as a workman to labor for souls." Parents should examine their sons to determine whether they had "natural faculties for the ministry." If so, then these young men "should be reared from the first to be ministers: but whatever may be their appointed sphere in life, they will be educated especially to be promoters of the kingdom of Christ." A son set apart for the ministry "should be made familiar with the fact that his parents have set him apart from all worldly and sinful pursuits to be a servant of God . . . He should be taught from infancy to look upon himself with mysterious awe as a consecrated thing, and on God's service, as his destiny." These young men should be taught from their earliest days to minister to their "younger brothers and companions" and to seek to promote the cause of Christ financially by setting apart "a portion of his little funds to the mission and the Bible causes." And this childhood training, Dabney urged, should then be "accompanied with all such education as will best equip him for the glorious work." After using several biblical arguments to promote this end, Dabney appealed to his auditors, urging them to "give our children to God and let us educate them for his service, and not for the world."[33]

One of Dabney's most well-known sermons promoted the cause of foreign missions. Invited by the Presbyterian Church's Board for Foreign Missions to deliver the sermon for its 1858 annual meeting, Dabney took John 4:35 as his text. Desirous to provide missionary impetus for his auditors, Dabney offered two major points. The first demonstrated that those "heathen" around the world who died without Christ would be eternally damned. Though non-Christians around the world may have their own religions, Dabney argued, they did not seek after the true God, but rather were trapped in idolatry and superstition. These "infidel schemes" did not provide an atonement adequate to meet the need of human sinfulness and could not produce the "great want of the human soul, moral renovation"; nor could they offer the divine grace necessary to overcome native depravity. Men and women who were "slaves" to this false teaching were "perishing forever" and desperately needed to have the gospel preached to them:

for "while we sit here deliberating in cold debate, somewhere in this field of death every second of time marks the dying gasp of a human being! Hark to the fatal beat!" In divine providence, however, the mid-nineteenth century was the most propitious age since the beginning of the church for the preaching of the gospel in foreign lands. Human ingenuity, evidenced in new forms of mass communication, the decline of universal monarchies, the rise of English as a *lingua franca*, and the relaxation of hindrances in Roman Catholic and Muslim lands, pointed to that age as the best opportunity since the first century for the advancement of the gospel. Christians must seize this opportunity, Dabney proclaimed, for "if we waste this summer which seems at length returning, after so long a winter, so tedious a spring, and so many capricious frosts blighting the rising promise of the church, when will the third harvest for the world return?" Dabney's sermon drew high praise from at least one quarter: John Broadus, soon-to-be professor of New Testament and homiletics at Southern Baptist Theological Seminary, claimed that it was "one of the most powerful sermons with which he was acquainted."[34]

As a professional minister, Dabney was called on to preach at funerals. Early in his ministry at Tinkling Spring, he preached a funeral sermon for a Mrs. McComb Sr. from Matthew 6:19–21. He opened the sermon by observing that "I am never in the habit of saying much about the dead [for] two reasons. [First,] the dead person himself if he could speak from the other world would deprecate it . . . [Second,] I am not willing to propose the best saint to you as an absolute model." This declaimer was fairly standard fare in a Dabney funeral sermon. He would then move to "improve this occasion to cultivate true heavenly-mindedness, which we trust she tried to cultivate. Let us, not merely imitate her and be satisfied to do only as well as she, but let us, relatives, brethren, neighbors, try to obey the command she tried to obey and lay up treasure in heaven." Later in his ministry, when he served as co-pastor at College Church in Hampden-Sydney, Virginia, Dabney preached a funeral sermon from Genesis chapters 43 to 46. He observed that this text was appropriate for "the commemorations of the death of A. W. P. [for his] resemblance in these filial virtues." And yet, after a brief observation regarding this young man's life, Dabney turned his attention to "urging the value of the filial virtues on the young Christian." Dabney's pre-eminent funeral sermons were those he preached during the Civil War; of these, none was more famous than his 1863 memorial sermon for Stonewall Jackson entitled "True Courage."[35]

In terms, then, of his responsibility to preach the Word of God week by week as a professional minister, Dabney succeeded. In fact, his reputation as a preacher was quite high in the decade before the Civil War and earned him an invitation to succeed James W. Alexander as pastor at Fifth Avenue Presbyterian Church in New York City. In later years, Dabney's reputation as a preacher suffered a bit in comparison to the popular Presbyterian ministers of the age, particularly B. M. Palmer and Moses Hoge. He did not write many new sermons while he was co-pastor of College Church, and those he did write were often geared toward seminary students for chapel services and homiletic exercises. His great opportunity to impress his Presbyterian "fathers and brothers" as a preacher, when he retired as moderator of the Southern Presbyterian General Assembly in 1871, was used instead to lambaste the Northern Presbyterians' "broad churchism." In addition, after the war, the style of preaching in the Southern Presbyterian church moved away from doctrinally heavy sermons to a more "practical style," rendering Dabney's sermonic approach passé. Still, during his years in Tinkling Spring, Dabney was accounted a man to be reckoned with in the pulpit—zealous, didactic, and powerful in proclaiming the gospel of Christ.[36]

Dabney as Prospect

As his reputation grew within the Synod of Virginia, Dabney was soon offered positions of significance. One of his more important positions was as an elector for Union Theological Seminary. Upon the death of Samuel Graham in 1851, the directors and electors gathered the following May to select a replacement. As Dabney contemplated the approaching meeting, he confessed to his brother that he felt as though he was in a difficult position. The leading candidate, as far as he was concerned, was his brother-in-law, B. M. Smith, and Dabney felt the weight of difficulties with regard to Smith. On the one hand, Dabney wrote that "if I vote against him, it will be unpleasant, and though he is not fool enough nor anxious enough for the place to feel it, other people will imagine a thousand causes why a man should vote against a near connexion." On the other hand, "if I vote for him there will be another class who will say it is because of the connexion, and will revive the charge of an ecclesiastical family clique." Adding to these difficulties, however, was the more fundamental problem that Dabney did not believe Smith to be suited for the role of seminary professor. "I doubt if he is the man to conduct the highest branches of education for a profession such as ours," Dabney observed. "He lacks prudence and dignity. His speaking and writing are too flippant and his mind too hasty and confident. He is very ready and acute and if he had been rightly educated and rightly trained to permanent habits of thinking, his mind would have been very discriminating. But he is prone to take a snap judgment on a subject. When he has thus made up his mind, he will defend his ground very acutely and plausibly, often with very plausible sophistry, but he is as apt to be wrong as right." In the end, though, Dabney confessed that "Smith, with all the objections to him, will be the best of a bad choice."[37]

A surprising thing happened at the meeting, however. Among the electors, a movement began to elect R. J. Breckinridge, well-known minister and theologian from Kentucky, to the position. Dabney believed that these electors knew that Breckinridge would not accept, but that it was only "a ruse to delay the election of Smith, to whom they were opposed." Though Dabney did not have the objections to Breckinridge that he would develop a few years hence, still he believed the entire election to be a "farce." Dabney voted for Smith, who lost the election to Breckinridge by one vote. In the end, Breckinridge declined the proffered position, and the following year began Danville Seminary in Kentucky. After this meeting, Dabney began to position himself for the faculty opening.[38]

In July 1852, Dabney wrote a lengthy article for the *Watchman and Observer* on Union Seminary and theological education. In the article, entitled "The State and Claims of Union Theological Seminary," Dabney argued that the seminary deserved the support of Virginia Presbyterians for several important reasons. First, he held that Union Seminary was committed to simple theological education, rather than "literary novelties." Union Seminary's faculty was committed to "the interpretation of the Word, and the preaching of the body of divinity" as "their main, their every day work." Because this was the case, presbyteries could trust that students attending Union would have "the foundation of a good drilling in the old-fashioned, customary branches of theology." For accomplishing this work, Dabney held that Union Seminary's moderate size was a blessing and not a curse. Further, he argued that Union Seminary was vital for creating a supply of students "training in our own limits" who would satisfy "our own home destitution." As national issues began to create an intellectual demarcation between the North and the South, the necessity of a home education was increased. Indeed, he held that "the man educated at home, amidst the men with whom he is to act, the modes of thought and feeling he is to meet, the institutions he is to live under, has a double chance for success." Finally, Dabney believed that Union Seminary was a necessary bulwark against the concentration of power in a single institution, such as Princeton Theological Seminary. "Suppose such an institution [were] training all or nearly all the ministers of our church, and consequently becoming the fountain of literary and theological opinion for the whole church," Dabney wrote. "The result would be most un-Presbyterian and dangerous, even while this school remained orthodox." And if this school were to begin to teach heresy, such an institution "might spread its poison unresisted through the whole body." Hence, Union Seminary was vitally necessary and deserved the support of the Synods of Virginia and North Carolina.[39]

This article drew wide praise and notice throughout the synod. Soon, Dabney's friend Moses Hoge, the prominent minister of Second Presbyterian Church, Richmond, Virginia, began strategizing to bring Dabney to the seminary. Hoge, as one of the seminary directors, had spent a great deal of time thinking about the school. He believed that what was necessary was for the seminary's electoral college to "select some young man of promise, or at least some man in the very prime of life, for the chair of church history." That could be no one other than Dabney himself. Then Hoge asked, "But will such a man accept?

Can one be found willing to stake his reputation and prospects of future usefulness on the fortune of an institution, which in the opinion of the public can never flourish, while Dr. Wilson remains in the theological chair?" Hoge's plan was to elect two professors, one to assist Wilson in theology and the other to teach church history. These professors would then spend a great deal of time "in the saddle," taking the cause of the seminary throughout Virginia and North Carolina. Such a plan would attract solid talent to the seminary faculty, such as Dabney himself, and would revive interest in the seminary throughout the synods.[40]

Though Dabney later claimed that he "was not a candidate, did not desire it, and knew nothing of the movement" to elect him to the chair of church history and government, that claim appeared to be disingenuous. As Hoge himself admitted in May 1853, he had "done so much toward getting you to go to Union Seminary," both behind the scenes with the directors and with Dabney himself. Likewise, Dabney confided to his brother in April 1853 that "there is a possibility of my never living in my new house much, after all. The prospect of my removal is now exceedingly uncertain." Yet Dabney's later assessment of his election was probably correct: "I was 33 years old, as a dernier and almost desperate resort, as none of the big Yankees would condescend to take it." When the electors met for their 1853 meeting, they unanimously elected Dabney to the chair of church history, seeing him as an alternative to the less popular Smith. Dabney received the news in his cornfield, "with my hired negro replanting corn. My wife sent a boy to call me; he called saying Mrs. D says come to the house: who do you suppose is elected professor at U.T.S.? Who? She says you are. In much astonishment I went to the house when she gave me an official letter." While Dabney made a great show that he was in "perplexity" and desired to remain at Tinkling Spring, his language smacked more of strained disinterestedness, an attempt not to appear ambitious and overreaching. For Dabney had purposefully placed himself as the most available and best-educated potential faculty member, and had worked with Hoge to gain the position for which he was truly fitted.[41]

While Dabney gave the seminary's offer due consideration, not wanting to rush to judgment and appear too ambitious, he entertained letters from his friends, urging him to take the position. In particular, he heard from his friend William White, minister in Lexington, Virginia, who claimed that "I regard the position to which you are invited as more important than any pastoral charge in the land. And I am free to say that your habits, tastes, and general qualifications fit you for the station." Finally, toward the end of May, Dabney decided to go to the seminary. He notified his brother Charles William, saying, "I found that I could not see my way clear to refuse and this led me to conclude that I had better accept at once . . . Ever since the die has been finally cast, I have felt perfectly cool about it and have not been visited with that repentance you foretold." Dabney told his congregation after he had made up his mind, and "they took it in very good part, and as my friends tell me, there is not a man in the congregation who is angry, though some appear to be really grieved." When the presbytery agreed to dissolve his pastoral relation with Tinkling Spring, they adopted a minute for their records that memorialized Dabney's pastorate in words that had to be pleasing to him:

> They sympathize deeply with the church in being deprived of a pastor beloved in no ordinary degree, and whose ministry had been so universally acceptable, and so blessed of God, and which promised, under the smiles of the Head of the church, to be still more abundantly useful . . . The Presbytery would also express the pain they experience in parting with this beloved brother, and faithful fellow laborer in the vineyard, who had endeared himself to them in no ordinary degree.[42]

This was the final piece of comforting evidence, as if he needed more, that Dabney had achieved his goals in Tinkling Spring. He had arrived at the church untested and uncertain that he could manage a congregation so large. He left with words of affectionate regard ringing in his ears. And throughout this time, Dabney had conducted himself as a professional minister should—leading a revival and a church-building program, guiding his session through difficult church discipline cases, overseeing a school, visiting his members, and above all preaching high-quality sermons each Lord's Day. Also during this time, Dabney established his own household, over which he would serve as master, with a wife, two sons, and slaves. He had bought and sold property and had begun to gain real wealth. Over time, the Tinkling Spring pastorate would be viewed by Dabney as a kind of "golden era"—his first pastoral charge and a group of people for whom he felt real affection. Yet Dabney's ultimate goal was to achieve a position of prominence within his fast-growing denomination, to be a "gentleman theologian" in a denomination that prized gentility and theology. The call to Union Seminary meant one thing: at thirty-three, his life was just beginning.

3

Professor

*D*abney arrived on the scene at Union Seminary to find a school that was nearly defunct. Only eleven students had enrolled the previous term. Morale was so low that fellow professor and mentor Francis Sampson told Dabney that "if the stream did not turn, he should in 1854 quit the seminary forever." But Dabney and Moses Hoge had a plan to revive the seminary. After Dabney was elected as a professor, he could conduct lengthy fund-raising and recruitment tours for the seminary in Virginia and North Carolina. Hoge was confident that these tours would "strengthen every interest of our church" as well as increase the reputation of the seminary. Dabney would devote several summers to fund raising and recruitment in the seven years before the Civil War. He summed up his labors during these years by observing:

> I studied and taught my department with great vigor; made laborious tours every vacation, at my own expense, one year (1855) as a collector for the additional endowment, raising just $3000, the other years visiting churches, colleges, and universities, preaching, making our Seminary known and canvassing for the right sort of students . . . It is no boast to say that the revival of the seminary's influence under these circumstances was chiefly my work.[1]

Dabney's initial position at the seminary was professor of ecclesiastical history and polity. His course, in good Reformed fashion, took up the history of God's people from Old Testament times to contemporary days. As a result, not only did Dabney use the Old and New Testaments as texts, but his main text was Johann Mosheim's *Institutes of Ecclesiastical History*, supplemented by several other books, including the old standards, Humphrey Prideaux's *The Old and New Testament Connected* and Archibald Alexander's *A History of the Israelitish Nation*. Dabney believed that Mosheim was, "on the whole, about the best class book. Heavy, objectionable on many grounds, but yet learned and weighty, and introducing the student to the wide literature of the subject." For church polity, Dabney mainly developed his own material, supplemented by Francis Turretin's *Institutes of Elenctic Theology* and John M. Mason's *Essays on the Church of God*. In Dabney's lectures, the first half of the course was devoted to church history, tracing the development of the church and its doctrine through the ages, while the second half focused on church polity issues. There was little original in the material for either history or polity—the former was as much a course about the history of doctrine as about church history, while the latter was mainly a vindication of Presbyterian polity against independent and, especially, prelatic forms of church government. Though Dabney's lectures were not original, they were very well received. His friend C. R. Vaughan urged him to "never listen to any proposition to change your present position, either for a church or another chair. Write a Church history. This, in my judgment, is your work." Another friend, William H. Foote, reported, "I understand that your labors are very acceptable; that your lectures are listened to with deep interest, and that your example of study and investigation is impressing the students favorably, both as to yourself and as to their personal duties."[2]

Perhaps the most original statement in the lectures was Dabney's moderation on the controversial topic of *jure divino* (divine law) Presbyterianism. During the 1850s, the Old School Presbyterians were convulsed by a series of debates between Charles Hodge, the Northern doyen, and James Henley Thornwell, the Southern dynamo, on whether Scripture explicitly revealed the form of church government that Christ as King over his church required, particularly as it related to matters of church boards and ruling elders. While Hodge accused Thornwell of espousing a "hyper-hyper-hyper High-Church Presbyterianism," and Thornwell disputed whether Hodge's position was even Presbyterian, Dabney consistently walked a middle way between the two.[3] For example, in his lectures on church government, Dabney asked whether any form of church government was *jure divino*. In reply, Dabney distinguished two senses in which the claim to divine law for church order could be made. On the one hand, it could stand for the idea

> that the Bible contains guiding principles for Church government of inspired authority, that it is the duty of all visible churches to follow these principles, and that those churches who follow them are more after the divine mind and more adapted to man's true good, but yet those that follow them not are not thereby unchurched, but may be yet true though erring visible churches.

This point Dabney affirmed. On the other hand, divine law could mean "that a form of visible church government is so laid down in Sacred Scripture by inspired authority that those who do not apply are no visible churches." This Dabney flatly denied for several reasons. First, he pointed out that no denomination could claim more than a part of its government from the Bible. Because this was the case, the movements away from Scripture were ones of "policy and utility how far these additions may be carried." Second, Dabney noted that Scripture itself never makes the claim for church order set down by divine fiat. In addition, Dabney argued that such a divine law would "exalt the external form above a part of gospel truth." Church order would thus become "essential to salvation," which is contradicted by the spirit of the gospel itself. Next, Dabney held that a church might produce good spiritual fruit even though its government departed from the revealed form, namely, Presbyterianism. In particular, he held up the Episcopalians, Methodists, and Moravians as examples of those God had used though they practiced erroneous church order. Finally, Dabney recognized that "to be consistent in this dogma, we should have to

refuse all communion in the ordinances of all churches having different forms from ours, rebaptize their members, and reordain their ministers." There was a definite outline of church order contained in Scripture, which was Presbyterianism, but it was not so required as to
excommunicate those who were not Presbyterian.[4]

Dabney used this logic when he jumped into the debate over ruling elders in an essay published in the *North Carolina Presbyterian* in
the fall of 1860. Against those who argued that the office of ruling
elder was merely an appointed office that may or may not exist in the
church, Dabney argued that the office of ruling elder was explicitly
revealed in the definite outline of church order contained in Scripture.
This definite outline in Scripture pictured a church that had two
offices—elder and deacon—and two orders in the office of elder—
preaching elder and ruling elder. In fact, Dabney held that preachers
were only presbyters, not because they preached, but because they
ruled. If ruling elders were, in fact, a human invention, something that
the church thought was a good idea, then the church should simply
abolish the office as a "human invention," for "it is rebellion against
our Master's better wisdom to introduce so fundamental a modification of his institutions." While Dabney would not "push the notion
of a divine warrant to extremes," he did believe that the office of ruling elder was part of the revealed church order and, as such, should
be maintained within the church.[5]

Dabney was not only involved in teaching and fund-raising during these years. He was also stamping out rumors and innuendos that
threatened to affect the seminary's revival. After the death of his colleague Francis Sampson in 1854, Dabney's brother-in-law, B. M. Smith,
was elected to the chair of Oriental literature. During these early years,
Smith struggled to match the reputation and eloquence of his prede-
cessor. Toward the end of his first year of teaching, the students began
to murmur to such a degree about Smith's pedagogy that the noise
eventually reached Moses Hoge, who wrote to Dabney to inquire about
the matter. Hoge reported in a letter marked "confidential" that he
had heard that "the University students, especially, regard Mr. Smith
as incompetent to instruct, especially in Greek, and that they intended
to leave Union Seminary and go to Danville." The students also com-

plained that "Mr. Smith would commence a rambling, scattering lecture at 11 o'clock, and keep on until one of the students would slip out and ring the bell for dinner." Hoge urged Dabney to write in "entire frankness" in order to calm his disturbed spirit about this apparent unrest at the seminary. Dabney immediately replied that he had heard something of the matter. The complaints were that Smith was pushing the first-year students too fast, "that the lessons were so long, they had little time for anything but constructing the text," and that Smith was not giving the students any exegesis. Dabney warned Hoge to do what he could to squash the rumors, because "from what I have seen of Smith's temper and feelings about his seminary connexion, I should think that such reports, if they reached his ears, would produce his immediate resignation." Eventually the rumors died down, and the seminary began to grow slowly until the Civil War.[6]

On Theological Education

As a result of his long-standing involvement in theological education, Dabney expended a great deal of thought on its nature. Even before he went to Union Seminary, but particularly during his thirty-year tenure there, Dabney repeatedly defended the Presbyterian ideal of an educated ministry. He believed that a common theological education was vital for the church to maintain its doctrinal and cultural unity. He warned that if the church admitted poorly trained ministers into leadership, Presbyterians would "lose our doctrinal unity." The church would become a "broad-church," just like Baptists and Methodists—Calvinism and Arminianism, as well as other discordant doctrines, would be proclaimed from the same pulpit, and the rich heritage of the Reformed faith would be lost. It was obvious to Dabney that those pastors who lacked seminary training would entail "a considerable (comparative) liability to partial error, mistakes, and injury of the church and of souls." One proof of this inherent liability was "the great apostasy of prelacy and popery," which "was wrought precisely on that plan of a partially educated ministry." If Presbyterians wanted to send a mixed doctrinal message or to slide off into popish heresy, then they only had to loosen the requirements for ministerial training. "The only human way to avoid the tendencies to 'broad churchism,' " Dabney claimed, was strict Presbyterian theological education, the imbibing of "the Presbyterian and orthodox idiosyncrasy of mind." Only as "doctrinal affinity in the correct creed is propagated through the whole body" would the Presbyterian church be safe.[7]

Dabney was also concerned to maintain a cultural unity through a common theological education. He had long promoted Southern education for Southern ministers to serve Southern pulpits. Though some Southerners longed for a Northern education, Dabney claimed that this desire "deserves no more respectful treatment, than the notion of the foolish Miss, that a fashion must be pretty because it comes from Paris." Observation of the other professions forced Dabney to conclude that "the most solid success has usually been realized from the efforts of the native born and home-educated talent." The minister trained at home "amidst the men with whom he is to act, the modes of thought and feeling he is to meet, the institutions he is to live under, has a double chance for success." By contrast, those who went north to train at Princeton Seminary rarely came back home. The Southern church ought not to send her ministerial candidates away to Princeton, Dabney held, nor should she expect any help from any of the Northern seminaries. Rather, theological education for Southern pulpits ought to be done in the South.[8]

Imbibing the nascent professional ideal of the nineteenth century, Dabney defined the Presbyterian ministry as a professional task on a level with medicine and law. Dabney believed that there was "a close analogy between the professional preparation of the lawyer and the theologian. Both courses of study are special and professional," essentially graduate programs pursued after a general collegiate education. Further, in order to reach the higher classes, Presbyterian ministers had to be cultured and educated; and the seminary course produced "as highly educated a man as any M. A. of any University." Dabney confessed that the minister "may not have gone so deeply as that M. A. into the niceties of Latin, philosophy and prosody, or the shadowy regions of the calculus." Theological education, however, provided the minister with "a far nobler and broader culture" than that received by the university graduate. Presbyterian ministers should not embrace a lower standard of professional training than lawyers or doctors. "Society is steadily demanding a raised standard of preparation from lawyers and physicians," Dabney claimed, "The other professions are advancing largely; it is no time for ours to go back." The plain minister who was merely "well acquainted with his English Bible" was not sufficient to reach the professional classes. "Our world is also full of authors, legislators, lawyers, physicians, scientists, historians, antiquaries, philosophers, all equipped with the resources of learning," Dabney observed. If the Presbyterian minister was to accomplish his "missionary duty," he had to be as well equipped as the group he sought to reach. "The strength, usefulness, and respectability of the Presbyterian Church are chiefly due under God to her standard of education in her ministry," he believed.[9]

In addition, Presbyterian ministers, in order to serve the professional classes, generally had to come from the higher classes. Dabney claimed that the quality of Northern ministry had "deteriorated" because "so many persons of lower breeding and mercenary views" had been admitted. By contrast, in the South, Presbyterian ministers "must be gentlemen in bearing and principle." While this necessity did not shut the door on those in the "lower classes," it did mean that such men labored under a disadvantage and those received into the ministry would be of "innate nobility," raising "themselves by an invincible energy to the grade they deserve." By demonstrating self-discipline and energy in self-improvement, those few ministers who ascended from lower classes demonstrated that they belonged with and could minister to their social superiors.[10]

After the Civil War, Dabney sensed that theological education was struggling to accomplish its task. As a result, he urged several reforms in order to revise Presbyterian theological education, summarized in a "Memorial on Theological Education." This memorial appeared first as a series of articles in *Central Presbyterian* in 1866, and then was revised and presented to the General Assembly in 1869. Dabney's memorial opened with a proposed reform that sought to rectify problems with the theological curriculum and seminary structure. For example, he complained about the "multiplication of courses and professors in some of our theological seminaries." With the adoption of the

German model of higher education, specialization plagued the theological seminary. "Seminary education is expanded upon the surface; but it becomes correspondingly superficial," Dabney observed. The result was that, rather than drilling students in basic theological knowledge and the original languages, students gained "an ostentatious smattering of many specialties, with a temper more conceited and less humble and manly, without any deep acquaintance with the great masters of theological thought of previous generations and the great problems of theological science." The multiplication of courses meant that less time could be devoted to core courses, both in teaching and in studying the material. Rather than recitations, the courses were reduced to lectures that provided "a comprehensive, but brief course of lectures upon the heads of divinity." The result was that "the candidates in the seminaries . . . are likely to receive some weak, homeopathic dilution" of the theological *loci*. Likewise, the multiplication of faculty members meant that distinction would come by innovation and, eventually, heretical teaching. In the same way that German universities became unfaithful through the "over-specializing of studies and this demand upon their teachers to 'do new work,' " so theological education in America could travel the same path toward unfaithfulness.[11]

The chief example of specialization, to Dabney, was the trend toward including physical science as part of the theological curriculum. In 1866, Dabney was particularly concerned about the newly created Perkins Professorship of Natural Science in Connexion with Revelation at Columbia Theological Seminary. Dabney argued against science as part of the theological curriculum for three reasons. First, scientific instruction as part of theological education would be too shallow to be profitable. Next, a course of scientific instruction within theological education would prove "mischievous" to the entire seminary community. Not only would such instruction pander to the pride of theological novices, but it might provide a conduit for theological deviation to enter the seminary. Finally, Dabney believed that the nature of the relationship between science and theology was a disputed matter that was not covered by the Westminster Standards. As a result, specialized scientific training ought not to be an independent part of the church's theological education.[12]

Instead of the new and novel, Dabney promoted a simplified Presbyterian theological education. What theological students needed, he believed, was "three or four able and faithful professors, enough good books for practical use, and thorough-going sources of deep reading, strict recitation, frequent writing, and well-considered lectures upon the leading lines of sacred science." After the basic theological knowledge had been acquired, then would be the time for specialization. One way that Dabney hoped to accomplish the task of theological education was to restructure the seminary into three separate schools—theology; ecclesiology and church history; and biblical literature, covering both Old and New Testaments. Each professor would conduct a separate school, responsible directly to the board of directors and not to the other professors. Students, in turn, would "be allowed to take such schools as they find convenient, under judicious advice, and consume as much or as little time in completing their studies as they need." There would be no central curriculum; rather, each professor would make his course "so rich that no mortal, whatever his preparation or talent, could complete it in less than two years." Such a plan would give students flexibility in planning their theological education, allow students to take courses from different seminaries based on superior teaching, and provide students with "the very best education in the least time, by taking in each seminary only those schools which are most approved." In addition, Dabney believed his plan would allow for closer examination of the students by the professor in charge, rather than by the board of directors or some other outside party. Such a plan also meant that it was not possible to follow the trend toward including "practical training in parochial duties" in theological education, which Dabney deemed "a failure." He thought that seminary training should be restricted to intellectual labor and "thorough mental culture." If ministers were to gain pastoral skills, such training would have to occur "under the pressure of pastoral responsibilities," not in the seminary classroom.[13]

Presbytery exams for ordination were a second area that Dabney believed to be ripe for reform. He complained that presbyteries were not doing their jobs in examining licentiates for ministry. Rather than grilling potential ministers in the areas demanded by the Book of

Church Order, presbyteries assumed that a seminary certificate was a sufficient sign of acquired knowledge. The presbytery examinations then became "a merely decent form, instead of an actual and thorough test of attainments." This, Dabney argued, made the seminary faculty the de facto presbytery, displacing the actual presbytery from which the licentiate came. It was painfully obvious that not everyone who completed the seminary course was necessarily fit to be a Presbyterian minister. Yet unfit men were being admitted into ministry by overindulgent presbyteries. "It is wholly forgotten," Dabney charged, "that we are a religious Commonwealth, governed by a written constitution, and that every Presbyter is sworn to execute that constitution with exactness; that a certain grade of scholarship is there required; and if this requisition is found impolitic and unwise, the only proper, the only honest course is, to seek first an amendment of the constitution." The presbytery had to tighten up its examinations in order to ensure that the constitutional standard was met.[14]

Presbyteries were also abusing the clause in the constitution that allowed them, in "extraordinary cases," to ordain men who did not have the requisite educational background. Dabney claimed that the fathers of the church had intended by "extraordinary case" to refer to a "candidate who possesses the extraordinary intellectual and spiritual qualifications, acquired in a secular career, [who] is allowed to stand his examination, and if qualified, to receive immediate licensure, without being required to study divinity two whole years under some approved divine." But the presbytery was still required "to examine him upon all the studies which are required of inferior and younger students." What was occurring in some presbyteries was far from this practice; the result was that "the credit of our ministry" was being lowered. "The door into our ministry is already made too wide," Dabney complained. Presbyteries ought to narrow the doorway into the ministry so that the church's ministry might be filled by the best-equipped and highest-quality men.[15]

Dabney's solution to the problem of relating the seminary to the presbytery was for the theological seminaries to serve as "the teaching agent of the Presbytery to train its candidates." The presbytery, by contrast, was "the master, the judge, the father of all candidates for the ministry, whether licensed or unlicensed." The seminary as the agent ought not to usurp the responsibility of the master; rather, seminary faculties ought to be entrusted with keeping "accurate records of each student's diligence in study, in equitation, and in attention to the ordinances of religion." The seminaries would simply pass this information on to the presbyteries. "Let it give no diploma," Dabney held. "Let it pass no decree of rejection on any." The presbytery was the church court that was entrusted with the approval or disapproval of ministerial candidates. Because this was the case, Dabney entreated, the presbytery ought to make its exams thorough and set the standard high. "Let us elevate the terms of admission," he believed, "and we shall see more men of elevated character seeking the sacred office." If presbyteries would simply do their constitutionally assigned task of strict ministerial examination, then the problem of the paucity of ministers would be reversed. The honest ambition of righteous men would be fired to enter the ministry because it would be viewed as a holy and difficult honor to gain.[16]

A third reform of theological education that Dabney desired was for the Presbyterian General Assembly to cede the management of all the church's seminaries to the synods geographically connected to them while retaining general oversight and a final veto over synodical action. After the Civil War, the directors of Columbia Seminary attempted to transfer control of that seminary to the General Assembly of the Presbyterian Church in the United States, which in effect would have made Columbia the "national" seminary of the Southern church. Dabney opposed Columbia's action, not only because it created difficulties for his own Union Seminary, but also because it was "virtually a revolution of the principles of the whole church on this question." Before the division of the Old School church in 1861, both Union and Columbia had been under synodical control—Union overseen by Virginia and North Carolina, Columbia by South Carolina, Georgia, and Alabama. If Columbia were to come under the control of the Assembly, Union would be forced to do the same or else to compete with its sister institution on an uneven playing field. Better to emphasize local control, Dabney counseled, so that each seminary would be supported and governed by local ministers and churches.[17]

The multiplication of seminaries under local synodical control would also assist in preserving the church's orthodoxy. Dabney argued that "whenever the course of events shall elevate any of our seminaries into a dangerous centralizing institution, we shall be the enemies of that centralization." In particular, Dabney warned that Princeton Seminary, as the former national seminary for Presbyterians, could become once again "the central and dangerous institution." Dabney feared that a central institution could become heterodox, which would result "in corrupting the opinions of its ministry." While heresy at Princeton seemed preposterous because it was "the very flagship of Calvinism, the prime enemy of heretics," yet Dabney warned that the endowments and professional attractiveness of that seminary would entice those motivated by "unsanctified ambition." By maintaining multiple small institutions with limited faculties, Dabney believed that orthodoxy would be maintained and ambitious heretics checked.[18]

Dabney's Intellectual World

Of course, the best educational structure in the world would not solve the problem of orthodoxy unless the seminaries themselves were sound. And the way to ensure the soundness of the schools was to promote sound men to the most important chair: didactic and polemic theology. In 1859, the trustees made Dabney the adjunct to Samuel Wilson, having him bear the entire teaching load for the theology department. Dabney remained the nominal subordinate until Wilson's death in 1869. But everyone knew that Dabney was the prominent man in the department and that he was in the intellectual sphere where he belonged. Students were in awe of Dabney's depth of learning and thoroughness of teaching. "Dr. Dabney is a colossus, an intellectual giant and impresses you with the idea that he is of prodigious strength at the first meeting," one student wrote home. But they also appreciated Dabney's kindliness as a teacher. In a reminiscence written by Peyton Hoge in 1890, he noted that "there could never have been any teacher more considerate to ignorance, more patient with dullness, more kindly in correction, and more gentle in reproof, than was this great man." In a similar manner, W. S. Lacy claimed that "for clear views of truth, considerations more or less positive, and a system of theological belief, robust, reasonable, and warm with life, I am altogether indebted" to Dabney. He was the great man whom everyone recalled from their seminary days and with whom everyone wrestled.[19]

Dabney's influence came from the way he drew his students into his intellectual world. Dabney's intellectual world was characterized by the rationality that was the keynote of nineteenth-century American theology in the South. This rationality led American theologians to emphasize a natural theology based on human reason and consciousness. Drawing from the Scottish moral philosophers—Thomas Reid, Dugald Stewart, and their successor William Hamilton—American theologians claimed that all truth was unitary. Natural and biblical revelation were "two books" that pointed to the one true God. Biblical Christianity was not threatened by scientific endeavor, but rather encouraged the investigation of God's handiwork. Natural philosophers (as physical scientists were called) shared basic principles and assumptions with moral and mental philosophers, namely, that the capstone of God's creation was humankind; therefore, human beings could look inward and find in the working of the mind the axioms by which the entire universe worked, a universe created and sustained by God. When human consciousness was carefully studied, certain intuitive or primary truths were discovered that served as the basis of all other thought and activity. The way to discover these laws or truths was through a rigid application of logical induction as taught by Lord Francis Bacon. This Baconianism was a fixture of nineteenth-century American theology and continued on in twentieth-century American evangelicalism.

The chief aspect of Dabney's realist epistemology was its rationality or orderliness. The way of knowledge was "just as regular in [its] operation" as other observable phenomena. For Dabney, the cornerstone of his theory of knowledge was the law of causation. Causation, which Dabney deemed to be "of most fundamental importance to theologians," was "the doctrine of common sense . . . When the mind sees an effect, it intuitively refers it to some cause, as producing its occurrence." Common sense also knew intuitively that there was "a power to produce" the effect. Because of the strictures of David Hume, many empiricists had doubts about causation, claiming that the mind simply drew an association, which did not actually exist, between a perceived cause and its effect. Dabney, following Thomas Reid, argued strenuously that causation was the ground of human experience, not the consequence of it. "No experience of the fact that a given antecedent had produced a given consequent so far as observed, could logically produce the conviction that it would, and must do so everywhere, and in all the future, if it were not sustained by an intuitive recognition of cause and effect in the sequence," he claimed. Though experience did not create the mental association between cause and effect, it did play a role in correcting and limiting human belief in causation. If causation were denied, science would be impossible: "It is only because our judgment of cause is a priori and intuitive, that any process of induction, practical, or scientific, can be valid or demonstrative." Dabney went so far as to confess that the law of causation was "the very key of nature."[20]

Although Dabney affirmed the great importance of causation, he hesitated to affirm strict uniformitarianism. Dabney believed that "nature is uniform just so far as the same powers are present and her uniformities are nothing but the necessary results of the permanency of substances and powers." But he asked, "Does nature, in fact, present an aspect of uniformity?" The correct answer was: "Far from it." Nature itself provided several examples of "unexpected and unintelligible" phenomena that shattered belief in uniformity. Perhaps the real reason Dabney wanted to avoid a strict uniformity of the law of causation was to provide room for supernaturalism in the form of divine intervention at creation. Thus, in his debates in the 1860s and 1870s with James Woodrow, then Perkins Professor of Natural Science in Connexion with Revelation at Columbia Theological Seminary, Dabney attacked the uniformity of natural laws and analogies from those laws to the origin of all creation. Christians who believed the biblical account of creation had to confess that God had created all things and then allowed natural laws, including causation, to begin their work.[21]

For, in fact, the law of causation was grounded in the being and providential will of God. Like Reid again, Dabney affirmed "providential naturalism"; that belief in God's providential control of all things made belief in causation and other natural laws rational. Remember that Dabney claimed that an intuitive belief in causation not only affirmed the connection between cause and effect but also asserted that there was a "power" that caused the effect. That power was God: "It is only when we assume that there is a Creator to the created, that there is an intellect and will; and that, an immutable one, establishing and governing these sequences of physical change; that the mind can find any valid basis for the expectation of law in them." God had a divine design, a "final cause," for all creation that provided the basis for confident exploration of the laws of nature in the present. Without belief in God and in God's final cause, "inductive science" had no "foundation whatever." In fact, Dabney was convinced that "the logic of the atheistic physicist is mad." A thorough-going materialist had no basis for scientific endeavor unless he was happily inconsistent with his own basic principles.[22]

Not only did a denial of God and God's final cause leave the materialist without a basis for science, but a denial of innate powers did as well. While rejecting John Locke's claim that the mind had innate ideas, Dabney argued that the mind had innate powers, "which a priori dictate certain laws of thought and sensibility, whenever we gain ideas by sensitive experience." These innate powers developed "certain abstract notions and judgments" as well as discerned which "cognitions are first, immediate intuitive, and [which are] second, derived or illative." Proper reasoning, then, traced cause and effect inductively back to "the ultimate fact, an intuition of consciousness." From that primary, intuitive truth, Dabney believed that deduction was a legitimate logical procedure in order to understand all of God's truth. The only thing necessary to convince men and women that they possessed innate powers was an honest inspection of their own consciousness.[23]

Dabney claimed that three marks of an intuitive truth distinguished it from a derived thought: intuitive truths were primary, necessary, and universal. Intuitive truths were primary because "they are not derived or inferred from any other truth, prior in order to proof to them; but are seen to be true without any dependence on a premise." Intuitive truths were also necessary; to negate these truths "would lead to a direct contradiction." Thus, an intuitive truth followed the so-called law of noncontradiction. Finally, intuitive truths were universal. All honest, "sane" men and women believed that these truths were primary: "All people that are sane, when the terms of their enunciation are comprehended with entire fairness, and dispassionately considered, are absolutely certain, the world over, to accept them as true." The fact that some human beings may reject certain truths that Dabney deemed to be primary and intuitive bothered him little. After all, human corruption and native imperfection could easily account for the inability of some to recognize certain primary truths. "Still the fact remains," he declaimed, "that there are first truths, absolutely universal in their acceptance, on which every sane mind in the world acts, and always has acted from Adam's day, with unflinching confidence." Dabney pointedly followed this by affirming, "On that fact I stand."[24]

Dabney's affirmation of intuitive truths and realist epistemology led him to insist upon "Baconian" or inductive methodology. Inductivism's "main use" was "to enable us to anticipate nature." If human beings were to exert "beneficial power" over nature, men and women had to learn nature's patterns. "To be able to produce the given effect we desire, we must know the natural law under which that effect arises," Dabney averred. Discovering the power behind a cause—the heart of inductive demonstration—was the way to gain scientific truth. The method of gaining knowledge of those natural laws was through inductive logic and analogy. The "correct definition" of inductive demonstration was always a "syllogism, whose major premise is the universal necessary judgment of cause, or some proposition implied therein." For Dabney, "the syllogism gives the norm of all reasonings." The syllogism had several permutations through which it could go in order to provide inductive demonstration. Dabney approved of five methods—agreement, difference, a combination of difference and agreement, "residues," and corresponding variations—each of which could provide an inductive proof.[25]

Inductive demonstration was not complete until the individual gave "due honor to the doctrine of final cause." Dabney held it as axiomatic that "every physical effect has also a final cause." That final cause was rooted in the divine will: "To assume that God always has some designed rational end for all his creatures and actions, this surely is not pre-sumption," Dabney exclaimed, "but only the necessary respect for his wisdom." What God's purpose actually was could not be discovered ultimately by finite human minds; to doubt that God did in fact have a purpose for all his creation, however, was to forsake "the main guide of induction." The regular laws of nature could be intuited only as a result of a prior belief in the divine power that stood behind those laws. "The doctrine of divine purpose, and that of the stability of the law of true causes, are the answering parts of one system of thought," Dab-ney held. It was no wonder that Dabney believed that the doctrine of final cause was "the meeting-point of theology, philosophy, and the inductive logic." Either one embraced belief in a final cause for all cre-ation, which was nothing less than "God's constancy to his own ends," or one was reduced to "absolute fatalism" with Herbert Spencer and Auguste Comte. There was "no other alternative."[26]

With such strong language on behalf of teleology, it is easy to under-stand why Dabney felt that the whole edifice of the Christian faith was threatened by evolution. The theory of evolution confused "the notions of fortuity and causation." By eliminating final cause from creation and substituting blind chance, evolutionists denied that creation was the function of any intelligence whatsoever. Dabney believed that if there were no divine purpose or divine personality, then the law of causation could not be a valid intuition. If causation was not valid, then a human being could not trust his or her own consciousness; there was no order in nature, but constant flux, which was random or fated by an impersonal force; science and knowledge were impossible; and life was an absurdity. Such a disordered, nihilistic vision was abhor-rent to Dabney; as a result, he repudiated any move against teleology. He even went so far as to admit that even if the theistic evolutionists' case was granted, "teleology is as apparent as ever"—there had to be a Mind that stood behind the evolutionary process. "Nature is uni-form," Dabney claimed, "neither chaotic nor fatalistic, because she is directed by a Mind, because intelligence directs her unintelligent phys-ical causes to preconceived, rational purposes . . . Nature is stable, only because the counsels of the God who uses her for his ends are sta-ble." Such a belief in divine order led Dabney to claim that "none but theists can consistently use induction," which was akin to saying that none but theists could be scientific. Only those, such as Dabney, who embraced Scottish realism and inductive methodology could hold on to belief in both God and true science.[27]

Conservator of the Old School Tradition

Dabney not only introduced his students to the rationality of Scottish realism and natural theology, but also communicated the basic divinity of Old School Presbyterianism. Indeed, he reveled in his position as a conservator of the Old School tradition. In his sermon as retiring moderator at the 1871 General Assembly, Dabney stated that "it has been the fixed principle of Presbyterianism in all its better days, that its teachers must subscribe to its honored standards in the strict sense of the system of doctrine which they embody." Thus, Dabney claimed that Southern Presbyterians stood for strict subscription to the Westminster Standards. "We think we have a 'thus saith the Lord,'" Dabney proclaimed. "We are . . . honestly convinced that every point of our orthodoxy is received from Christ and his apostles." Because the Westminster Confession was an accurate summary of what Jesus and the apostles taught, to deviate from it at any point was the beginning of apostasy from the true faith. In an essay commemorating the 250th anniversary of the Westminster Assembly, Dabney compared the Westminster Confession to an arch in which "the removal of any one [stone] loosens all the rest and endangers the fall of the whole." In the same way, the Westminster Standards were an organic whole; to deny one part was to do harm to the rest of the system. "It is for this reason," Dabney wrote, "that the Confession will need no amendment until the Bible needs to be amended." Strict adherence to an unchanging creed was the way to maintain orthodoxy in the South.[28]

Equally important to Dabney's conservation of the Old School tradition was the influence of Francis Turretin. Like the courses of Charles Hodge at Princeton Theological Seminary and James P. Boyce at Southern Baptist Theological Seminary, Dabney's systematic theology course at Union Seminary relied heavily on Turretin's magisterial *Institutes of Elenctic Theology*. One student recalled that in Dabney's theology class, Dabney would assign a topic with a set of questions and readings for the students to pursue, mainly from Turretin in Latin. The following class period would be taken up with a recitation, in which Dabney would "quiz" the students "unmercifully, sometimes himself taking the position of the errorist and putting us to the defense of the true doctrine." After that, the students were then expected to write a paper, answering the assigned questions with reference to the class material already covered. When the papers were turned in, Dabney would read his own paper on the assigned topic, after which the process was repeated. Dabney's lecture "would make us all feel, day by day, the feebleness of our grasp of the subject and the immense amount we had to learn."[29]

As a result of his teaching methods, it would be expected that Dabney's theology bore the tincture of the older Reformed divine. The structure of Dabney's *Syllabus and Notes of the Course of Systematic and Polemic Theology* followed Turretin's *Institutes* fairly closely; the deviations occurred when Dabney addressed a topic of particular concern in the nineteenth century—for example, he added a section on the "sources of our thinking," which was his summation of Scottish realism, and two sections on evolution and the new science. One of the most surprising differences was that, while Turretin devoted a lengthy section to the doctrine of Scripture, Dabney did not deliver a lecture on Scripture's inspiration and authority. Rather, he was content to address that doctrine briefly at the end of a protracted treatment of reason's role in religion: "I need only add, that I hold the Scriptures to be, in all its parts, of plenary inspiration; and we shall henceforward assume this, as proved by the inquiries of another department," that is, the seminary department that taught "Biblical Introduction." Another striking difference was that while Turretin spent an entire locus on the doctrine of the church, Dabney treated only the sacraments, leaving church polity issues to the seminary department that taught "ecclesiastical polity." Not only did Dabney's theological structure sometimes differ from Turretin's, but he also sometimes disagreed with Turretin's positions, in particular his formulation of the doctrines of providence and imputation. By and large, however, Dabney stood for the Reformed scholasticism of Turretin and the Westminster Assembly, giving his theology a cast similar to that of his Princeton contemporary, Charles Hodge. Dabney believed that the Reformed faith was the only correct version of Christianity; it could not be improved upon. After all, Dabney reasoned, "there can be but one right system. All others, so far as they vary from this, are wrong." As a result, "revealed theology cannot be a progressive science" and cannot gain new truth. Once the Reformed faith was recovered by Calvin, Turretin, and the Westminster divines, there was no further need to innovate but rather to conserve the tradition.[30]

Still, it is interesting that his students most frequently remarked on the moderation of Dabney's theology. For example, former student Peyton Hoge observed that "while [his] Calvinism was thorough-going and intense, it was essentially moderate. While his intellect could not tolerate the fallacies of Arminianism, and his reverent faith reconciled from its rationalist tendencies, he had as little patience with the over-refinements of the scholastic theologians." As examples of this moderation, Hoge pointed out that Dabney preferred the term *preterition* to *reprobation* in describing how God decreed to deal with the non-elect. In addition, Hoge claimed that Dabney had no patience with supralapsarianism, which he saw as "an over-refinement." Dabney also opposed the Princeton theology's emphasis on immediate imputation because he believed that the distinction went beyond the Westminster Standards. Biographer Thomas Cary Johnson further remarked on Dabney's moderation: "He was a moderate, but thorough-going Calvinist, believing himself in thorough harmony with the doctrinal portion of the Westminster Standards." Because the Standards exercised a chaste moderation on several conflicted issues, Dabney did the same.[31]

Dabney's attachment to the Old School tradition led him to emphasize certain doctrines that he deemed to be vital to the Reformed faith. Chief among these was biblical authority. Though Dabney assumed biblical authority as a working principle in his lectures on systematic theology, he vociferously argued for it in his occasional writing. In particular, Dabney attacked biblical critics, such as W. Robertson Smith, who had cast doubt on the inspiration and authority of Scripture. Smith, Dabney charged, employed "the loose and rash methods of the most skeptical school of criticism" upon the Old Testament canon. By following the proponents of "infidel criticism"—such as Karl Graf, Julius Wellhausen, and Abraham Kuenen—Smith committed himself to the maxim that "the true critic must admit neither the possibility of the supernatural nor of inspiration." This maxim was fatal to biblical criticism: "If God has indeed given his church a true inspiration and supernatural helps, and has meant his Bible to record such gifts, then the expositor who sets out to explain the Bible from the prime assumption that such gifts cannot possibly exist, must infallibly go amiss." In addition, Smith's avowal of biblical inspiration was weak, claiming for the Bible the same "views of truth as the soul attains by the exaltation of its religious consciousness." This position placed no essential difference between the inspiration known by a biblical writer such as Isaiah and a profound preacher such as George Whitefield. Because Smith failed to evaluate biblical inspiration and the supernatural preservation of Scripture correctly, his criticism promoted a mild form of historicism, which Dabney deemed to be unacceptable. To claim that the biblical writers were conditioned by their historical and cultural context meant that it would be impossible "to discriminate the fallible human coloring from the infallible divine light" in the Bible. The only possible result of Smith's criticism was "virtual infidelity," and that was why Dabney judged his work to be "thoroughly untrustworthy."[32]

Instead of bowing to the alleged expertise of infidel critics such as Robertson Smith, Dabney urged his fellow Presbyterians to go to the Bible itself, which witnessed to its own divine origin. Dabney believed that "the contents and proposed end of revelation" demonstrated its divine origin. Unlike the scriptures of Islam, the Qur'an, Dabney claimed that the Christian Bible was in "perfect harmony" with natural theology—that God exists and rules the world by providence and moral law. In addition, the Bible accurately portrayed the human condition and provided an explanation of "how a ruined and polluted creature could be found amidst the handiwork of a creator whom we must believe to be at once omnipotent, benevolent, and holy." The Bible told about not only the depravity of humankind but also the good news of salvation. That the books of the Bible presented this material with "marvelous consistency" throughout was "enough to show that they all came from one source and that divine." Dabney also believed that the Bible's consistent presentation of Jesus Christ evidenced its divine origin. A commonsense reader of the Bible accepted its presentation of Jesus of Nazareth as God in human flesh who came to save sinners, rather than believing that the Bible was a fiction crafted by "a company of liars." Finally, Dabney claimed that the Bible's divine origin was vindicated by the lives of Christian people. The message of the Bible—salvation through faith in Jesus Christ—had been demonstrated to be true through the lives of Christians for almost two thousand years. These lines of evidence, Dabney believed, were enough to establish the divine character of the Bible to the honest common sense of most men and women. What was required, then, was for human beings to submit to the Bible's authority, to believe in Jesus Christ, and to live all their lives in accordance with biblical directives.[33]

Dabney also developed the doctrine of providence as a key part of his theology. He held that God "bears a perpetual, active relation to" the world by which God sustained and governed "all His creatures and all their actions." God directed all this in accordance with his "eternal will" so that even the evil in human lives worked according to God's plan. No human being was excepted from God's providential control; rather, "by a mode which is perhaps beyond the cognizance of the human reason, [providence] secures the action designed by God's intelligent purpose, from each created agent, in strict conformity with its nature and powers." The reality of God's sovereign control ruled out mechanistic ideas about the world, but it did not violate the real "property which creatures have of acting as second causes." There was a concursus between God and human beings that preserved the real action of both and yet gave God priority. Belief in divine providence was not fatalism; instead, providence "establishes the agency of second causes; for it teaches that God's method and rule of effectuating events only through them . . . is as steadfast as His purpose to carry out His decree." Thus, providence impelled human beings to action, not passivity. Such providential control provided Christians with the impetus to pray, Dabney held: "prayer implies a Providence."[34]

Dabney, as a Calvinist, was a staunch defender of the "five points of Calvinism." In a little booklet on those doctrines, Dabney observed that study of all non-Calvinist systems led one to conclude two things:

that any debate over Calvinism would revolve around "whether man's original sin is or is not a complete and decisive enmity to godliness" and whether "man's ruin of himself by sin is utter and the whole credit of his redemption from it is God's." Dabney held firmly that human beings were corrupted by original sin, an "evil quality" that pervaded the totality of human existence. He did not mean that human beings were "from their youth as bad as they can be" or that "they have no social virtues towards their fellowmen in which they are sincere." Rather, the moral natures of men and women underwent "an utter change to sin, irreparable by" themselves as a result of the fall. Thus, human depravity evidenced itself "in a fixed and utter opposition of heart to some forms of duty, and especially and always to spiritual duties, owing to God, and in a fixed and absolutely decisive purpose to continue in some sins . . . especially to continue in their sins of unbelief, impenitence, self-will, and practical godlessness." This human depravity produced an "actual guilt" that Dabney defined as "the debt of penalty to law arising out of transgression." God, the holy lawgiver, was affronted by violations of divine law—God's righteousness demanded retribution; God's justice, satisfaction; and God's holiness, renewed purity.[35]

Human beings, however, were unable to satisfy the retributive justice and penal wrath of God. Their own corruption was under judgment; nothing they could do would satisfy the wrath of God. Yet God was not content to allow all humankind to fall under divine judgment. Instead, in mercy, God made a way whereby he might be reconciled to sinful humanity and still retain his principles of righteousness, justice, and holiness—God provided a substitute for sinners in Jesus Christ, who died on the cross in order to bear the sins of his people and to satisfy the retributive justice of God. In the crucifixion event, Dabney claimed, "it is the actual guilt of sinners . . . which is transferred from them to" Jesus. Thus, the problem of actual guilt, arising from depravity, was dealt with at the cross. What was required in order to know that God had removed one's guilt and reconciled the individual to God's own self was faith in Jesus Christ, Savior of sinners.[36]

Dabney believed that this "penal substitutionary theory" of the atonement was the keystone of Christianity. "There is scarcely a leading head of divinity which is not changed or perverted as a logical consequence of this denial of penal substitution consistently carried out," Dabney taught. Forsake the penal substitutionary theory of the atonement and other key doctrines were sure to go: God's distributive justice; God's immutability; the doctrines of original sin and justification; the nature of faith; the doctrines of adoption and perseverance; and the church's teaching on the eternal punishment of the reprobate. Most important, however, was what the denial of the penal theory of the atonement would do to the doctrine of providence. If there was no special providence in Christ's sufferings, then the problem of evil would forever remain an "insoluble mystery." Such an idea was unthinkable to Dabney. The scoffer against Christianity would have his objections answered in "our doctrine of redemption through Christ's substitution, and nowhere else." God permitted evil in the world and suffered with that evil in order to demonstrate his glory through the cross-work of Jesus. Dabney exclaimed exultantly, "The Messiah is our complete theodicy!" Divine providence was saved through the penal substitutionary activity of Jesus.[37]

Dabney also defended the doctrine of election. Because human beings are totally depraved and unable to save themselves, God must take the first steps. God, the eternal, omnipotent, sovereign first cause, chose men and women out of the mass of justly damned humanity to be saved. And God did this for his own glory as well as for reasons that God has not revealed to humankind. The rest of humankind God was pleased to pass by and to leave in their sins. Though many believed election to be a harsh doctrine, Dabney affirmed it as "the sweet one . . . the blessed inlet to all the salvation found in this universe." Human beings, because of their sins, ought to bear the just punishment of God. But God's grace provided "the sweet and blessed source of all that is remedial, hopeful, and happy in earth and heaven." This was the crowning doctrine of the Bible, one that grounded other doctrines such as providence, the covenant, and especially the perseverance of the saints. Because God's election was immutable, sovereign, and unconditional, those who experienced regeneration would certainly be preserved until the end of their lives.[38]

Finally, the doctrine of the spiritual nature of the church was a vital Old School doctrine for Dabney. Though he did not address ecclesiology as part of his lectures on systematic theology, Dabney stood staunchly for the spirituality of the church in his occasional writing. The spiritual nature of the church was part of Dabney's understanding of the separation of church and state. The state and the church belonged to different spheres. The state was responsible to secure the "secular rights" of citizens through three functions: taxation, punishment, and defensive war. The church, on the other hand, was responsible to proclaim the gospel and to persuade men and women to believe through three functions: preaching, right administration of the sacraments, and discipline. Because the church was a spiritual institution, it could not bear "penal power" or be "armed with civil pains"; the state could not coerce men and women to embrace a particular religion. Both violated soul competency, the idea that "God holds every soul directly responsible to Himself" and that "no one shall step in between" the individual and God. Likewise, the church's pulpit and courts were not to involve the church in secular matters to which the Bible failed to speak definitively. The church's responsibility was to declare the duty of men and women in particular moral issues and then leave their consciences free. And while Dabney thought that some of his fellow Southern Presbyterians took the spirituality doctrine too far at points, he was in general agreement with them on the nonsecular character of the church.[39]

The spiritual nature of the church had been viewed by recent historians, such as E. Brooks Holifield, as merely a "protective gesture during the slavery controversy." While it certainly protected Southern masters from abolitionist logic in their church pulpits and provided the main complaint of Southern Presbyterians against their Northern co-religionists after the Civil War, the doctrine of the spirituality of the church also appeared in venues where it could not be construed as a protective gesture. For example, Dabney appealed to this doctrine during antebellum discussions of Presbyterian parochial schools. He believed that "it was the Church's duty to instruct parents how God would have them rear their children and enforce the duty by spiritual sanctions; but there its official power ends." Moreover, church courts, whether local sessions or presbyteries, were "not suitable bodies to govern a school." Secular education involved church courts in matters that were not strictly spiritual; hence, parochial education was "an illegitimate usurpation of parental rights and a violation of liberty of conscience." Thus, while the doctrine of the spirituality of the church played a major role during the debates over slavery, the non-secular character of the church came into play on other public issues.[40]

Life, Death, and Ministry in Southside Virginia

It would be a mistake to suppose that Dabney's entire life was taken up with teaching ministerial students. Rather, these early years in Hampden-Sydney were filled with life and ministry, as well as disappointment and tragedy. Of course, Dabney was busy writing, assisting Moses Hoge and T. V. Moore with the early direction of *Central Presbyterian,* as well as overseeing the *Presbyterial Critic* with his Baltimore friends Thomas E. Peck and Stuart Robinson. He was also busy preaching as a pulpit supply, first at New Store Church in Buckingham County, Virginia, then at College Church, Hampden-Sydney. Eventually, the ministry at College Church would evolve into a co-pastorate with his brother-in-law, B. M. Smith. College Church was a relatively small congregation, with about 150 communicant members. As a result of Dabney's preaching, the Sunday congregations soon grew to such a degree that the church was forced to build a new sanctuary in 1860. The "curious old College Church" with its "Saxon arches of brick" could have been remodeled to seat the white portion of the congregation, if the church was willing to "exclude the negroes." But "the session said no for they must be provided with settings, just as well as their masters." Dabney dusted off his architectural drawings from Tinkling Spring and superintended the building of the new church house. When the facility was completed, it could seat almost 800 worshipers—500 seats for the white masters on the floor and 300 for the African-American slaves in the balcony.[41]

Dabney also had opportunity to serve the church as a commissioner to the General Assembly, which convened in 1856 in New York City. It was the first time that Dabney had traveled to the North. He took his two sisters, Anne and Betty, with him, and sought to experience as much of the "grand city" as he could. Shortly after arriving, he attended a concert at the Academy of Music. He was in awe of the houses, which were like "palaces." He also took his sisters on a steamboat excursion that was sponsored jointly by the Old School and New School assemblies. He attended tours of the Merchants' Exchange, Trinity Episcopal Church, and the Dusseldorf Gallery, where he was particularly moved by a painting by De La Roche. In the midst of the sightseeing and shopping, Dabney also conducted some of the church's business, and made important contacts for the future. He met James Henley Thornwell for the first time, and later observed that "he is a common looking, little stoop shouldered man. But he has a fine mind. His manners are very simple, friendly, and natural." Dabney was pleased that the Union Seminary report went smoothly, though he was distressed that the Assembly in principle made R. J. Breckinridge's Danville Seminary a "seminary of the whole church," urging Presbyterian churches throughout the country to donate to its endowment. He was further distressed by the corresponding Congregational delegates from Massachusetts and Maine "who gave us a dose of abolition." When the moderator thanked them for their words, Dabney "thought the old man showed himself nearly as much an abolitionist as they. The worst of it was, he speaks as the mouthpiece of the Assembly." But by and large, Dabney kept his mouth shut and observed the doings of the "big guns."[42]

In the midst of these activities, Dabney experienced new stresses in his home life. His third son, Charles, was born on June 19, 1855, but tragedy struck his two older boys. Within a month of each other, both died of diphtheria, a disease that attacks the throat and air passages and causes the sufferer to suffocate. Watching his two oldest sons die deeply affected Dabney, as it would any loving parent. His younger son, Jimmy, died first, suffering with the illness for about a week. Even until his death, he was "intelligent," Dabney reported to his brother, "and his appealing looks to us and the physician would have melted a stone." After that, Bob, who had been sick first but appeared to be on the mend, became progressively worse until he died as well. The double blow shook Dabney to his core. "This is strange, perhaps inexplicable. Death has struck me with a dagger of ice. He has not only wounded, but benumbed," he admitted. While he struggled to trust

God, asking God to allow him to "see the blows blessed to myself, my kindred and my friends," still he confessed that the only real comfort during this time was his work. To escape his home with its attendant sickness and sorrows and to throw himself into teaching was a consolation for which Dabney was thankful.[43]

Dabney would later have three other sons born to him: Thomas on September 5, 1857; Samuel on June 8, 1859; and Lewis on August 11, 1865. Thomas would himself die of diphtheria in 1862, but the other three boys would survive to adulthood, with Charles becoming a university president and Samuel and Lewis both attorneys in Texas. Undoubtedly, though, the preeminent relationship in the Dabney home was between Robert and his wife, Lavinia. Their relationship was one in which Dabney clearly saw himself as the "patriarch," but willingly acceded to Lavinia's wishes and desires most of the time. In fact, in the few letters that remain between husband and wife, Dabney was downright passionate. From New York during the 1856 General Assembly, he wrote, "As soon as I saw your handwriting I tore the letter open and began to read it in the midst of the great crowd which throngs that place at every hour, forgetful of the pickpockets, curious eyes, and everything else." His greatest regret was that his wife was not with him in New York: "I see a great many things which are extremely interesting, but I am not happy except for a few minutes when I forget myself. My soul goes hankering after my Binney and Charley." At the end of a lengthy fund-raising tour for the seminary in 1858, Dabney wished "for rest, rest, sweet rest, in your arms." The only pleasure that Dabney derived from the tour was "counting off the days and when one ends, of saying, well, this brings me one day nearer to my Binney! . . . I love you more than ever: and every year my judgment, as well as my love, tell me what a treasure you are to me." By most accounts, theirs was a good marriage, a union of two different personalities into one life. That did not mean, however, that Lavinia was completely subservient to Dabney's whims. Already noted was her determination to be with her sister during the birth of her first child. Likewise, though Dabney favored the use of corporal punishment, Lavinia would sometimes intervene: "Often when Dabney began to reach for a stick, Lavinia, whom her boys never saw lose her temper or speak harshly, would quiet him with a softly-spoken 'Oh Mr. Dabney' and lead the small offender discreetly away."[44]

As a result of his growing reputation, Princeton Seminary made several attempts to add Dabney to its faculty. In part, this faculty recruitment must be viewed as part of a larger Princeton strategy to maintain the unity of the Old School church in the face of impending civil war; at the same time Dabney was being wooed to join as professor of ecclesiastical history, B. M. Palmer was being sought for the pastoral theology professorship. Still, Charles Hodge made a serious run at Dabney for Princeton. After explaining plans for reorganizing the teaching loads at the seminary, Hodge tried to be his persuasive best: "Now, my dear sir, would that I could sit down by your side, or even at your feet, stranger as I am, and beg you, with many prayers and supplications, to consent, should God see fit to call you to come and help us in our great sorrow and need." Because of the strained timetable that Hodge and the Princeton directors were on, he urged Dabney to allow his name to be put up for election. "Is it, my dear sir, too much to ask nothing, to beg you simply to be silent and wait to hear what God, by his church, or through his providence, or by his Spirit in your own heart, may say?" Hodge asked.[45]

Yet Dabney was not content merely to do nothing and to "be silent." After offering several subsidiary reasons for not accepting the Princeton professorship, Dabney concluded that the one weighty question was where he might do the most good for Christ and the church. "I cannot avoid the conviction that, so far as our fallible wisdom can judge," Dabney wrote, "the post of superior usefulness for me is here" at Union Seminary. The reason for this was simple: "by going away I shall inflict an almost fatal injury on a minor interest of the church in order to confer a very non-essential assistance on a major interest of the same church." While Princeton would be able to supply its faculty needs from several prominent portions of the church, Union Seminary in 1860 was just beginning to solidify, enrolling thirty-six students. If Dabney's goal of providing Southern ministers for Southern churches was going to be a reality, then he needed to stay at Union Seminary. As a result, though he was grateful for the consideration, Dabney rejected Hodge's offer. But the story did not stop there—for Princeton's directors decided to nominate him anyway, contingent upon General Assembly approval. Dabney was quite upset, repeating several times in a letter to A. T. McGill that "with my present views of duty, I could not go to Princeton if elected by the General Assembly, and . . . I see nothing in the future which is likely to change them, at this time." In the end, the Princeton matter was dropped.[46]

Though Dabney did not go to Princeton, he cherished the invitation to the end of his long life. Throughout his ministry, however, he despaired of the disparity between Union and Princeton. During his thirty-year tenure at Union Seminary, Dabney taught 465 different students; by contrast, during the same thirty years, Charles and A. A. Hodge trained three times as many students, 1,594. Even worse to Dabney's mind, the Princeton theologians schooled 150 Southern-born candidates—over thirty percent of the entire number that Dabney taught.[47] This superiority of Princeton over Union provided no small measure of frustration for Dabney. While he never desired to make Union Seminary as large or even as influential as Princeton before or after the war, Dabney did want Southern institutions to provide Southern education for Southern ministers. In the days before the Civil War, Dabney argued this very point. He believed that the "very existence of the Union . . . depended upon the maintenance, not only of political, but of social equality; for when we are felt to be inferiors, our political equality will soon be assailed." As a result, "every sentiment of patriotism, every attachment to the Union, as well as our state pride, pleads with us, to put an end to this intellectual and commercial vassalage." In order to make the North respect the South, it was necessary for Southerners to assert "our social independence." That meant the building up of "home institutions," such as Southern theological seminaries. "He is no true Virginian," Dabney claimed, "who does not give the preference to the institutions of his native State, on this ground, when other things are at all equal. As Presbyterians, we are patriots; and should for this reason, stand manfully by our own seminary." Dabney was a true Virginian who stayed by his seminary, even when flattered by calls elsewhere. That commitment would be tried by the fires of the days ahead.[48]

4

Patriot

When Dabney mounted the steps up to his pulpit at College Church, Hampden-Sydney, Virginia, on November 1, 1860, he was determined to act as a moderating force in the growing national crisis. Once the Democrats had divided at their fateful summer convention in Charleston—Southerners siding with the incumbent Vice President, John C. Breckinridge, Northerners following Senator Stephen Douglas—it was obvious to Dabney that Lincoln would be elected. But Dabney did not believe that Lincoln's election furnished a sufficient cause for secession; in any case, he believed that secession had to be concerted in order to be effective. Still, the secession agitation was frothing over in Deep South states such as South Carolina. In order to calm the fire-eaters in South Carolina as well as Virginia, Dabney decided to use the Synod of Virginia's appointed fast day in order to teach his auditors what Christian patriotism demanded.

Christians should be most patriotic, Dabney claimed, because the peace of one's country was vital for the success of the gospel. Christ's kingdom was dependent, in part, on the politics of earthly kingdoms; if there was national peace, then the gospel could sound forth and do its good work. As a result, Christians should fear internal political convulsions and war because the gospel cause would be harmed. Men and women would be distracted from the claims of the gospel by politics; families would be scattered by war; and civil liberties would be restricted by standing armies and the requirements of internal security. All this would inevitably lead to restrictions on the gospel ministry and would postpone "the movement of the world's redemption . . . and the enthroning of the Prince of Peace over his promised dominion." Even worse, Christianity would be shown to be impotent to affect the lives of people in real time. Though the churches boasted of the recent revival of 1858 and of the power of Protestantism in the land, a civil war would bring tremendous guilt on the church, "second only to that of the apostate church which betrayed the Savior of the world; and its judgment will be rendered in calamities second only to those which avenged the divine blood invoked by Jerusalem on herself and her children."[1]

Hence, Christian patriots ought to seek the good of their country through prayer and confession of sin. Southerners, in particular, ought not to confess the sins of "fellow citizens of another quarter of the Confederacy," but their own—worldliness, luxury, profanity, and, especially, acts of vengeance. If Southerners did not confess these sins, then God might chastise them through convulsion and war. "Often has his manifold, wise, and righteous providence permitted an unjust aggressor to make himself the instrument wherewith to lash his sinning people," Dabney proclaimed. Not only was prayer and confession necessary, but Christians ought to consider the way in which they used their votes and influence. Dabney held that Christians should "carry our citizenship in the kingdom of heaven everywhere, and make it dominate over every public act." That meant electing politicians who were good and honest men, not demagogues; and supporting newspaper editors who spoke the truth and who did not seek to fire people's passions. "Declare that from this day no money, no vote, no influence of yours shall go to the maintenance of any other counsels than those of moderation, righteousness and manly forbearance," Dabney counseled. Finally, Christians should study the things that make for peace. Dabney desired for his audience "to grant all that is right and ask nothing else." If they did, peace would return to the country.[2]

Though Dabney's sermon was distributed throughout the country in pamphlet form and hailed by friends in both North and South, privately he was diffident about the prospects for peace. While Dabney earnestly believed that war would be disastrous for the gospel, and he sincerely worked to delay the war and to conciliate passions, he had long believed that civil war was probably inevitable. In 1851, after the passage of the Compromise of 1850, Dabney told his brother Charles William that the South should begin to "unite ourselves better and prepare ourselves better for resistance to the next outrage." Preparation meant, at the very least, the development of independent economic relations through trade with Europe and a thoroughly biblical proslavery defense. By 1859, preparation also meant a thought-out position on secession. In another letter to his brother, Dabney urged that if the South were to secede, the effort had to be concerted and based on a genuine constitutional violation. When the time came for secession, Southerners needed to be calm and "avoid ultraisms in order not to carry unnecessary odium and to set ourselves right in the sight of God, who has to dispense our fate, and of man." Finally, preparation meant that Southerners should store up arms for a potential conflict. As Dabney reflected later in life, "When our enemies came near electing their man in 1856, we should have taken warning and spent the interval of Buchanan's weak, pacific administration 'arming to the teeth.' This neglected, we should have remained quiet when Lincoln went in, and employed the respite at last in arming for defense." Hence, Dabney's public patriotic attempt to conciliate Northerners should be read against his private reflections on the necessity for preparation for civil conflict, reflections that stretched back ten years before the fall of Fort Sumter.[3]

Even more, Dabney's patriotism should be read against Southern preoccupation with masculinity and honor. Historians working in the train of Bertram Wyatt-Brown have argued that Southern culture based itself on the standards of honor and shame. Most often, the ethics of honor was related to a premodern, Stoic ideal, in which individuals saw themselves subject to the moral taboos of a community, and particularly to that society's patriarchy. This code of honor placed one in relation to others within a given society. Elites (town squires, for example) were given the most honor and esteem by others; peers were also given respect and honor; but those who were on social rungs below oneself (poor white males, women, and slaves) could not possess honor. In the case of African-American slaves, these were the most dishonorable of all, for they did not and could not possess self-determination, a key requirement for the honorable man. In order to be deemed a person of honor, one had to demonstrate valor, especially in seeking revenge upon dishonoring slights. Honor depended on others' opinions and often required violence in order to be maintained. In times of peace, if one's honor was impugned, the way to regain it was to seek revenge through the violent means of the *code duello*. By prizing honor above life itself, one gained or regained honor. As a result, men in an honor-driven society prized times of war, when displays of valor on the field of battle were the quickest way to gain honor and reputation.[4]

This code of honor was pictured best in Southerners' favorite novel, Sir Walter Scott's *Ivanhoe*. As the Jewess Rebecca related the scenes of the battle around Font-du-Broef's castle to the injured Ivanhoe, the knight's impatience to be in the midst of the battle raised the question of honor. Ivanhoe felt keenly that by not participating in the battle, by being "passive as a priest, or a woman," while others were "acting deeds of honor," he was dishonored. For a knight such as Ivanhoe, "We live not—we wish not to live—longer than while we are victorious and renowned." Rebecca mocked this lust for honor as unworthy, for after one was dead on the field of battle, nothing remained. In response, Ivanhoe cried, "What remains? Glory, maiden, glory! which gilds our sepulchre and embalms our name." Again, Rebecca replied that glory was worthless for one who was dead, for every other affection was buried in the grave with the hero. Ivanhoe's response was impatient, but spelled out the ideal of chivalry and honor to which the later American South held: "Thou wouldst quench the pure light of chivalry, which alone distinguishes the noble from the base, the gentle knight from the churl and the savage; which rates our life far, far beneath the pitch of our honor, raises us victorious over pain, toil, and suffering, and teaches us to fear no evil but disgrace." Ivanhoe concluded his speech by rhapsodizing, "Chivalry!—why, maiden, she is the nurse of pure and high affection—the stay of the oppressed, the redresser of grievances, the curb of the power of the tyrant—nobility were but an empty name without her, and finds the best protection in her lance and her sword." General Lee could not have said it better himself. This was the ideal of honor that characterized Southerners as they fought on the Civil War killing fields.[5]

Because Dabney was in the "passive" class of "priests," who were coupled together with "women" as those who were not honorable, he and his other ministerial brethren attempted to redefine honor, transforming it from a Stoic ideal associated with hierarchy and violence to a standard actuated by piety and faith in Jesus Christ. Certainly, those who died on the field of battle gained honor; but those who feared God above all things, including death, were the ones who gained true honor. Hence, Lee, Jackson, and other Southern heroes were honorable not merely because they were valorous in battle, but because they were Christians who feared God. Further, because Christianity was necessary for genuine honor, ministers could be honorable men as well. Although ministers may not be found on the leading edge of the battle and may find their congregations dominated by women, these facts did not make them dishonorable. Rather, because ministers upheld the only path to true courage in the face of death—namely, faith in Jesus Christ—they, too, were honorable men. By transforming an ideal that had once led Southern masters away from Christianity into one that was fused with Christian requirements, Dabney and other ministers hoped to gain social control over their male congregants as well as carve out social respect for themselves as men of honor.[6]

Though Dabney attempted to redefine the issues of manly honor and Christian patriotism, most Southerners still believed that honor was gained by facing down violence and death without fear on the field of battle. This in turn raised pressing questions for Dabney—how could a minister of Jesus, the Prince of Peace, gain honor on a field of war, killing those who professed faith in Jesus? The tension between his role as minister and the call of martial honor would plague Dabney throughout the war. While Dabney mixed the callings of minister and soldier for five brief months, for the most part he was far from the front lines of the war, either ministering in the back of the army with the surgeons or at home caring for his household. Dabney's opportunities for honor were few, and his sense that he was somehow dishonored by his failures and inactivity during the war caused him great frustration and, in the end, intense bitterness.

Dabney's intense love for his country also made the line between the sacred and the secular hard to maintain. While Dabney attempted to distinguish between what he did in his official capacity as a minister and what he did as a private citizen, it appeared that he and other Southern Presbyterians gained their entrance into the political debate and exercised their cultural authority as *ministers*, not as private citizens. This ambiguity of the minister's authoritative role was particularly apparent in their use of the religious papers. Ostensibly "private" organs free from ecclesiastical control, religious newspapers provided ministers with their most direct communication with a large audience. And these respected "elders in Zion" spoke from their authoritative capacity as ministers to the important public issues of the day. Often, these ministers crossed the lines from the sacred to the secular, from merely denominational concerns to issues of national moment. Even Dabney bewailed the blurring of the lines between secular and religious newspapers on the eve of the Civil War. In a January 1861 letter to Charles Hodge, Dabney argued:

> I felt, and still feel, that it would be best, if possible, to maintain that line strictly; and to have all our ecclesiastical journals adopt the policy which has been pursued thus far by the Philadelphia *Presbyterian*. Hence, upon receipt of your essay, I ventured to write to the editors of the two papers in our section (Richmond and Fayetteville) urging them with all my weight, to make no discussion on this subject in their columns.

Yet, as Dabney confessed, "They have both to my regret acted on different views, pressed to it doubtless, in part, by the great difficulty of keeping back other assailants any other wise by occupying the lists themselves." Dabney himself, however, also acted on different views; his April 1861 letter to Samuel I. Prime, which was deeply political, was published in the *Central Presbyterian*. The lines between secular and sacred were blurred by the powerful forces at work in the Civil

War. But the lines were also blurred by the difficulty of reconciling Christian devotion to one's country with loyalty to a "kingdom not of this world."[7]

"On the State of the Country"

Like other Old School Presbyterians—most notably Charles Hodge, James Henley Thornwell, R. J. Breckinridge, and B. M. Palmer—Dabney attempted to shape Presbyterians' response to the political issues of the day. From 1856 until Virginia seceded in 1861, Dabney sought to moderate passions among Southerners and represent Southern opinion to Northern conservatives. To be sure, Dabney was under no illusions about Northern opinion. He knew that most Yankees were implicitly "free soil," but he also assumed that they would work for peace in order to preserve the federal union. In the short term, Christians ought to lead the way in moderating the passions aroused by talk of secession and war; if they failed in this duty, civil war was inevitable, with disastrous consequences for all involved.

Dabney perceived that the nation was proceeding rapidly toward crisis and wrote an 1856 editorial for the *Central Presbyterian*. He warned that "our common country is in danger of *disunion*." The potential disunion was due to the abolition frenzy, Dabney held. But abolitionism had transmuted into something far more dangerous: "the grave, pervading, national question of *Free-soil*." The majority of Americans were committed to keeping the new territories free from slavery, while the slaveholding minority demanded the right to take their slave property into the expanding West. These principles—free soil and slave power—were in "irreconcilable opposition." The national union was being divided into sections, and the end result would be that "the whole North will be arrayed against the whole South, on a question which each supposes essential to its honor, its religion, and its existence." Over the question of free soil, Dabney prophesied, the nation would go to civil war, a bitter contest characterized by the "hot indignation of mutual outrage." Christians should not allow political debates over free soil to destroy the national union, a political compact that promised peace for the gospel and the expansion of the kingdom of God. Rather, Christians should pray for their common nation, refrain from debates that stirred up "national passions," and confess their national sins. Such moderation was Dabney's strategy for preventing the South from entering a disastrous war that would lead to the destruction of its social and economic system as well as to dangerous days for the gospel.[8]

Dabney continued to write on these issues, seeking to moderate passions and provide a middle way for Virginia Presbyterians. In 1858, he sent another essay to Moses Hoge, editor of the *Central Presbyterian*, on the rising "Free Soil agitation." Dabney confessed that "my fears may seem extravagant, and consequently, the whole article, which those fears have educed." He believed, however, that "only one step more is needed to make an angry rupture [between the sections] inevitable, and to the verge of that we have come, viz., the active adoption of retaliatory legislation by the southern states." Hence, Dabney offered his essay as a way of conciliating national passions, hoping that it would circulate both in Southern religious papers and in the *Presbyterian*, with its editorial offices in Philadelphia. But it does not appear that this appeal was published.[9]

After spelling out his views on secession to his brother in 1859—requiring that it be concerted and constitutional—Dabney voted for John C. Breckinridge in the 1860 national election, "fully expecting to be beaten" and sure that Lincoln and the Republicans would seize the White House in the face of the divided Democrats. Yet Dabney reiterated his belief that Lincoln's election did not provide a sufficient reason for war or for immediate secession. Writing to Hoge after South Carolina seceded, Dabney declared, "I regard the conduct of South Carolina as unjustifiable towards the United States at large, and towards her Southern sisters, as treacherous, wicked, insolent and mischievous. She has, in my view, *worsted* the common cause, forfeited the righteous strength of our position, and aggravated our difficulties of position a hundredfold." Just a few days before this letter, Dabney had written to his mother, "As for South Carolina, the little impudent vixen has gone beyond all patience. She is as great a pest as the Abolitionists." Dabney's frustration with South Carolina was due to the fact that she had violated the two planks of his secession policy: the state failed to consult other Southern states before seceding and she made the election of Lincoln the sole cause for her action.[10]

After South Carolina seceded, Dabney continued to work for a peaceful resolution to the national crisis, both publicly and behind the scenes. Publicly, he wrote another appeal for peace addressed to Christians throughout the nation, which he circulated during the fall and early winter of 1860. While many Virginia Presbyterians signed the appeal, eventually published in March 1861 in the *Central Presbyterian*, other Southern Presbyterians failed to sign. Most notably, James Henley Thornwell believed that the effect of Dabney's appeal "would be to delay the secession of the South, and, as that is inevitable, the sooner it is brought about the better." Thornwell believed that Southern honor was deeply offended by Lincoln's election; submission to the free-soil Republicans was an unacceptable degradation that would lead to virtual slavery. Dabney and other Virginia Presbyterians disagreed with Thornwell's view. In the appeal, Dabney reiterated his belief that evangelicals should do all in their power to moderate national "passions" and mediate the dispute that seemed inevitable. This appeal was signed by most of the prominent Virginia Presbyterians, and some not-so-prominent ones, including T. J. Jackson, professor of artillery at Virginia Military Institute.[11]

Dabney also worked for peace privately, exchanging several letters with Charles Hodge. The letters, written between December 1860 and February 1861, made plain the wide divergence between the North and South, even within the Old School church. Dabney and Hodge disagreed over the nature of free soil and particularly over the rights of the South to carry slave property into the new territories. While Hodge claimed that slavery was a creation of "local law" and could exist only within the sphere of that locality, Dabney believed that slavery existed in the South as a result of the work of "Divine Providence" and constitutionally secured rights to property. The two theologians also disagreed on whether the United States Constitution allowed secession. Dabney held that it did because the compact had been made by sovereign states; Hodge, on the other hand, argued that Southern claims that "any state has the legal and moral right to secede from the Union and to reclaim all the federal property . . . within its territory" represented "an intolerable wrong." The entire exchange led Hodge to realize "the difficulty of mutual understanding and of a satisfactory accommodation." Dabney, however, came away from the exchange convinced that, though Northerners were resolutely free-soil, they would stand for Southern rights to slave property within the federal union.[12]

All of Dabney's labor for peace was ultimately for naught. After Fort Sumter had been reduced to rubble, Lincoln had issued his call for 75,000 troops in order to "crush the rebellion," and Virginia had withdrawn from the federal union, Dabney joined the secession forces. As a declaration of his new commitment, Dabney wrote an open letter to his friend and editor of the *New York Observer*, Samuel I. Prime. The letter, which Prime refused to print for fear of New York mobs, and which was subsequently printed in the *Central Presbyterian*, was belligerent and warlike. Dabney opened by vindicating himself and Virginia, claiming that "the guilt lies not at our door." When Dabney first saw the dangers of disunion in the distance, four years earlier, he had sought to bring about reconciliation. Virginians had continually sought peace and endured wrong, "until endurance ceased to be a virtue." All of Virginia's "demands for constitutional redress have been refused," and now "the infamous alternative has been forced upon her, either to brave the oppressor's rod or to aid him in the destruction of her sisters and her children, because they are contending nobly, if too rashly, for rights common to them and her." To Dabney, this was coercion. As a result of the federal government's attempt to coerce both Virginia and the rest of the South, "in one week the whole State has been converted into a camp."[13]

Dabney blamed Northern conservatives for this turn of events. Northern conservatives seemed oblivious to the possible effects of civil war. The war would leave the North "with a consolidated Federal Government, with State Sovereignty extinguished, with the Constitution in ruins, and with your rights and safety a prey to a frightful combination of radicalism and military despotism." Furthermore, a war would forever affect relations between the sections—it would "shed rivers of treasure and of more precious blood" and "plant the seeds of national hatred which are to bear fruits in other wars for centuries." The only goal that Northerners could have for such a war would be "the conquest and subjugation of free and equal States!" In amazement Dabney declared that "the North undertakes to compel its *equals* to abide under a government which they judge ruinous to their rights!" This was nothing less than slavery; the North sought the "submission" of the South, transforming "sovereign States" into "helpless slaves, in the last resort of their own servants." These were the monstrous designs of the North, demonstrating that "this much-lauded Federal compact" was "a horrid trap" that Virginians "do well to free ourselves and our children from," even "at the expense of all the horrors of another revolutionary war."[14]

If the North argued that the South had started the war by firing on Fort Sumter, Dabney claimed that the North had become an aggressor when it transformed the fort, "intended lawfully for [South Carolina's] protection," into a "means of her oppression." Firing on Sumter "was an act of strict self-defense" that was justified in the face of the war movements of the Lincoln government. Thus, it was the North's fault that her flag was fired upon, that South Carolinian troops seized Sumter forcibly, and that this murderous war to reconstruct the federal union was occurring. All this, even though it was a war that "the constitution confers no power to wage . . . This war has no justification in righteousness, in any reasonable hope of good results, in constitutional law. It is the pure impulse of bad passions."[15]

It is important to notice themes of honor and patriotism in Dabney's declaration of war. He had advocated peace until it was no longer a "virtue," until the edge of "dishonor" was reached. Rather than responding in violence to reclaim honor, Virginians like Dabney declined "all acts of self-defence" in order to seek peace. But with Lincoln's call for troops it was obvious that the North sought to subjugate equals and to make them "helpless slaves"—ones who were so degraded that they were not capable of self-government. This was the ultimate dishonor. Importantly, Dabney even shifted to gendered language to make his points—the North thought Virginia was a "decrepit" old woman, whose "breasts were dry" and whose mind was gone, but in fact, Virginia was "a Minerva radiant with the terrible glories of policy and war." Dabney believed that the North was dishonoring the South, claiming that it was an effeminate and degraded region that required subjugation by force. As a result, patriotism required violent talk in order to regain masculinity and honor—Dabney jeered that those who disliked his letter could "seek their revenge of me . . . at that frontier where we shall meet them, the northernmost verge of the sacred soil of Virginia." There on the front line of battle, manly honor could be gained and the passions of patriotism rewarded.[16]

Dabney's letter was eventually published in pamphlet form and solidified the support of other Virginians for the new Confederacy. Yet to understand how the events of the week after Sumter transformed his perspective on secession and on a potential civil war, one only has to hear words written five days after this letter to Prime. Dabney, who had previously preached the horrors and difficulties of war, now saw "many things which make me hope that it may be the will of a good Providence that we shall be spared the sufferings and crimes of a great war, or at least defeat." Lulled into believing that the North had no will to fight and no generals to fight for her, lulled into believing in the superiority of Southern arms, intoxicated by patriotism, Dabney concluded, "Such a people cannot be conquered."[17]

"Our Parson Is Not Afraid of Yankee Bullets"

Once Virginia joined her Southern sisters, the young men of Dabney's church and seminary classroom volunteered at once, joining the 18th Virginia Volunteers.[18] Dabney decided to leave the pastoral work at College Church to his co-pastor, B. M. Smith, and to seek a chaplain's commission for the summer in order to "watch over our young men." Dabney received a state commission and followed the regiment to northern Virginia. Sharing the tent of chief surgeon Dr. Richard Welton, Dabney ministered to the regiment throughout the summer and participated in the Battle of First Manassas. His ministry had some measure of success; he heard from the regimental colonel that "he dated his conversion to my ministry especially from a Thanksgiving sermon I preached the Thursday night after the Battle" of Manassas. The Stonewall Brigade camped near the 18th Virginia; Dabney had opportunity to renew his acquaintance with one of the heroes of First Manassas, the recently minted "Stonewall" Jackson. Dabney was related to Jackson by marriage—they had married Morrison cousins—and knew each other more through shared contacts than personal acquaintance. Jackson's Lexington, Virginia, pastor, William S. White, was Dabney's longtime ministerial friend, and Jackson had signed Dabney's final appeal for peace just months prior to First Manassas. In the months after the battle, however, Jackson and Dabney "began a friendship which led to strange results."[19]

During these four months with the Virginia regiment, Dabney struggled with harmonizing the duties of patriotic manhood and his calling as a minister. Repeatedly, he had to assure his womenfolk that he was not participating in the fighting. For example, Dabney wrote his sister that "I hope you all are not permitting any apprehensions for my safety [to] distress you. I am not so romantic in my ideas as to think of mixing up secular and sacred callings." If battle was to come, Dabney assured, he would be found in the back with the surgeons. Such a position was "harrowing indeed to the sympathies," but still was "exposed to little danger under any circumstances, either of being killed or taken." Later Dabney wrote to his mother, assuring her that "I am a non-combatant, and intend to remain so. I have persisted in refusing to get any uniform or side arms." And after the battle of First Manassas, Dabney urged his sister to relate to their mother that "I do not intend to expose my life to any danger: I do not consider it my duty." Still, for Dabney to find his place at the back of the battle was an affront to Southern ideals of honor and manhood. While Dabney's religious duty may have been to avoid danger, he found that the duties of honor "required" him to ride as an orderly for the regimental colonel during the battle, a fact that he did not relate to his mother and sister. Reconciling manhood, honor, and his Christian vocation was no easy matter for Dabney.[20]

At the end of his summer's term, over the objections of his brother Charles William, who appealed to patriotism, manhood, and honor while urging Dabney to remain with the army, Dabney returned to his place at Union Seminary. Fourteen students remained, and the seminary directors "had ordered to keep the seminary open." As he proceeded to train the remaining students in the seminary course, he attended the Synod of Virginia meeting in Petersburg, where he helped the synod to withdraw from the Old School Presbyterian church. After the synod meeting, Dabney contracted his first of several bouts of camp fever. Though elected to go as a commissioner to the formative assembly of the Presbyterian Church in the Confederate States of America, he was felled by the sickness. He ended up in bed for several months and "had no part in the organization of our church government there."[21]

Although Thornwell and B. M. Palmer set the tone for the first Assembly, Dabney had prepared an address for the new church that stood in marked contrast to Thornwell's more famous "Address of the General Assembly of the Presbyterian Church in the Confederate States to All the Churches of Jesus Christ Throughout the Earth." While Thornwell made the case for separation from the Northern Old School Presbyterian church first by emphasizing the Northern church's breach of the spirituality of the church, Dabney believed that the separation between Northern and Southern Presbyterians was profoundly political. His address arraigned the 1861 Gardiner Spring Resolutions, which led to the division in the church, as not only "unfeeling . . . and discourteous" to Southerners, but also "unrighteous, unconstitutional, and, in its own nature, divisive of the church." The resolutions effectively made political secession akin to "the sin of rebellion" and liable to church censure. The Spring Resolutions involved the church in a merely political matter, since "the obedience which our brethren render to the governments of their several states cannot be a proper subject for church censures, because it was the proper result of the relations they owed to those governments and to the federal government." The state government was "the original one" with the authority "nearest to the citizen." Citizens owed ultimate loyalty to their states; when Virginia seceded, it would have been rebellion for Dabney *not* to have followed his state. By making state loyalty a chargeable ecclesiastical offense, Northern Old Schoolers put Southerners in an impossible position.[22]

Furthermore, the Spring Resolutions did not represent sound politics, Dabney proclaimed. The resolutions displayed hostility toward secession, while failing to recognize that "the constitution of the United States was formed by independent and equal states, for the common and equitable good of all the parties alike." The constitution was a compact among sovereign states to join in a union that would cede to a "general government the direction of those concerns which were common alike to all." With the election of Lincoln, a sectional party seized the government and destroyed the "fundamental intent" of the constitution. A new union was substituted in place of the old. As a result of this momentous change, "it is preposterous to say that we whom our constitution still made freemen and equals could not righteously exercise our option to accept or refuse these new terms of union, preposterous for Americans whose government is formed on the right of people to choose." By withdrawing "from the connexion which was thus perverted," the South determined that it was better to sever the union than to submit to tyranny.[23]

Dabney pointed out that the subsequent actions of the federal government demonstrated that secession was the correct course. The federal government "waged war against the states without the authority of law, and attempted their forcible coercion . . . in the face of the fact that such powers were intentionally withheld after mature deliberation by the fathers of the constitution." It armed fortresses and navies to subdue those who had helped to pay for those military defenses. The North had "kidnapped and confiscated the slaves of the southern people" and utterly "overturned" the decisions of the Supreme Court. The federal government had violated the writ of habeas corpus and other constitutional protections "by a multitude of arrests without legal warrant." The end result had been that "the government of the United States now exhibits the monstrous inconsistency of trampling upon every valued right and principle of its constitution, in the pretended effort to preserve the authority of that constitution." The Civil War, Dabney charged, was motivated "by lust for sectional domination, by the rage of disappointed rapacity, by revenge, hatred, and mortified pride."[24]

By reciting these facts, Dabney believed that he did not violate the spiritual nature of the church. He merely brought these facts to bear in order to "defend the liberty of conscience of the people of God." Because the Northern church had attacked its fellow believers in the South in the name of politics, Dabney held that a political defense of Southern actions was permissible and necessary. There were occasions when a church court had to consider political matters in order to "determine the nature of the act." Moreover, in line with the doctrine of the spirituality of the church, Dabney did not desire the Old School Assembly to "wield its ecclesiastical power of its members in the North to constrain them to favor us." Rather, he only meant to carry one point: that Southern Presbyterians could not "be subjected properly to church censure for yielding allegiance to the Confederate States at the prompting of their own judgments, because they have therein done no sin." Because the Northern church had made loyalty to the federal government a term of communion, Southern Presbyterians had "no option consistent with good conscience, except to dissolve all ecclesiastical union with the Presbyterian Church in the United States."[25]

The differences between Dabney's and Thornwell's declarations were stark. Whereas Thornwell carefully preserved the doctrine of spirituality of the church, Dabney rested his defense of Southern action on the political propriety of secession. Believing that it was proper to introduce political doctrine in order to judge "the nature of the act," Dabney cleared Southern secession at the bar of history and political economy, at least for those sympathetic to his argument. Of course, Southern Presbyterians did not have an opportunity to judge Dabney's case. Because of his camp fever, he was unable to attend the historic meeting at Augusta, and his address was filed in his papers for historians to read.

During this same winter, Dabney's beloved sister, Betty, died on the same day Jefferson Davis was inaugurated as president of the Southern Confederacy. In a reminiscence written shortly after her death, Dabney recorded Betty's passing in excruciating detail and his role in almost effeminate terms. While Betty was "manfully" facing death, the ultimate destroyer, Dabney nursed her and went to such lengths that, as she lay dying, he "got on the bed behind her, and raised her on my bosom, sustaining her head in my hand." Dabney held his sister on his lap until she expired; then he "tenderly resigned her form, which lay like the graceful willow, wilted and bruised, and placed her beloved head on the pillow, that her eyes might be decently closed." Betty, without the aid of drugs that would numb the pain, had faced death and entered into eternity manfully, while Dabney and his kinfolk pierced the air with "wailings" and "uncontrollable grief."[26]

Around the same time as Betty's death, the Confederate government passed its conscription law, claiming the few students still at Union Seminary. Perhaps remembering his deceased sister's patriotic love "for the honor of Virginia," Dabney was interested in seeking another tour in the army as a chaplain and had been told by General D. H. Hill, a fellow Presbyterian, that he could have a position in his division. In the meantime, Stonewall Jackson had sent his wife away from Winchester to stay with her cousin, Dabney's wife, Lavinia, at Farmville. Jackson, as a result of his wife's intercession, offered Dabney the position of chief of staff of the Second Corps in the Army of Northern Virginia. Dabney thought the offer to be "almost preposterous," but with Mrs. Jackson at his table and J. M. P. Atkinson, president of Hampden-Sydney College, in favor of the move, Dabney gave it more consideration. He was not sure how to harmonize his calling as a minister of the gospel and a position as a staff officer in a corps that was charged with destroying the Yankee host. He went to visit Jackson at Swift Run Gap in April 1862, prepared to explain how unfit he was for the position offered and to secure a chaplain's commission in the corps. But Jackson "overruled all objections, [and] allowed me two days to [read] Halleck's articles of war . . . And he thrust me into the office."[27]

For the next five months, Dabney mixed the callings of Confederate soldier and gospel minister. In his ministerial calling, he preached on Sundays, when Jackson was not engaging the enemy, and apparently had opportunities to preach at other times. But in his military calling, Dabney helped the army kill the "enemy." Jackson's other aides did not care much for the theological professor. Fellow staff officer Henry Kyd Douglas believed that Dabney was "an excellent officer in camp" but was not equal to situations in the field. Further, Dabney did not fit in with the other aides; on the march to Richmond, when the young officers longed for dancing and women, they were pleased that Dabney was with Jackson because "he was too old, and too reverend, and to unelastic to fit in such a crowd." There was also some jealousy among the staff, for many believed that the younger Sandie

Pendleton should have been elevated to the position of chief of staff instead of Dabney. The distaste was mutual—he believed that the young aides "were too bumptious and self-sufficient." Slowly, as he learned his duties, he gained the respect of Jackson's corps, drawing the comment from one colonel, "Our parson is not afraid of Yankee bullets and I tell you he preaches like the Devil."[28]

Dabney served Jackson throughout the rest of the Valley Campaign, and then during the defense of Richmond. "I began to find out pretty soon, that my constitution and health were wholly unfit for such campaigning as Jackson's," he complained. The general "postponed his own comfort, and required us to postpone ours with an absolute, not to say a needless rigidity." Although he had the privilege of eating "at the same table, and most frequently sleep[ing] in the same room" with Jackson, Dabney's health failed. By the end of the Richmond campaign, Jackson insisted "upon my taking a sick leave from Harrison's landing, which I did not ask for." Dabney suffered from camp fever once again, a sickness "which brought me to death's door." The illness forced him to resign his commission, which Jackson accepted "with great reluctance, regarding me as the most efficient officer on his staff."[29]

The appraisal of Dabney as an officer was mixed. While Jackson apparently believed that he was a good officer, and Dabney would later claim that he was a key player at the Battle of Port Republic as well as during the Richmond campaign, later historians have not been as kind. Henry Kyd Douglas pointed out that Dabney had no military training, and that he had only been in the field a total of five months, having no experience for the work of chief of staff. "While he did his duty faithfully," Douglas admitted, "he could not be of any service to the General in such an emergency; and as for training a staff to its duties he knew nothing about it." Recent Jackson biographer J. I. Robertson Jr. hammered Dabney, claiming that he "had proved to be a misfit at army supervision" and was "overmatched" while trying to supervise the Second Corps' march to Richmond.[30]

Likewise, there was little testimony to Dabney's effectiveness as a chaplain. J. William Jones did not detail Dabney's chaplain work at all, though he reproduced a picture of him in *Christ in the Camp* and noted his effectiveness as a preacher during his time as Jackson's chief of staff. Though Dabney served as a chaplain during the summer of 1861 and made missionary tours during the winter of 1864–65, Jones did not list him in his chaplain's roster, nor did Dabney list himself in a roster he prepared at the end of the war. It did not appear that Dabney participated in the "Great Revival" of 1862–63, having left the army months prior. He did not record any autobiographical reflections on revival preaching in the army or stirring responses to his sermonic performances. In sum, Dabney's career as a Civil War chaplain and soldier is difficult to assess with accuracy because he did not participate long enough in either office to be noticed.[31]

Defending Virginia and the South

Yet Dabney was frustrated by his apparent failure as a staff officer. Not only did his short-lived service raise questions about his manhood and honor, but this second bout of camp fever nearly killed him. He received a doctor's clearance to remain at home and recover, and Jackson officially accepted his resignation in September 1862. In the midst of his pain, frustration, and loss, Dabney was determined to retrieve his manhood and honor by fighting for his country with his pen and not with the sword. In writing the book *A Defence of Virginia (And Through Her, of the South)*, Dabney attempted to justify to himself that the "labors of the scholar, while more humble, are no less necessary to the welfare of our country, than those of the solider." While the book originally served as a defense of slavery aimed toward England as a potential Southern ally, it was also directed to issues arising in the Presbyterian Church in the Confederate States of America. At the founding of the Southern Presbyterian church, James Lyon, a prominent minister from Columbus, Mississippi, was chosen to write a pastoral letter on slavery that would be sent from the Assembly to all its churches. The letter was not ready until 1863, and when Lyon presented it to the Assembly, he shocked a number of ministers by denying the biblical propriety of slavery and urging a series of reforms. The Assembly debated Lyon's paper and then sent the letter back to a committee with instructions to revise the pastoral letter and present it to the 1864 Assembly. Lyon modified the letter, but several continued to oppose its message. Lyon urged the Assembly to stand for his proposed reforms of slavery or else abolition would be the assured result. But the Assembly appointed another committee with Dabney as its chair. By the time the new committee was prepared to issue its pastoral letter, the war was over and the issue of master–slave relations was moot. Yet the fact that the Southern church even doubted whether slavery was a biblical relation also activated Dabney's pen on its behalf.[32]

Based on articles that Dabney had written twelve years earlier for the Richmond *Enquirer*, *Defence of Virginia* took four years to reach press because of a series of mishaps. First, Dabney had intended to dedicate the book to Jackson, but Stonewall's ill-timed death after the Battle of Chancellorsville prevented the general from receiving that honor. Then, intending to publish the book in England as a project of the Confederate government, Dabney sent the manuscript to his friend Moses Hoge, who was in London. Hoge apparently forwarded the manuscript to the Confederate authorities in England, but they did not publish the manuscript. Dabney was convinced that this publication failure was due to the influence of A. T. Bledsoe, who he believed was jealous for the success of his own book on slavery. Dabney did not give up on publishing the book; he even prepared an "Advertisement to the Reader" in 1864, explaining the circumstances of its creation and delay. Yet *Defence of Virginia* did not appear until after the war through the agency of the New York publisher E. J. Hale, with the blessings of Robert E. Lee. While the book did not sell well, it was viewed as an able defense of Southern slavery; the United Confederate Veterans eventually placed it among the first ten books that served as constitutional defenses of Southern rights.[33]

The burden of *Defence of Virginia* was quite simple: to demonstrate that slavery per se was not a sinful social and economic relationship. In order to prove this single point, Dabney ranged widely through historical, biblical, and economic arguments. Historically, Dabney reviewed the history of the African slave trade, blaming England, and especially New England, for its existence and praising Virginia for dismantling the trade. Dabney made the dubious claim that

Virginia's "citizens have been precluded by Providence from the least participation in" the slave trade. Such a claim ignored that slave trade was not restricted to slaves coming from Africa to America; rather, even after it became illegal to import slaves, Virginians profited quite handsomely from the slave trade, transmitting Virginia slaves to the west and Deep South through their slave markets in Richmond and Alexandria. But the entire thrust of Dabney's historical argument was to paint New England's "hypocrisy" in broad strokes: "The structure of New England wealth is cemented with the sweat and blood of Africans." This historical review extended to a history of the abolitionist movement, which Dabney claimed was equally hypocritical. While berating the South for holding slaves, the North did nothing for its own recently emancipated slaves. Dabney charged the Northern states with neglecting the welfare of emancipated slaves; failing to grant them civil rights; allowing blacks to live in "shocking decadence, vice, and misery"; protecting themselves with self-serving language; demonstrating a genuine repugnance for freed blacks themselves; and forgetting that the Northern gradual abolitionists had recognized slaveholders' property claims.[34]

Dabney also offered a legal argument for the propriety of slavery. Remembering, perhaps, Charles Hodge's argument that slavery existed solely as a result of municipal legislation and that territories held in common for all the states—slave and free—could not be used as slave states, Dabney argued vehemently that slavery "was in full accordance with the law of nature and nations as then recognized by the States and the federal government, and had universal recognition by the force of general law." Hence, slavery was not the exception to federal law; rather, it was established by federal law, Dabney believed. Instead, the exception to federal law was "free soil" as established by local municipal legislation. Further, because slavery was a federally established social and economic relation, slavery by right could go into federally held territories. Thus, Dabney concluded that not only was the Northern abolitionist argument hypocritical, it was not even constitutionally correct.[35]

By far, however, the longest and most important arguments that Dabney offered in defense of Virginia's peculiar institution were biblical. "Our best hope is in the fact that the cause of our defence is the cause of God's Word, and of its supreme authority over the human conscience," he believed. "For, as we shall evince, that Word is on our side, and the teachings of Abolitionism are clearly of rationalistic origin, of infidel tendency, and only sustained by reckless and licentious perversions of the meaning of the Sacred text." In order to demonstrate that the Bible was on his side, Dabney first defined what he meant by "slavery." According to Dabney, slavery was "the obligations of the slave to labor for life, without his own consent, for the master." Thus, the master had rights to "the involuntary labor of the slave" and was allowed to take whatever steps deemed necessary in order to secure that labor. Slave labor was viewed as property that could be valued, yet the slave's person—his personality or soul—was not the master's property, but instead belonged to God. The fact that some masters abused the slave system did not invalidate the social relation. In fact, Dabney claimed a "strong abhorrence and reprobation of all such unlawful abuses of a lawful institution." Nor did he believe that all people everywhere should live in the social relation of master–slave. He even went so far as to admit that "there is true evil in the necessity for" slavery, not in the social relation itself but in the depravity of the laboring classes that required slavery as "the useful and righteous remedy." But for the African race, which God had placed in America, "slavery was the righteous, the best, yea, the only tolerable relation."[36]

Dabney's thesis was that "the Bible teaches that the relation of master and slave is perfectly lawful and right, provided only its duties be lawfully fulfilled." In order to demonstrate this, Dabney ranged widely over Old and New Testament texts. Dabney began with Genesis 9, a key text in the apologetics for American slavery. There Dabney observed that while the curse of Ham and his son, Canaan, did not justify African slavery, it did provide "the origin of domestic slavery." God had provided slavery, according to Dabney, to remedy "the peculiar moral degradation of a part of the race." Because God had sanctioned slavery for Ham and his posterity, slavery could not be sinful, he concluded. Dabney also considered Abraham and Isaac as a slaveholders. God clearly had not disapproved of Abraham's slaveholding, he argued, because God extended the sacrament of circumcision to include Abraham's entire household—male sons *and* male slaves. Also, God told the runaway slave Hagar, who belonged to Abraham, to return to her master and submit herself to him when she had run away. Another series of Old Testament texts that Dabney examined were the Mosaic laws. He tried to demonstrate that, because God had "expressly authorized" slavery in the Old Testament, it was "innocent" to hold slaves "unless it has been subsequently forbidden by God." Finally, Dabney pointed out that slavery was mentioned twice in the Ten Commandments, "in modes which are a recognition of its lawfulness." Both the Fourth and the Tenth Commandments explicitly mentioned slavery: the Fourth commanding masters to allow slaves rest and worship on the Sabbath, the Tenth forbidding covetous attitudes toward another's slaves. The most incredible Old Testament argument that Dabney made, however, was that God was a slaveholder—in both Numbers 31:25–30 and Joshua 9:20–27, it appeared that God claimed a "tithe" of slaves akin to a tithe of grain or cattle. Hence, God could not have taught that slavery per se was sinful because God himself held slaves.[37]

While Dabney claimed that the inspired arguments of the Old Testament should be enough for Christians, still he believed that the New Testament also sanctified the master–slave relation. Though he held that the "mere absence of a condemnation of slaveholding in the New Testament is proof that it is not unlawful," he did not rest his case there. He pointed out that Christ had applauded the faith of the slaveholding centurion in Matthew 8:5–13. Further, the apostles had failed to act against slaveholding as a moral evil. In fact, slaveholders were prominent members of the early church, and the apostolic writers specifically instructed them about how they were to treat their slaves (e.g., Eph. 6:9; Col. 4:1). Finally, Dabney pointed to the apostle Paul's letter to Philemon, claiming that not only did Paul not rebuke Philemon for slaveholding, but he also returned Philemon's runaway slave Onesimus to him, apparently recognizing Philemon's property rights in his slave.[38]

Though Dabney believed that the biblical argument in slavery's behalf was the most important, he went on to demonstrate from political economy and ethics as well why slavery was a permissible social relation. Although slavery was not the *sine qua non* for a just society, Dabney believed that it was the best possible relation of white capital and black labor in the nineteenth-century South. While the rest of the world knew unrest between labor and capital, the South had solved this predicament "by making labor the property of capital and thus investing it with an unfailing claim upon its fair share in the joint products of the two." Southern labor relations were peaceful, providing a true boon for economic conditions. Instead of the grinding labor system of the North, where blacks were starved, abandoned, and forgotten by capitalists, the South cared for African Americans by making them part of the household, providing them sustenance and a place to live. Dabney claimed that Southern masters expended large amounts of money, which would have been used on luxuries if they had lived in the North, in order to maintain the slaves. If the masters resorted to the "birch" or the whip, it was only to make their farms more efficient. In addition, Southerners were more prepared to care for others in their community because they already extended themselves for their slaves. Southern masters recognized their obligation to care for the poor, such as their slaves. The result of the Southern slave system was that the laborers of the Old South "were the best fed and clothed, so they were the most athletic, the most skilled, the most effective and the most cheerful agricultural laborers in the world." Instead of the grinding oppression that Northern immigrants knew, in Dabney's bucolic vision the Southern slave was cared for and worked efficiently.[39]

"If Thou Mayest Be Made Free, Use It Rather"

At first glance, it appears that Dabney carried his central point: that the Bible did not appear to condemn the social relation of slavery as sinful. Yet Dabney's defense of slavery was plagued by several problems. First, Dabney conveniently ignored or explained away several passages that mitigated against slavery. For example, Deuteronomy 23:15 commands Israelites not to return slaves who had run away from oppressive foreign masters; instead, these former slaves should be allowed to live among the Israelites in one of their towns as freedmen under their protection. Dabney approved of Moses Stuart's interpretation of the text, holding that this had nothing to do with Hebrew slaves, but only foreign slaves, and that the reasons for this law were obvious: "the bondage from which he escaped was inordinately cruel, including the power of murder for any caprice; and that to force him back was to remand him to the darkness of heathenism, and to rob him of the light of true religion, which shone in the land of the Hebrews alone." Because this text dealt with "foreign" slaves, Dabney held that it did not apply to the American South. But to read this text in a different way would lead one to a much different conclusion, one that was in line with Northern opponents of the Fugitive Slave Law. For slaves that escaped to the North *were* escaping a bondage that was "inordinately cruel, including the power of murder for any caprice." To return slaves to the South *was* to remand them to oppression and potential death. Further, it is not entirely clear that the South was the land of true religion for black slaves. As historians Erskine Clarke and Eugene Genovese have demonstrated, it was not until the 1840s and 1850s that slaveowners took seriously their responsibility for evangelizing their slaves, and missions to African Americans still received widespread opposition until the Civil War. Hence, Northern opponents of slavery could easily read this text and conclude that they were commanded by God not to return fugitive slaves, but to grant them a place in Northern society.[40]

Further, even if one granted that slaves in the American South were not "foreign" but similar to Hebrew slaves, then African-American slaves should have been subject to the biblical law of jubilee. Leviticus 25 specifically commanded that every fiftieth year was to be consecrated in order to "proclaim liberty throughout the land to all its inhabitants." Hebrew slaves were freed, fields lay fallow, and property was returned to its original owners. Freedom was the ultimate goal of the year. And the reason for the jubilee year was to remind God's people that "it is to me that the people of Israel are servants. They are my servants whom I brought out of the land of Egypt: I am the LORD your God." Yet when Dabney discussed the issue of the jubilee, he focused on the fact that foreign slaves were not liberated. But he contradicted himself here—either African-American slaves are "foreign" or they are akin to "Hebrew" slaves, but they cannot be both. Slaves either had the biblical right to escape from bondage or were to be set free from bondage every fifty years. God's ultimate design was not slavery, but freedom.[41]

Another text on which Dabney performed hermeneutical gymnastics was 1 Corinthians 7:20–21. There the apostle Paul clearly stated that if the opportunity arose for the slave to gain his freedom, doing so was the preferable course. Dabney initially admitted the force of the language in the text. But then he attempted to mitigate the text's import by claiming that "we must remember the circumstances of the age, in order to do justice to his meaning." First, Dabney said that slavery had been much more harsh in the first century. Second, first-century masters "were accustomed to require of their slaves offices vile, and even guilty." Third, first-century society offered a way of social mobility for a "freedman" and his family. Fourth, the master and his slave were of the same skin color; after a few generations, no one could remember that the ancestor had been a slave. These four conditions of first-century slavery were markedly different from those of nineteenth-century Virginia. Dabney held that slavery in his day was comparatively mild; slaves were overseen by Christian masters; there was no possibility for social mobility once the slave was "deprived from his master's patronage"; and the slave, being black, would be "debarred as much as ever from social equality by his color and caste." Thus, Dabney's appraisal was that "freedom to the Christian slave here, may prove a loss." This line of reasoning, however, failed to overturn the apostle's claim that freedom was preferable to slavery *for the Christian slave.*[42]

In addition, Dabney completely discounted New Testament texts that appeared to argue for an egalitarian and multiracial society within the church, a place where there was "neither Jew nor Greek, there is neither slave nor free, there is neither male nor female, for you are all one in Christ Jesus" (Gal. 3:28). Ephesians 2 argues that the dividing wall of hostility between racial lines—Jews and Gentiles—has been torn down by the power of the resurrected and exalted Christ. And Revelation 4–5 presents a powerful picture of the "ransomed people [of] God" who come "from every tribe and language and people and nation," a glorious mosaic of every race under heaven worshiping God as his "kingdom and priests." Dabney did not deal with this line of argument at all in *Defence of Virginia*, although he would strenuously deny it in the postbellum period as African Americans sought ordination within the Southern Presbyterian church.[43]

Next, in his defense of slavery, Dabney also failed to reckon adequately with abuses of slavery, ones that he had willingly recognized in the past. In 1840, after a couple of years of overseeing his mother's slaves, Dabney wrote to a friend, "It seems to me that there could be no greater curse inflicted on us than to be compelled to manage a parcel of negroes. Whatever may be the influence of slavery on the happiness of the negroes, it would most effectually destroy that of the master, if they were all like me." In part, the difficulty for the master, he held, was the range of abuses that plagued slavery. Slavery was a system

> where the black is punished with death for an offence for which a white man is only imprisoned a year or two; where the black may not resist wanton aggression and injury; where he is liable to have his domestic relations violated in an instant; where the female is not mistress of her own chastity; where the slave is liable to starvation, oppression, and cruel punishments from an unprincipled master.

These abuses, which also included "the domestic slave trade," made slavery a problematic enterprise and liable to the charges brought by abolitionists.[44]

Eleven years later, Dabney's view of the abuses had not changed. Dabney confided to his brother that if slaveholders wanted the support of the Bible, then they had to "pay a price. And the price is this: they must be willing to recognize and grant in slaves, those rights which are a part of our essential humanity, some of which are left without recognition or guarantee by law, and some infringed by law." Dabney told his brother that "we must come out and grant that our right to hold slaves does not include a right to make them break the Sabbath or to keep them ignorant of moral and religious duty, or to make a husband guilty of the sin of separation from his wife for other cause than fornication or to violate the chastity of a female by forcible means." Unless Southern masters granted these rights, Dabney believed, they could not defeat the abolitionists.[45]

Yet by the time he wrote *Defence of Virginia*, he saw these abuses as unimportant or generally nonexistent, contradicting his earlier opinions: "The popular apprehension of the slave's condition and treatment, spread throughout Europe and the North *is utterly false*." First, in the past Dabney had admitted the problems of slavery, such as the slaves' deplorable illiteracy. In *Defence*, he reversed himself and claimed that

> it is our solemn and truthful testimony, that the nearly universal temper of masters was to promote and not to hinder [the mental or religious culture of slaves]; and the intellectual and religious culture of our slaves met no other general obstacle, save that which operates among the laboring poor of all countries, their own indifference to it, and the necessities of nearly constant manual labor.

This, of course, ignored laws throughout the South that made it a crime to teach slaves to read and outlawed churches ruled by black pastors. Second, Dabney had previously decried the way black slaves were forced to work on the Sabbath; in *Defence* he claimed that

> the law protected the legal right of the slave to his Sabbath, forbidding the master to employ him on that day in secular labors, other than those of necessity and mercy. Instances in which slaves were prevented by their masters from attending the public worship of God, were fully as rare among us, and as much reprobated as similar abuses are in any other Christian country.

Third, in the past Dabney had believed that blacks were subjected to inhuman punishments, even death; by the time *Defence* was published, he held that "the slave whose life was assailed might exercise the natural right of self-defence, even against his own master." Of course, a slave might have exercised self-defense, but he would have been severely punished for doing so, sent "down the river" to the notorious slave-trading dens of New Orleans, or even lynched. Fourth, Dabney had admitted the government's failure to protect slave marriages; yet in *Defence*, he rationalized this failure, claiming that the master was the authority in this area, that the government could not interfere in the master's dominion, and that the master did not often exercise his power to break up slave families—which was patently opposed to the facts. Finally, Dabney had freely admitted the great problem that existed between white male masters and black female slaves. Yet, unbelievably, in *Defence*, he claimed that the crime of white men raping black female slaves was "unheard of on the part of white men amongst us." Part of the reason the crime was "unheard of" obviously was that black women had no rights to press charges against white masters. To claim that white masters did not use their power over "the chastity of the female slave" was willful propaganda of the highest order and manifestly untrue. These abuses were not mere blemishes on the slave system, as Dabney claimed; rather, they arose out of the relationship of power that existed between master and slave, and signaled the deeply problematic character of the "peculiar institution."[46]

Most difficult, however, was how Dabney's argument for slavery in the "abstract" merged with race-based slavery. Even if he could defend slavery in the abstract as an acceptable social relation, which seems questionable, his intense racial prejudice against African Americans nullified his entire argument. Dabney claimed that black slaves "were what God's word declares human depravity to be under the degrading effects of paganism." In Africa, blacks were "living but one remove above the apes around them." Even though some had been brought to America and placed under the influence of the gospel, slaves were still prone to particular vices, such as "lying, theft, drunkenness, laziness, waste." In short, African Americans were "morally inferior" and degraded, unfit for freedom and self-governance. As a result, Dabney conjectured that slavery was useful for restraining blacks from "damaging" themselves with freedom: "We certainly are not required by a benevolent God to ruin [the slave] in order to do him justice!" In fact, "Africans among us had a right to the protection of bondage." Equally important, Southern slavery avoided the problem of amalgamation. Though he was committed to the biblical testimony that all humankind was made "of one blood," Dabney believed that African Americans had become "a different, fixed *species*" of the human race, "separated from the white man by traits bodily, mental and moral, almost as rigid and permanent as those of *genus*." By separating the races, and by subordinating blacks, there would be no fear of a "hybrid race, stamped with all the feebleness of the hybrid, and incapable of the career of civilization and glory as an independent race." Therefore, unlike proslavery apologists such as George Fitzhugh, Dabney saw Southern slavery not simply as a system of social relations between masters and slaves in the "abstract," but as a racial system that singled out whites as the only allowable masters, blacks as the only possible slaves.[47]

"God's Sermon to Us"

While *Defence of Virginia* languished in England during the last years of the war, Dabney was occupied with another writing commission. Because he had already memorialized Stonewall Jackson in a powerful sermon after the general's death in 1863, and because he was both a relative and a former member of Jackson's staff, Mary Anna Jackson asked Dabney to write a biography of the Confederate chieftain. Dabney spent the rest of the war on his *Life of Jackson*—researching the battles, visiting Mrs. Jackson, securing Jackson's remaining papers, and writing the manuscript. The resulting biography was Dabney's longest-standing literary monument and one of his chief glories. Twentieth-century historian Douglas Southall Freeman accorded to Dabney the honor of being the "first distinguished Confederate biographer." And Dabney later viewed himself as the keeper of Jackson's memory and the authority on Jackson's life and military career. He even engaged in several debates over details from the general's career.[48]

Yet Dabney's *Life of Jackson* revealed as much about Dabney as it did about Jackson. The parallels between the two men were hard to miss—loss of fathers early in life, childhoods spent in rural settings and agricultural activity, a lifelong interest in ethics and politics, conversion to the Presbyterian church, adherence to the States' Rights wing of the Democratic Party, and commitment to slavery. Yet the differences were obvious as well—while Jackson was a single-minded soldier who seemed energized in the midst of battle, Dabney barely survived battle for the five months he was in Jackson's army. Jackson denied himself everything that would keep him from the enemy, a discipline that Dabney found far too harsh. Above all, while Jackson's manhood and honor thrust him into battle, Dabney edged into the background and spent the majority of the war at home in Farmville, Virginia. Jackson met his death reconnoitering the no-man's land between Union and Confederate troops in the dark night after the first day of Chancellorsville; the last days of the war found Dabney hiding in the woods between Petersburg and Appomattox, fearful of capture. Jackson was the Christian soldier-hero who displayed "true courage," an ideal to which Dabney longingly aspired.[49]

Thus, Dabney saw more in Jackson than a man or a brilliant military tactician. Jackson was "God's sermon to us, his embodied admonition, his incorporate discourse, to inculcate upon us the virtues with which he was adorned by the Holy Ghost; and especially those traits of the citizen, the Christian, and the soldier, now most essential to the times." The sermon that God preached through Jackson was that the truly heroic man, the truly courageous man, the truly honorable man was the one who was "the best Christian." For Jesus Christ himself was "the divine pattern and fountain of heroism. Earth's true heroes are they who derive their courage from him." According to Dabney's way of thinking, although he may have spent the war recovering from illness and avoiding the battle lines until he returned to Petersburg during the siege to supply the pulpit of Tabb Street Presbyterian Church, he was as heroic, as honorable as Jackson himself—for they both feared Jesus Christ above all else. This redefinition of honor and manhood, which culminated in Dabney's *Life of Jackson*, was Dabney's attempt to rationalize his avoidance of the war and to reclaim his manly honor.[50]

Opinions of the biography were mixed. Mary Anna Jackson claimed that Dabney's portrayal of Jackson during his "battle-frenzy" was "so unlike" her husband; she later penned her own, more sentimental, reminiscences of him. Likewise, Robert E. Lee wished that Dabney had toned down the defense of slavery and secession that made up a large part of the book. *Central Presbyterian* editor William Brown suggested that the part of the biography which "equated the criminality of northern aggressions with the crucifixion of Christ approached blasphemy." Dabney struggled to get the manuscript published in England, had difficulties sorting out royalty payments, and was generally disappointed with sales of the book. Though Jackson's subsequent profiler, G. R. Henderson, praised Dabney's biography, the most recent biographer of the Southern general found Dabney's work riddled with confusion of fact as well as hyperbole. Still, the work remains an important fixture in the historical understanding of the war. Dabney recognized that this would be the case. "It is more certainly true," he observed in his preface to in *Life of Jackson*, "that if contemporaries do not write, with such partiality or impartiality as they may, it will be impossible for any other historian in posterity, to write a truthful narrative. None but eye witnesses and actors can contribute the facts, which are to be the materials of future history." Also, he was convinced that future historians would want to know "not only what men did, but how they felt." It was the deep feelings and patriotic passions that sometimes failed to do Dabney credit as a biographer and historian.[51]

"Unconquered, Unconquerable, and Forever Alienated"

Dabney never got over the Civil War, and he frankly could not understand his contemporaries who later did reconcile with the "enemy." The war was the dividing line of his mental history and the most significant event of his life. The Civil War brought about division in his church and nation, the creation of new religious and political institutions, the destruction of cherished hopes for political independence, and a series of justifications for religious and political separatism. While before the war he had been Virginian first, American second, after the war Dabney was Virginian first, Southerner second, and American maybe. The war brought about a transition from nationalist to sectionalist, from Constitutional Unionist to Secessionist. He consciously identified himself with the South that had existed before the war, and tried to remind his later New South brethren of the principles of that older South. It was Dabney's duty of honor and Christian patriotism to be loyal to the principles of the cause, even when the Old South was unpopular, and finally sentimentalized and rendered irrelevant. He became exactly what he had warned Charles

Hodge that the South as a whole would become: unconquered, unconquerable, and forever alienated.[52]

Why Dabney became so embittered while countless other Southerners reconciled themselves to defeat and participated in a growing sense of national reconciliation during the 1870s and particularly the 1880s is hard to understand. Perhaps some of Dabney's bitterness was legitimate, aroused by the suffering brought about by the first modern war fought largely in his native state—Dabney's friends and relatives were the suffering ones, and his soul burned in indignation against those who had caused the suffering. And perhaps Dabney's bitterness also derived from the way Reconstruction played out in Virginia—the hypocrisy of the Northern victors coupled with the corruption of the Conservative Party that seized control of the Virginia Assembly in 1869. But at the root of Dabney's intense bitterness was the dishonor he felt by not taking his part at the front lines of the war. In 1864, Dabney wrote to a friend in his old congregation at Tinkling Spring, "Every time I hear of the fall of a friend among our valuable young men I feel a shock of grief and indignation. I feel that there is a sense in which they have died for me, and in my stead, for my defence, and that of my home and little ones, and that their sufferings and blood are the price of my safety." Home was the place for women and children, not for those patriots who defended their country. Yet Dabney spent most of the war at home, playing the role of "an old hen" while his wife was sick in 1864. And with the exception of the five months he had served as Jackson's chief of staff, the times when Dabney had been near the war were spent in the back of the army, not in the front lines proving his manly mettle and gaining honor. Confederate soldiers felt the fire of the enemy, saw the enemy's gallantry as well as their own heroism, and reckoned that though the North had superior supplies, both sides in the war fought for principle and honor. As a result, those who actually fought believed that reconciliation with the North was between equally honorable parties, a sentiment that existed during the Reconstruction period and became general during the 1870s. However, for those such as Dabney, who spent most of the war away from the front lines and who were not able to assert their manly honor in martial ways, the North was a corrupt and dishonorable foe; to lose to such unworthy enemies and then to reconcile with them was the abandonment of principle, honor, and manhood. The only way for noncombatants such as Dabney to maintain honor was to continue to hate the "enemy." As Dabney confided to fellow Presbyterian D. H. Hill, "The only choice we have is to teach the Southern people to hate the Yankees, or else, to be all Yankees together."[53]

After the war, most of Dabney's students greatly admired and feared him, but they recognized that this was the one issue on which Dabney had become "narrow" and "implacable"—his attitude toward his former Northern enemies. One former student, Samuel Hall Chester, who later became the secretary of the foreign missions committee of the Southern Presbyterian church, observed that Dabney "became so embittered by the ruthless methods of Federal officers like Sheridan and Sherman, and the efforts of Congress to impose Negro rule on the South that he almost went off his mental balance. Being once taken to task for the violence of his denunciation of these leaders, he made no reply, but preached the following Sunday on the text, 'Do not I hate them, O Lord, that hate Thee?' " While Dabney believed that Christian patriotism and honor required him to remain loyal to his principles and the past, such a loyalty would make him increasingly lonely as the South experienced Reconstruction and sought to make itself new.[54]

5

Presbyterian Partisan

The end of the war filled Dabney with apprehension and depression. As historian Charles Reagan Wilson observed, "In the post-Appomattox period, [Dabney] developed a disturbing vision of the religious and moral effects of Confederate defeat. With apocalyptic imagery and prophetic warnings, he portrayed the post-bellum South as a fearful land for a religious man. For Dabney, defeat created a dark night of the soul so troubling that it took all his human will to calm his doubts." Wilson's observation was not hyperbole. The early years of Reconstruction in Virginia overturned all the eternal verities of Southern civilization, and brought into question Dabney's moral universe. As he wrote to his mother in 1868, "The labors of my life seem to be like marks made on a sandy beach for the rising tide to wash away." Northern control and African-American rule, coupled with Southern destitution, made Dabney feel as though the world was a "wilderness . . . with plenty of wild beasts in it."[1]

This fear and gloom, brought on by a sense of dishonor caused by "submission" to Northern rule and "degradation" to the position of slaves, made Dabney wonder whether "there is any other country on earth, where the prospect would not be better for Virginia society and Virginia Christianity's making a permanent impress for good." Like other former Confederates, Dabney extensively explored the possibility of emigrating from America to another country, particularly Brazil. As early as August 1865, Dabney mentioned emigration both to his brother Charles William and to his friend Moses Hoge. To Hoge, Dabney wrote, "From all I see, the only chance to save any of the true Christianity of the South is to transplant it as quick as possible . . . I fear the only way to save Virginia is to take her out of Virginia. My ambition never has been to leave Virginia to go to the Yankees, and now it is to take Virginia, along with myself, away from that race." Dabney corresponded extensively with Confederate General Jubal Early about the possibilities of emigrating, with the correspondence reaching a fevered pitch in the early months of 1867. While many "Confederados" did make their way to Brazil, taking their Presbyterianism with them, Dabney's mind eventually turned more and more to remaining at home, and the idea of emigrating faded out of view.[2]

The issues at home were pressing and demanded Dabney's energies. While the North had gained the upper hand politically through the force of arms, Dabney sought to maintain a distinctive Southern civilization, not by emigrating to Brazil, Australia, or New Zealand, but by strengthening the Southern institutions that remained. Primarily, that meant strengthening the Southern Presbyterian church, now formally known as the Presbyterian Church in the United States (PCUS). In fact, during the war, Dabney participated in ecumenical efforts that sought to forge a single Presbyterian church in the South. While not completely successful—the Associate Reformed Presbyterians, for one, resisted the efforts of the PCUS—Dabney's vision for a united Southern Presbyterian church arose from the belief that the church would be the safeguard of Southern morals as well as doctrine. As he would later argue, Dabney believed that the only "bulwark against the flood of Yankee innovations in religion and morals" in the South was the Southern Presbyterian church. By creating one Southern Zion in a united Presbyterian church, he thought that Southern civilization could be preserved. As a result, Dabney served as the point man in the effort to reunite the Southern Presbyterian church, derived from the Old School branch of the national church, with the United Synod of the South, which had sided previously with the New School.[3]

Dabney's efforts to create a single institution to preserve Southern religion and civilization also meant that the church increasingly became a public sphere, where religious arguments carried implicit and explicit political meanings. As historian Jack Maddex perceptively noted, in the postbellum period Southern Presbyterians' rivalry with Northern Presbyterians became "a surrogate for politics." By forging one Southern Presbyterian church, and by keeping the Southern church separate, Dabney tried to maintain a sense of sectionalism in the reunited country. It was primarily in the PCUS, not in monuments or Confederate Day speeches, that Dabney sought to preserve Southern identity.[4]

While Dabney enlarged the borders of his Southern Zion to include former New School Presbyterians, he made certain that those borders excluded both African Americans and Yankee Presbyterians. Dabney's arguments against ordaining African Americans in the Synod of Virginia not only defeated the short-term possibility of racial reconciliation and black leadership within the church, but also set the "racial orthodoxy" for the Southern Presbyterian church for over a hundred years. Motivated by racial prejudice in place of biblical reasoning, Dabney's defense of segregation was a completely indefensible moment in his career. Likewise, his arguments against fraternal relations with the Northern Presbyterian church smacked more of self-interest than sound biblical rationale. Dabney refused to consider friendly relations with Northern Presbyterians until that church repudiated the 1861 Spring Resolutions and its notorious 1865 "Pittsburgh Orders," required tighter subscription to the Westminster Standards, and reaffirmed the Old School principles that had apparently been lost in the reunion of the Northern New and Old School branches in 1869. He also opposed the Pan-Presbyterian Alliance, which first met in 1877, because the Reformed churches that made up the Alliance were "latitudinarian" in their doctrinal standards and "abolitionist" in perspective. While Dabney was able to hold the line against any form of racial reconciliation, he was not as successful in his battle against fraternal relations with the Northern church—in 1882, New South Presbyterians within the PCUS repudiated his position. This battle against the Northern church did more to damage his reputation than any other action, and would ultimately be the impetus that relegated Dabney to the margins, both ecclesiastically in his loss of influence within his church and geographically in his "exile" to Texas.

Yet Dabney's agenda for the church during this period was not entirely negative. He recognized that the Southern church could not remain static and rest on its supposed purity. Rather, the PCUS had to be active in taking the gospel to those who needed to hear it. As a result, Dabney was deeply committed to foreign and domestic missions. Among his dearest correspondents during the postbellum period were Edward Lane, foreign missionary to Brazil, and E. O. Guerrant, home missionary to eastern Kentucky. In his correspondence with these two former students and friends, Dabney displayed a vital interest in sending the "pure Gospel" of the Reformed faith to the "darkest regions" of the earth. This was the only way in which the Southern Zion would remain a vital force—by the laborers' going into the world that was like a field "white unto harvest" to reap gospel fruit. By building up Southern Presbyterianism, the church would continue to shape Southern culture and maintain itself against the vain religious, political, and social philosophies of the dreaded "Yankees."

One Southern Presbyterian Zion

When the Southern Presbyterian church formed in 1861, it expressed a desire for fraternal relations and merger with several other churches of "like faith and order" within the borders of the Confederacy. The first church to join with them was the Independent Presbyterian Church. Located mainly in South Carolina, the tiny communion that emphasized congregationalism and some New Divinity doctrines had first entered into merger discussions with the national Old School Presbyterian church in 1857. At that time, reunion was rejected by a group led by James Henley Thornwell and R. J. Breckinridge, who claimed that the ordinations of the Independent Church ministers were invalid. Motivated by the exigencies of the war, however, talk of reunion started again, and the Independent Church was received by the larger church in 1863. One of the unusual aspects of the union was the unrecorded understanding that the peculiar doctrines of the Independent Presbyterian Church were to be tolerated, while officially the union

136

was based on subscription to the Westminster Standards as containing the system of doctrine found in the Scriptures.[5]

Perhaps this reunion laid the groundwork for the reunion of the Southern New School Presbyterians, called the United Synod of the South, with their former Old School brethren. While the Independent Church was a small body in South Carolina, the United Synod was a significant group with over a hundred fifty churches and almost twelve thousand members, located mainly in Virginia, Tennessee, and Mississippi. Originally siding with the Northern New School for procedural reasons more than doctrinal ones—though there were significant doctrinal sympathies with the New Divinity—the Southern New Schoolers were forced to withdraw from the New School church in 1857, after the national body declared that slaveholding was an offense liable to church discipline. While members of the United Synod had attempted in 1858 to effect a merger with the Old School church, they were rejected by a group led by Thornwell and J. B. Adger, and forced to go on their own. Not until the war started was interest in a reunion between the two parties renewed.[6]

Dabney and Hoge were among the few who were interested in reunion with the Southern New School as early as 1857. Shortly after the Southerners returned from that pivotal New School Assembly that essentially forced them out of their church, Dabney wrote an editorial for the *Central Presbyterian* that stood as the Virginia Old School "position" on reunion with the New School. Dabney claimed that "we have no hesitation in avowing our conviction that a reunion with us, on the proper basis, will *for them* be the wisest, safest, and happiest solution of the difficulty into which our New School brethren have been driven by the unrighteous action of their late Northern associates." He offered several arguments and sought to assuage fears that the Southern New School would have about joining with the Old School. In addition, Dabney promised that "should this union be formed, we have no humiliations to impose on our brethren commonly known as New School, no concessions to demand of them, but expect to meet them as equals." Intimated also was the promise that the Southern New Schoolers would not have to agree with the Old School's actions in excising four synods in 1837, and that the examination for

New School ministers received in the Old School church would not touch on the doctrinal points that had divided the two groups. After these essays were published, Hoge told Dabney that "our editorial entitled 'Our Position,' is making a great sensation in the New School camp." Hoge had received several assurances that leading Virginia New Schoolers approved of the essay. Emboldened by this positive reception, Hoge urged Dabney to write a second essay that set forward the way in which the New School could be received into the church. In compliance, Dabney urged in the *Central Presbyterian* that it was just for the Old School to seek to examine those who would be entering their presbyteries, but that New Schoolers had nothing to worry about, for the Old School desired a union with them, ending the "odium and sin of perpetuating the division."[7]

At that point, reunion was rejected and the Southern New School became the United Synod of the South. But the Civil War brought on a new situation that made merger between the United Synod and the Southern church desirable for both sides. Once again Dabney, supported by his West Hanover Presbytery and the East Hanover Presbytery, was in the lead on the issue. The 1863 General Assembly, in response to an overture from these two presbyteries, appointed a committee of correspondence to meet with the United Synod, chaired by Dabney. The United Synod did the same, and the two committees met at First Presbyterian Church, Lynchburg, Virginia, in July 1863. Dabney dominated the meeting, essentially having the plan of union drawn up beforehand. The report, which was released to the Presbyterian newspapers in November, consisted of six articles, the most important being the first, which touched on the doctrinal basis of the union. While both churches claimed "to sincerely receive and adopt the Confession and Catechisms of the Presbyterian Church, as containing the system of doctrines taught in the Holy Scriptures," the report recognized that there were several areas of difference between the two groups. Thus, the article set forth a declaration, penned by Dabney, "to manifest our hearty agreement, to remove suspicions and offences, to restore full confidence between brethren, and to honor God's saving truth." The declaration focused on six areas—the fall of humankind and original sin; regeneration; the atonement; justification; the nature of revival;

and the centrality of the visible church—that generally sought to balance Old and New School understandings of what the confession taught. The second and third articles of the plan of union dealt with the boundaries of various presbyteries and how the new presbyteries should be drawn. The fourth article urged union of churches in neighborhoods that supported both United Synod and General Assembly churches. The fifth article assured United Synod missionaries of continued support in the united church, while the final article provided for the ratification of the plan of union.[8]

Dabney's plan found critics in John Miller and B. M. Palmer, both writing in the *Southern Presbyterian Review*. Miller claimed that the first article of the plan, with its doctrinal declaration, was unnecessary, unconstitutional, unprecedented, and prejudicial to future discipline. Miller believed that if the plan were adopted, the declaration would operate like a creedal statement to which men would be required to subscribe. According to Miller, such a declaration was unnecessary because the Presbyterian church already required subscription to the Westminster Standards. In addition, to require subscription to another statement, without approval of the presbyteries, was unconstitutional and unprecedented in Presbyterian history. Further, a statement in addition to the Standards would be prejudicial to discipline because a minister under investigation could appeal to this declaration of the plan of union, which might or might not agree with the Westminster Confession. Above all, Miller appeared quite disturbed that a doctrinal declaration, essentially hammered out in a day, would be part of Presbyterian law without going through regular Presbyterian procedures.[9]

While Miller focused on the plan's procedural irregularities, B. M. Palmer took on its doctrinal and historical problems. Palmer first objected that the plan's preamble appeared to serve as "a virtual abjuration of all the principles so earnestly contended for in 1837." By claiming that the "former separations" brought about "dishonor" to Christianity, the plan of union denigrated the Old School, Palmer believed. In fact, the entire report lumped the Old School together with the New, impeaching "the orthodoxy of our own church in the imputation of errors which she is required to disown." Yet it was the New School that had been deviant in doctrine, Palmer charged, and still was—for in 1858, the United Synod had clarified its mode of subscription in order "to embody the fatal reservation of a subscription for 'substance of doctrine.' " Even more, this report shielded these New School men from declaring their true principles, which frustrated Palmer. "What we desire of these brethren," he declared, "is a plain straightforward adoption of the Church standards, in their simple and obvious import, without equivocation or reservation of any sort." Instead, the report bore the marks of "being a compromise between the parties negotiating . . . There is an antithesis pervading the entire document, a balancing of one view against another, which points to the two parties who are to adopt the instrument as plainly as though it were written, this is for you, and that in turn for you."[10]

After assailing the "quasi-symbolic character" that the declaration must assume in the united church, Palmer focused on three specific doctrinal issues on which he found the report unsatisfactory. First, Palmer believed that the section on imputation improperly allowed the position of mediate imputation. Second, the same section, which dealt with an individual's inability to turn to God, was stated in "language so incautious as to open the door for the importation of the worst heresies that can afflict the church of God." When the report claimed to reject "the error of those who assert that the sinner has no power of any kind for the performance of duty," it was speaking the language of the New Divinity, not the Westminster Standards. Palmer upbraided Dabney for allowing this language in the declaration: "Alas! that our brother should thus 'speak half in the speech of Ashdod!' Is not this the identical language in which the hereditary enemies of Calvinism have always endeavored to excite the prejudices of unthinking and uncritical men? And are not these the arguments by which the old theology has ever been assailed?" He also took a special shot at Dabney's fitness for the task of committee chairman, writing, "We venture to say that this painful embarrassment would not have been felt by our excellent brother in his theological chair at Prince Edward: but as a committee man at Lynchburg, he had a new and strange role to play, as the special advocate of New School opinions, and he works awkwardly in the harness." Palmer's third area of doctrinal question was on the atonement. He objected that the report claimed that Christ had not received the precise penalty due to sinners, but only one equivalent to it. Further, the report held that Christ's death had a universal design, with the result that his death was efficacious for only a portion of those for whom he had died. Rather than adopting such a flawed declaration, Palmer urged the church to pursue union with the United Synod through "a square and unreserved adoption of our acknowledged standards, in their obvious and literal import."[11]

By the time of the General Assembly, the battle lines were essentially drawn and the arguments well rehearsed. The debate took the better part of four days, with Dabney, Moses Hoge, and William Brown defending the plan of union, and Palmer and Adger speaking against it. Dabney's speech, which lasted three hours, responded to his critics. To Palmer's objection that the preamble signaled a defection from the testimony of the Old School in 1837, Dabney claimed that the "separations" referred to were "all those causeless and mischievous divisions in the South, divisions of hearts, of churches, of schools, as of my native congregation, that of the sainted Wharey, of the College Church, the Richmond Church, the Union Seminary, and a multitude of other churches," not specifically the division of 1837.[12]

Dabney then moved on to answer Palmer's specific doctrinal objections. Those who believed that Dabney revived the distinction between natural and moral ability failed to attend to the distinction he made between "ability" and "power." He claimed that the word "inability" in Calvinist theology "had a most sharply defined and specific meaning, as expressive of the lack only of one peculiar kind of power," whereas the word "power" was a general term with reference to ability "to make or receive any change." Hence, the statement in the report affirmed that human beings were completely unable to turn to God by their own volition, but asserted that they had power to do their duty in other arenas of life, a belief that Dabney claimed was universally held by Calvinists. Finally, on the atonement, Dabney claimed that the Westminster Confession did not take a position on the order of decrees—the long-standing debate among Calvinists over infralapsarianism and supralapsarianism. Indeed, he held that "if we impute our sequences to God, we plunge into error. The most we can comprehend is that God, in entertaining from eternity one part of this contemporaneous purpose, has regard to a state of facts as to that part destined by him to result from his same purpose as to other parts of his moral government." Further, the report simply said the same thing that the Bible said about the nature and extent of the atonement. While the nature of the atonement "has no limits," the atonement is "applied through this work of Christ precisely to those to whom it was God's eternal purpose to apply it; and that is, his elect." Dabney also defended the idea that, in Christ's death, one penalty was substituted for another, claiming this to be the standard position of all the authors of the Reformed faith. To close the speech, Dabney made reference to Palmer, uttering the wish that Palmer would be returned to his pulpit in New Orleans at the end of the war and that "during long and prosperous years may minister to that great city the glorious gospel of the Savior, until the fame of his genius, his sanctified eloquence, and his usefulness is borne on the white wings of her imperial commerce to the ends of the earth." The comparison between Dabney's graciousness and Palmer's criticism was invidious and worked to Dabney's favor.[13]

Dabney's committee report was referred to a new committee, chaired by James Lyon. This committee submitted the report to the General Assembly, but rewrote the first article to read that "the General Assembly and the United Synod declare that they continue sincerely to receive and adopt the Confession of Faith and Catechisms of the Presbyterian Church, as containing the system of doctrine taught in the Holy Scriptures." The declaration was done away with, in the fourth resolution of the committee, because the committee held that "the Assembly does yet judge that it is most prudent to unite on the basis of our existing standards only, inasmuch as no actual necessity for other declarations of belief in order to a happy union now exist[s]." The Assembly voted on this committee report, and the plan of union with the United Synod passed, fifty-three to seven, Palmer and Adger carrying only five other votes in addition to their own.[14]

Dabney won a great victory with this merger, but the reasons why he sought to unite with the United Synod remain unclear. His biographer, Thomas Cary Johnson, claimed that Dabney feared the proposed New School seminary to be established in Charlottesville, Virginia. With the potential faculty election of A. H. H. Boyd, a prominent New

School minister from Winchester, Virginia, who held strongly to the New England theology, the influence of the seminary could have been great. With the union of the two Synods of Virginia, the endowment for the proposed seminary would go to Hampden-Sydney College, and all future ministers would be trained at Old School seminaries such as Union. Dabney must have known, however, that prominent ministers in the United Synod *did* hold to the New Divinity, and that those ministers believed they were entering the church with essentially the same rights that the Independent Presbyterian Church had received—to teach their peculiar doctrines without fear of discipline. In addition, Palmer and Adger were correct: the declaration that Dabney had penned was broad enough to be affirmed by both Old and New Schoolers. For Dabney later to charge the Northern church with "broad churchism," after the 1869 Northern Old School–New School reunion on a similar basis as the Southern reunion, was hypocritical in this light. Perhaps the only way that he could rationalize the reunion with the United Synod was that the united Southern Presbyterian church would serve as a single Southern Zion, an institution that would preserve Southern religion, morals, and civilization in an increasingly hostile world. By enlarging the borders of the Southern Zion, Dabney hoped to preserve what was "best" about the South, with the result that his hopes for a united Southern Presbyterian church may have been less about the *church* and more about the *South*.[15]

The "Ecclesiastical Equality of Negroes"

Directly after the end of the war, the General Assembly of the PCUS began to consider what to do with the former African-American slaves in their churches. During the 1866 General Assembly, John L. Girardeau, who before the war had served as a missionary to blacks in Charleston, South Carolina, presented a paper on behalf of a committee on the relation of the church to the freedmen, which was later published in the *Southern Presbyterian Review*. Entitled "Our Ecclesiastical Relations to Freedmen," Girardeau acknowledged the basic unity of the human race and the unity of all true believers in Jesus; African Americans were one with whites as humans and believers. While they were slaves, social and ecclesiastical equality was out of the question. Once Reconstruction made the slaves equal in civil society, however, the question that "deserves to be considered . . . [is] whether we ought not to adopt such measures as will, at least to some extent, conform our relations to them to the existing order of things." The insuperable problem is that "the elevation of the colored people to *civil* equality with the whites, tends to produce in them a desire for *social* and *ecclesiastical* equality. This the whites will not be willing to concede." The solution to the problem was either to allow blacks to form completely separate organizations or to maintain a connection with blacks, setting up "branch" churches to allow whites to exercise some sort of oversight over blacks. Girardeau preferred the latter solution, while acknowledging that it faced its own difficulties. If white Southern Presbyterians allowed blacks to have partial oversight over their churches, this would lead them to desire full oversight over their own affairs, moving them outside white control. In addition, if black ruling elders were elected, they would be barred from white presbytery or synod meetings from fears of race-mixing, which would also lead them to demand separate church structures.[16]

The General Assembly was not prepared to act on Girardeau's report. Instead, the Assembly recommitted the paper to the committee and added four new members, including racial conservatives Samuel J. Baird and B. M. Palmer. The committee then offered a substitute paper and resolution, indicating that "it was highly inexpedient" to effect an ecclesiastical separation of the races or to ordain African Americans as elders or deacons. The solution that the committee offered was the licensing of African-American exhorters who could labor among their own people "under the supervision of the body appointing [them]." Northerners and Southern racial moderates assailed these resolutions. J. M. P. Atkinson, William Brown, and Thomas Peck engaged in a spirited exchange in the *Central Presbyterian* over the meaning of the Assembly's actions. Atkinson argued that the church should allow African Americans to exercise the full privileges of church membership within a single interracial church, including the opportunity to stand for the offices of deacon, elder, and minister of the Word. Brown believed that such propositions were radical and dangerous—not only would it fail to satisfy the freedmen, but Atkinson's plan would drive whites from the Presbyterian church. What was needed, according to Brown, was a separate church structure for blacks. Peck disagreed with Brown, believing that it was wrong to drive blacks away from the church into separate organizations. If a biracial church meant that blacks no longer sat in the balcony, according to Peck, then so be it.[17]

By the time the Synod of Virginia met in 1867, the question of the ecclesiastical standing of African Americans was at the center of debate. Dabney viewed the whole question as "the crotchet of ecclesiastical amalgamation with the negroes" that had drawn "Drs. Atkinson and Peck to their side; the latter two influenced more by the spirit of romantic magnanimity and self-sacrifice than by sound logic." While Dabney was absent from the debate, the synod passed a resolution that overtured the General Assembly "to declare that ordination to the work of Gospel ministry is to be given to all those who are called of God to and qualified for that work without respect of persons." When Dabney returned, his friends and former students desired him to speak to the resolution. In the afternoon, the resolution was returned to the floor. Dabney recalled that the resolution was a "shocking surprise" to him, and he "was outraged and about desperate. I knew that this negro amalgamation would ruin our church. I felt that it was a moment of life and death for the church. I resolved, therefore, to fight like a man striking for life or death, to drop every restraint, and to give full swing to every force of argument, emotion, will, and utterance."[18]

The result was later published as a pamphlet on the "Ecclesiastical Equality of Negroes." Dabney opened his speech by noting five reasons for his opposition to the synod's resolution. First, he deemed the topic as "unseasonable." While he essentially agreed with the action taken by the 1866 General Assembly in Memphis, Dabney wished that the matter had never been broached. The present was not the time to consider the matter—the South was not ready to deal with the issue, and the North would not credit the church for wrestling with it. Further, "I have had enough of declarations and manifestations," he declared, "of special interest in, and love for, the souls of 'the freedmen' under existing circumstances . . . I, for one, make no professions of special love for those who are, even now, attempting against me and mine the most loathsome outrages."[19]

Second, Dabney opposed the overture as "both incorrect and ambiguous." He believed that the General Assembly was plain and mainly correct: while all men were morally equal before God in creation and redemption, yet ecclesiastically they were unequal. The church could restrict church office from some "at the dictate of a sound discretion. This is scriptural truth." For Virginians to deny this plain meaning in the Assembly's action was itself incorrect. Further, the synod's resolution was ambiguous. Dabney himself affirmed that God's call and qualifications could come to black men, and if they were properly qualified, they could be ordained. But if the synod meant to affirm that an African-American man could be ordained "to teach and rule white people, and make him a co-equal member with myself in West Hanover Presbytery, to sit in judgment on the affairs of white churches and members," then "I am utterly opposed to you."[20]

A third reason that Dabney opposed the resolution was that it was impractical. The only effect of the synod's action would be to agitate white members of the Presbyterian church. In addition, ordaining African Americans would be the excuse needed to lower the ordination standards of the church, for no black man could ever be found who met "that high standard of learning, manners, sanctity, prudence, and moral weight and acceptability" that the Presbyterian standards required. Fourth, Dabney opposed the synod's action "because that race is not trustworthy for such position." African Americans were a "subservient race . . . made to follow, and not to lead." In addition, the black man's "temperament, idiosyncrasy and social relation make him untrustworthy as a depository of power." Finally, the synod's action sought "to bring a mischievous element into our church at the expense of driving a multitude of valuable members and ministers out."[21]

Yet the potential results of the action troubled Dabney even more than the action itself. For in a day when the church was the only place where white Virginians could meet and act "without the disgust of negro politics and the stain of negro domination," the leaders of the church meant to do nothing less than to foster "ecclesiastical amalgamation." Race-mixing in the churches would lead to social amalgamation and miscegenation. This was the goal of the devil himself, who was behind the reckless social change: to "taint the blood which hallowed the plains of Manassas with this sordid stream." By admitting African-American males into the sessions and presbyteries of the church, the synod was one step away from race-mixing, for "you must have this negro of yours reviewing and censuring the records of white sessions, and sitting to judge appeals brought before you by white parties, possibly by white ladies!" Amalgamation was the ultimate end of the synod's action.[22]

The synod could pull itself back from its disastrous action, Dabney proclaimed, if it would heed the Bible and the Presbyterian standards. Advocates of ecclesiastical equality for African Americans often quoted Galatians 3:28, claiming that the text meant that "because the blessings of redemption are common to all classes and races of true believers, therefore it follows, of course, that every privilege and grade of church power must be made common to them." Dabney, however, believed that the Bible argued against such a conclusion. First, though the blessings of the gospel in the Old Testament came to all believing Jews, God did not allow everyone to be priests but restricted the priesthood to the tribe of Levi. Second, though women were included in the blessings of Christ in texts such as Galatians 3:28, the apostle Paul elsewhere specifically excluded women from church office. Third, though former polygamists in the first-century church enjoyed the blessings of redemption, they were also specifically excluded from holding church office. Thus, Dabney argued that the Bible did exclude classes of believers from church office even though they knew the blessings of redemption.[23]

Moreover, the church itself had the right to exercise power in limiting office based on race and class and had exercised that right throughout its history. One example was that the ancient church had not ordained slaves even though slaves were admitted to church membership. Another example was recent Presbyterian history. For over a hundred and fifty years, the Presbyterian church in the United States did not ordain a slave. Yet no one had agitated to do so; no synod had declared that "color and race [presented] no barrier to ordaining a negro as the spiritual ruler of white men, provided he had the other qualifications." All of this recent agitation, to Dabney's mind, was pure hypocrisy—for there had been free blacks in the antebellum period, but no one demanded ordination for them. Not only did the church have the right to limit church office, the presbytery also had the right to examine every potential candidate's call to ministry. If the presbytery must credit every black man's sense of calling while rigorously investigating a potential white minister's divine call, this smacked of "abolition frenzy," the idea that blacks were "truer vehicles of the mind of the Spirit than . . . a white man."[24]

In conclusion, Dabney opposed "the attempt to establish a clerical equality between the two races, in the same churches and judicatories, as being bad for us and bad for them." Instead, he advised the synod to solicit blacks to remain members of white churches, with no hope of church office. If African Americans would not do that, then Dabney advocated the establishment of a separate church, "ecclesiastically independent of, and separate from, ours, but in relations of friendship and charity." In order to effect such a separation, Dabney desired the church to provide aid in church-building, ministerial training, and even ordination to enough men to form a separate presbytery, "when enough can be found possessed of constitutional qualifications."[25]

After Dabney's speech, one observer noted that the effect was powerful: "His audience was held in the agony of suppressed emotion . . . Some of the visitors were fairly alarmed. When he finished, we felt as men feel when a tornado has just swept by them. We drew a long breath to relieve the lungs." The synod rescinded its overture and substituted another, urging the General Assembly to "revoke the paper adopted by the last General Assembly on the relation of our church to the colored people, on the ground that the whole subject of licensing and ordaining persons to Gospel Ministry is by the constitution placed, in the first instances, in the power of the Presbyteries." The 1867 General Assembly heeded the Virginia Synod's overture and rescinded its resolution from the previous year. Thus, Dabney's speech served its purpose and turned the tide against racial equality within the Southern Presbyterian church. Other conservatives within the church complimented Dabney's speech. Stuart Robinson distributed copies of Dabney's pamphlet at the 1868 meeting of the Synod of Kentucky. "It is needless to tell you," Robinson wrote to Dabney about the pamphlet, "that I concur in your views of the tone which ought to be maintained . . . as far as a man of peace, like myself, can concur with a man of war like you." B. M. Palmer later remarked that he had been "long prepared to plant myself firmly on the ground which you have more rapidly and intuitively taken." Ultimately, the church provided for a separate, affiliated African-American Presbyterian church in line with Dabney's wishes. In addition, issues of race-mixing and white supremacy would be used to hinder reunion with the Northern Presbyterian church for the rest of the nineteenth century. Thus, Dabney's speech set the "racial orthodoxy" of the Southern Presbyterian church for the next hundred years.[26]

Dabney's racial orthodoxy, however, was not biblical orthodoxy. Far from proving his case that nonwhites were biblically banned from holding church office, Dabney revealed his intense racial prejudice. Particularly, Dabney's view of blacks as degraded and dishonorable was without foundation and especially troubling.[27] The apostle Paul specifically dealt with issues of racial origin in Galatians 3:28: "There is neither Jew nor Greek, . . . for you are all one in Christ Jesus." In Christ's church, there was no place for racial pride or superiority; in fact, Paul warned the Roman Christians not to be arrogant toward the Jews, who appeared to be rejected by God and distant from God's promises (Rom. 11:17–18). Further, God did not single out one group of people in the world as degraded and dishonorable—all humankind is degraded by virtue of sin and rebellion against God, and all need redemption through Jesus Christ. Such was Paul's argument in the first three chapters of Romans—Jews and Gentiles, blacks and whites, "the whole world" was held accountable to God because of sin, Paul claimed in Romans 3:19–20. Moreover, Paul did not restrict church office solely to converted Jews; rather, Paul instructed Titus to "appoint elders in every town as I directed you," even in Crete, a place that Paul later characterized as full of degraded and dishonorable people (Titus 1:5, 12–13). In the New Testament, the apostles did not restrict office based on racial markers, but appointed Jews and Gentiles alike to be elders over the one body of Christ. Dabney failed to see that the common waters of baptism and the common bread and cup of the Lord's Supper symbolized a new reality: the one body of Christ, made up of and ruled by those from every tribe, nation, and language.[28]

Fraternal Relations and Presbyterian Alliance

Dabney not only believed that it was important to keep African Americans separate within the church, but also believed that any form of friendly relations with the Northern Presbyterian church would be disastrous. Southern Presbyterians in general might have been willing to seek friendly relations with the Northern church at the end of the Civil War. But the 1865 Old School General Assembly meeting in Pittsburgh, inflamed by the assassination of Lincoln, issued its infamous "orders," claiming that the formation of the Presbyterian Church in the Confederate States of America was "unwarranted, schismatical, and unconstitutional." Further, the Assembly developed a plan to reconstruct the Southern churches, providing a means to reclaim ministers "when they properly acknowledge and renounce their errors." These errors included "aiding or countenancing the rebellion and the war which has been waged against the United States," propagating "the system of Negro slavery," and supporting the "doctrine of States Rights." The Pittsburgh Orders were confirmed by the following year's General Assembly and made reunion with the Southern church virtually impossible.[29]

While the Pittsburgh Orders alienated Southerners, the Northern Old School–New School reunion in 1869 provided a continuing reason for the Southern church to remain separate. As the Northern Old School Presbyterian Church became increasingly politicized during the war, the differences between the two Northern branches appeared less important. Added to the Old School change on social and political issues was the New School Presbyterians' chastened attitude toward Presbyterian polity. The only genuine issue that stood in the way of reunion was the problem of confessional subscription. A small group within the Old School, led by Charles Hodge, continued to advocate "strict subscription" to the Westminster Standards against the New School principle of "system subscription." When Henry Boynton

Smith, New School theologian at Union Theological Seminary in New York City, urged that the basis of reunion be "the adoption of the standards without note or comment," Old Schoolers caved in and reunited with the other Northern branch in 1869. Southern Presbyterians expressed profound concern about the "new church" formed by the reunion. One writer in the *Southern Presbyterian Review* contended that the united Northern church was an entirely new church, as was evidenced by its "diluted" doctrine and the addition of "a new Trinity" in its creed: "the union, the war, and the negro." Southern Presbyterians believed that they had to remain separate until the "Yankee" church repented of its political pronouncements made before the reunion and reformed its principle of doctrinal subscription.[30]

Dabney feared that the Northern church would attempt to draw the Southern church under its control. Writing to Moses Hoge in 1867, Dabney complained that the independence of the Southern church would "be lost after a time (partly betrayed by its own men, and partly overpowered by the Yankees)" and that in "thirty years" there would be "no such thing as a separate Southern Church." In 1870, the issue of Northern and Southern Presbyterian reunion came to a head at the PCUS General Assembly in Louisville, Kentucky. Dabney was elected moderator of the Assembly and discovered that a delegation from the Northern united church, led by former Old Schoolers Henry Van Dyke and J. C. Backus, had come to seek fraternal relations. Dabney was not certain how to receive "the 'affectional salutations' of those sneaking Radicals," and he decided to "pass them by with a few formal words of course, and a freezing punctilious politeness." After receiving the delegation's salutations and plea for renewed relations, Dabney gave a speech "without saying anything" and then referred the whole matter to the committee on foreign correspondence, headed by B. M. Palmer. The report issued by Palmer recommended that a committee be sent to confer with the Northern church on issues of church property, for the Southern church would never be "anything more than any other separate denomination, unless [the Northern church] disavowed all their political platforms and turned out all the loose broad church men." Surprisingly, when the Assembly went into a committee of the whole, the Palmer report met with opposition and was debated at length.[31] Fearing that the Assembly would reject Palmer's report and advocate fraternal relations with the Northern church, which Dabney believed to be the first step toward reunion, he raised his voice on the floor:

> I do not profess to be as good as some people; I hear brethren saying it is time to forgive. Mr. Chairman, I do not forgive. I do not try to forgive. What! Forgive these people, who have invaded our country, burned our cities, destroyed our homes, slain our young men, and spread desolation and ruin over our land! No, I do not forgive them. But you say, "They have changed their feelings toward us, are kind." And why should they not be kind? Have we ever done anything to make them feel unkind to us? Have we ever harmed or wronged them? They are amiable and peaceful, are they? And is not the gorged tiger amiable and peaceful? When he has filled himself with the calf he has devoured, he lies down in a kind, good humor; but wait till he has digested his meal, and will he not be fierce again? Will he not be a tiger again? They have gorged themselves with everything they could take from us. They have gained everything they tried to get, they have conquered us, they have destroyed us. Why should they not be amiable and kind? Do you believe that the same old tiger nature is not in them? Just wrest from them anything they have taken from us and see.[32]

Dabney's speech turned the debate. The committee of the whole was convinced that fostering friendly relations with the Northern church was not feasible. They appointed another committee to answer the Van Dyke delegation, once again headed by B. M. Palmer. The committee demanded the Northern church's thorough repentance and reform, in line with Palmer's earlier report. The end result, Van Dyke complained, was that the Southerners "stripped every leaf from the olive branch and made a rod of it to beat us with." Likewise, Charles Hodge later sniffed, "The idea of undertaking to erase from the records of past Assemblies all that is offensive to us or to others with whom we may have friendly relations is impracticable and absurd."[33]

Dabney hoped that the idea would remain absurd to the Northern church and that friendly relations would never occur. In order to reinforce the reasons why Southerners ought to remain independent, at the 1871 General Assembly Dabney preached his sermon as out-going moderator on the dangers of "Broad Churchism." Presenting the Southern Presbyterian church as the "last advocate of faithful sub-scription and a strict adherence to doctrinal purity in this land, and possibly in the Protestant world," Dabney assailed the Northern reunited church for failing to stand for strict subscription to the West-minster Standards. The Northern church stood for the principle of "comprehension" and "liberal subscription in doctrinal beliefs"—they wanted to lower the doctrinal standards "as to embrace in one denom-ination all whom we recognize as within the church catholic, and as holding the truths fundamental to salvation." Such latitudinarianism would leave the Northern church with "no distinctive testimony for Christ." Instead, the New School men contradicted the Old School men and canceled out the latter's witness. The Old Schoolers within the united church might have a glorious individual testimony, but the "broad church" principle left them without a "complete church testi-mony." Furthermore, the latitudinarian principle was impossible; even the most tolerant church expressed intolerance on some point, most frequently in issues left to Christian liberty. The end result of a broad church could only be peace bought "at the cost of a Sadducean indif-ference to truth." In the future, unity in the Northern church would be maintained through administrative structures supported by money and denominational preferment. If the Southern church were to con-tinue as the defender of strict subscription, it must avoid any move-ment toward reunion with the Northern church.[34]

Later, in an anonymous pamphlet, Dabney attacked the Northern church's "Presbyterianism, with the modern improvements." Those modern improvements were political in nature: the 1873 Northern General Assembly spent much time planning for the upcoming national centennial in 1876; its members took a day trip to Washington to pay their respects to President Ulysses S. Grant, who decided to go fishing instead of meeting Presbyterian parsons (to Dabney's great delight); and one of the Assembly's members claimed that "we owe allegiance to our country—first to God, and, secondly, to our country. Nail the flag just below the cross, and stand by it, and if need be, die by it."

But the most obvious political maneuver contemplated by the Northern Assembly was its desire to reunite with the " 'cursed children' of the South." The "Radical majority" wished to reunite with the Southern church "in order to extinguish them"; the Old School minority was "sorely in need of help to sustain the cause of Conservative orthodoxy." Southerners ought to know that the desire to reunite was not sincere—for if it were, the united church would retract its "usurpations"—and that they should not join a failed crusade on the part of the Northern Old School, Dabney urged. It was better for Southern Presbyterians to remain separate from those who mixed religion and politics.[35]

Dabney's pleas for ecclesiastical independence, however, were heeded for only a short time. By 1874, Southern Presbyterians were once again considering the matter of fraternal relations with the Northern church, setting up a committee of conference to meet with the Northern church in Baltimore. The following year, the church considered a new ecumenical endeavor, the Pan-Presbyterian Alliance. Both issues were anathema to Dabney and Palmer; but on the issue of fraternal correspondence, they were opposed by Dabney's dear friend, Moses Hoge, and brother-in-law, B. M. Smith, and on the Alliance, they were forsaken by their former ally, Stuart Robinson. Both the issues raised the ire of Dabney, who was convinced that any relations with the Northern church would spell the end of Southern Presbyterianism. In several essays on fraternal relations, Dabney argued vehemently against any communion with Northern Presbyterians, attacking along the same lines as he had in earlier warnings. He first reminded his fellow Southern Presbyterians why they were a separate church—it was due to the Northern Presbyterian "usurpations" that had occurred with the Spring Resolutions. The Northern church had "intruded into the secular sphere *for the purpose of invading* a right of private judgment," while Southern Presbyterians had resisted this intrusion by seceding from the Old School church. In addition, the Northern church claimed not only that Southern secession was the sin of rebellion, but that Southern slavery was also inherently sinful and that defenses of the system were both "heresy" and "blasphemy." Though it claimed that all past actions of the Northern Old School and New School Assemblies were "null and void," it would not retract its accusations of Southern rebellion. Until the Northern church repented of these "usurpations" of Christian liberty, there was no way that the Southern church could have profitable relations with it. "The omnibus Presbyterians have never even professed repentance. When they have done that, and have also evinced the sincerity of their repentance in a sufficient manner, it will be time enough to talk of 'fraternal relations.' " Dabney also accused the Northern church of reuniting on a "broad church" principle. The Presbyterian Church in the United States of America "had repudiated the noble doctrinal testimonies of 1837–38; allowed themselves to be absorbed by the New School; to be abolitionized; to be made a 'Broad-church'. Their doctrinal and ecclesiastical tendencies were manifestly unsafe."[36]

Dabney was not content with these arguments, recycled several times since 1868. He also argued that "we ought to have as little as possible to do with Yankee Presbyterians." If Southern Presbyterians were to pursue closer ties with the Northern church, they would be corrupted by their errors, not only doctrinal but also social, political, and moral errors. Southerners needed to realize that the only purpose Yankees had for reunion was "*to Yankeeize the South*." Relations with Northern Presbyterians not only would break down doctrinal and moral taboos, but also would raise the racial question once again. Dabney believed that "every sober mind must know that fusion would mean this: the convulsing and rending of our churches upon the question of negro equality in our church courts."[37]

Dabney argued against the Pan-Presbyterian Alliance in a similar vein. Claiming that the churches represented by the Alliance had been corrupted by abolitionism and latitudinarian principles, he warned that entrance into the Alliance would be a tacit admission that Southerners had been wrong to defend themselves during the Civil War and to continue their separation from the Northern church. These churches were "generally dominated by a truculent and infidel abolitionism," and they confounded "with the Protestant theory of constitutional republican right the insane leveller's theory of the frantic Lilburn of Cromwell's day or the atheistic radicalism of the Reign of Terror, and impudently call them by the same name." By joining with the Alliance, the Southern church confessed that its position on slavery was in fact sinful and embraced the positions of the North and the international Presbyterian and Reformed community. Moreover, cooperating with the Alliance was virtually entering into fraternal correspondence with the Northern church—an act that the church had consistently repudiated from 1870 to 1876. God had set the Southern Presbyterian church apart "to perform the high duty" of testifying for strict doctrinal subscription and the nonsecular character of the church. The doctrinal basis of a Presbyterian Alliance would be necessarily vague to accommodate the questionable orthodoxy of some Presbyterian groups and would produce a "most emasculated Presbyterianism." Not only would the doctrinal stance be vague and corrupting, but the purpose of the Alliance was "anti-Protestant and anti-Presbyterian." The Alliance's leaders envisioned it to be an international supreme court, to handle all cases referred to it by national general assemblies. This was "one of the essential elements of popery," Dabney charged, the establishment of a single catholic church. In short, the Alliance was a project that emphasized "formal union . . . at the expense of" doctrinal fidelity.[38]

The stance that Dabney urged his fellow Southern Presbyterians to adopt was "forbearing separation." The Southern Presbyterian church ought not to feign charity for her former oppressors and accusers. Rather, her duty was "forbearance and forgiveness" toward Northern church members. That meant that the Southern church should continue to avoid "unchurching, anathematizing or assailing them—from invading their rights, intruding into their congregations, or grasping their property." The church should not seek to retaliate against the Northern church for all the wrongs done, the slanders and false accusations. Rather, Southern Presbyterians ought to forbear all wrong but also be determined to remain separate. Such a strategy was "precisely the one which the Christian sense of every good man, and every prudent church court," recognized as providing "for the peace of the visible church, and the personal comfort and edification of injured Christians." All interchange of delegates with other denominations ought to cease completely until the Northern denominations repented from their base charges against Southern Presbyterians. The money saved from not attending ecumenical meetings could be used for building up Southern institutions and for saving Southern souls.[39]

But Dabney's positions on both the Pan-Presbyterian Alliance and fraternal relations with the Northern church were rejected. The church embraced the Presbyterian Alliance, sending delegates in 1877 and refusing to hear Dabney's protest at the following year's General Assembly. The far more bitter blow was the Southern church's overwhelming movement toward fraternal relations at the 1882 General Assembly in Atlanta. The Assembly had proposed fraternal relations based on a "concurrent resolution" with the Northern church, in which each would retract any harsh statements made about the other during the Civil War. Yet the Northern church did not retract its charges of rebellion and treason, stirring up the contempt of older Southern Presbyterians. Dabney claimed that the concurrent resolution was odious because it made "our church hypothetically confess a sin which she never committed, and which she has always held she never committed." Such an ecclesiastical adjustment was unmanly and dishonorable. Moreover, the Southern Assembly attempted to shut off any debate on the issue of fraternal relations, stigmatizing the older generation as "wranglers" and "old war-horses." Some had claimed, Dabney reported, "that the old men who were actors in the separation of 1861 are nearly all dead and gone; that the new men were not actors in that division; and therefore, it is time, or will soon be time, to drop the old testimony." All of this signaled to Dabney that the leaders of the movement for fraternal relations were "deserters of their own principles."

In order to remind the Southern church of the principles justifying its separate existence, Dabney once again rang the charges against the Northern church: the latitudinarianism embodied in the reunion of 1869; the violation of the spirituality of the church in the Spring Resolutions of 1861; and the Pittsburgh Orders of 1865, which had hurled the "fearful indictment of rebellion and treason" against the Southern church. The Southern church had consistently refused to have anything to do with the Northern church as a result of these three issues, standing as a testimony to "the spiritual rights of Christ's people in his spiritual kingdom." The Northern church had demonstrated in its failure to withdraw the charges of rebellion and treason that it was

still committed to the tyrannical, popish principle of the Spring Resolutions. Dabney observed, "This tells the sad story—that politics still
rule in that church; that really the breach of principle is not healed at
all; that the very central error which disrupted the church at first is
still unanimously held in that Assembly; that the same reason exists
for our maintaining our conscientious testimony, and our ecclesiastical independence."[40]

Dabney once again warned that the natural result of fraternal
relations was ecclesiastical fusion with the Northern church and that
the results would be far reaching. First, those who were moving
toward fusion had to recognize that they would split the Southern
Presbyterian church. There would be those who were "never going
to be traded off to the corrupters of American Presbyterianism and
slanderers of their fathers' virtues." A group loyal to Old School Presbyterianism would form a third denomination. Fusion would also
mean "the unobstructed triumph, among American Presbyterianism,
of the virtually popish and tyrannical principle of the Spring Resolutions." The Southern Presbyterian church would further "acquiesce
in becoming doctrinally a 'Broad Church' " that tolerated both the
Old and New Schools, and in surrendering "the committee system of
evangelism" and the Thornwellian position on eldership. Most importantly, fusion with the Northern church would lead Southerners
toward racial amalgamation and modern abolitionism. Dabney played
on Southern sexual fears, suggesting that "negro presbyters [would]
rule white churches and judge white ladies" and that the end result
would be "a mulatto South." That would be the "final perdition of
Southern society"—when the "rationalistic and skeptical features of
modern abolitionism" would be embraced by Southerners and
"domestic amalgamation" would be the result. In order to preserve
the South, Presbyterians must "*hold fast to our independence,* as our
sheet-anchor from ecclesiastical shipwreck." Dabney counseled that
Southern Presbyterians should "repudiate every entangling alliance
that endangers that independence" and then "go on our way, mind-
ing our own business." It would be better to remain separate from
the rest of Christendom than to admit fatigue and defeat in holding
to the old principles.[41]

However, Southern Presbyterians did not repudiate their fraternal relations with Northern Presbyterians, and they continued to discuss organic union to the end of Dabney's life. It was apparent that Dabney, along with other longtime Southern Presbyterian leaders, had become irrelevant to the entire debate as a younger generation of ministers sought reunion with the Northern church. Fears of the "Yankeeizing and Africanizing" of Southern Presbyterians and warnings of "ultimate apostasy," which would be the result of fusion, failed to bring the younger ministers in line. Richard McIlwaine, president of Hampden-Sydney College, attacked Dabney in harsh terms in the pages of the *Central Presbyterian*. Dabney, McIlwaine charged, thought that he was "too big or too pure or too anything else" to learn anything from "a Yankee, or African, or Hindoo, who is capable of helping him." Fusion with the Northern church was the necessity of the hour for Southern Presbyterians, McIlwaine believed; and it ought not to be delayed through "the influence of bad blood and Yankee-phobia and war recollections and illogical reasoning and mental phantasmagoria which are attempted to be palmed off as arguments." While McIlwaine's attack was repudiated by several Southern Presbyterians, including Dabney's longtime friend C. R. Vaughan, Dabney lamented that his time as a Southern Presbyterian leader had passed. That did not mean that Dabney changed his principles. To the end, he believed that the North "never understood us, do[es] not understand us, and never will understand us." As a result, the church should remain separate rather than allow the Northern church to embrace her in "the hug of death for southern Presbyterianism."[42]

Dabney was certainly within his rights to seek to prevent reunion with the Northern church based on doctrinal concerns; after all, in the Northern church, the infamous trial and acquittal of Chicago Presbyterian minister David Swing occurred in 1874, and the 1880s and 1890s would be marked by heresy trials of Northern Presbyterian seminary professors. It was not altogether clear, however, that Dabney was simply trying to preserve a doctrinally pure church. Particularly as fraternal relations came closer to being a reality, he tried to play the issue of race-mixing, arguing that reunion with the Northern church would create a racially impure church and produce a "mulatto South." If

Southern racial purity, referred to by the code words "Southern morals," was linked so closely with the independence of the Southern church, then Dabney's battle against the Northern church took on a different complexion, making it a less-than-worthy goal. Likewise, cultural solidarity, under the code words "Southern civilization," was an unworthy issue in the debate over fraternal relations. The gospel transforms cultural markers—such as circumcision and dietary laws—and brings into question cultural solidarity, a reminder of the "confidence in the flesh" that the apostle Paul "counted as loss for the sake of Christ" (Phil. 3:3–7). Dabney's arguments against fraternal relations and church union should have focused exclusively on the doctrinal deviations of the Northern church, epitomized in the debates at the end of his life on revising the Westminster Standards. While these arguments may not have swayed his more progressive brethren, they would have kept the focus on the only genuine basis for Christian unity: doctrinal agreement.[43]

Denomination-Building

Dabney was not content merely to oppose the Northern church. He recognized that the Southern Presbyterian church had to continue to grow in order to supply the intellectual and moral leadership needed in the South. Consequently, throughout his entire career, Dabney was a strong promoter of missions, both foreign and domestic. From as early as 1856, when he had the opportunity to spend a great deal of time with J. Leighton Wilson, the future secretary for foreign missions in the Southern Presbyterian church, Dabney cultivated an interest in missions. The Union Seminary legend was that "Dr. Dabney and Dr. Peck had . . . so much respect for Dr. Wilson, that when he visited the Seminary periodically, their manner of speaking of him to the students, even when their words were few, filled the student body with huge respect for Dr. Wilson and his cause, and gave great impetus to the missionary cause." This interest in missions continued to the end of Dabney's life. Some of the final articles he would write for church papers concerned funding for a Presbyterian college in Brazil and the faulty way in which the church conducted "domestic missions."[44]

160

Dabney's interest in foreign missions focused particularly on the Presbyterian mission in Brazil, headed by Edward Lane, a former Dabney student and a graduate of Union Seminary in 1869. Born in Ireland, Lane had come to America and studied at Oglethorpe University, the Presbyterian college of Georgia. After he graduated from seminary, he was licensed and ordained by West Hanover Presbytery, the same presbytery to which Dabney belonged. Lane then went as one of the first Southern Presbyterian missionaries to Brazil, where he labored until his death in 1892. Throughout Lane's life, Dabney supported the work in Brazil, perhaps because for a time he had considered emigrating with the "Confederados." Shortly after Lane arrived in Brazil, he asked Dabney to raise funds for a building for the Campinas College. Dabney complied, going on several fund-raising tours for the college. In 1870, he raised over $1,500 in Nashville for the work. Afterward, Dabney wrote constantly, advising his student on various matters related to the mission. When the mission experienced opposition within the PCUS in 1879, as a result of financial mismanagement by the foreign missions committee, Dabney continued to defend Lane's work and advise him accordingly. Upon Lane's death from yellow fever in 1892, Dabney was asked to write a character sketch of the missionary; the sketch was apparently never published. Shortly thereafter, Dabney made one final plea for the church to support fully the Campinas College in Brazil, not to abandon the college and the mission, but to continue to fund the work that Lane had done so faithfully for so long. In the decades after Dabney's death, Southern Presbyterians pointed to Brazil as one of their great early experiments in foreign missions.[45]

Dabney also had a long-standing interest in home missions, particularly after developing an abiding friendship with E. O. Guerrant, the founder of American Inland Mission. After Guerrant attended Union Seminary for a few sessions in the mid-1870s, the two men developed an abiding relationship. Guerrant hosted Dabney on a preaching tour of Kentucky in and around the Winchester area during the summer of 1875. Ever after that tour, Dabney continued to show a personal interest in the younger man, often urging him to take care of his tenuous health. In return, Guerrant invited Dabney to return to Kentucky several times, but Dabney graciously passed by the opportunities in both 1877 and 1879. When Guerrant was appointed the evangelist of the Synod of Kentucky, charged with laboring in eastern Kentucky, Dabney was quite pleased. "I have watched the evangelistic movement in your synod with great interest," he wrote. "I do not wonder that the choice of the church fell on you as their first evangelist: I should have chosen thus also." Dabney urged Guerrant to make sure to recruit students for the seminaries in his evangelistic meetings. After Dabney was in Texas, building up the theological school in Austin, Guerrant responded to a call from his teacher and secured $500 for the seminary in his various evangelistic meetings. And at the end of his life, Dabney confessed that "in looking back upon my active life it seems I must have been a very busy man. Yet my activities look small beside yours." Through this long-standing friendship with Guerrant, Dabney was able to encourage domestic missions and church-planting.[46]

These two relationships typified Dabney's approach to denomination-building. Fearful of centralized power, as typified in the excesses of the "omnibus" Northern Presbyterian church, Dabney focused on individual relationships with men whom he had known and trained. Even when their practice was far from what he would have personally approved, such as Guerrant's lax approach to Presbyterian doctrine and polity as well as his use of revivalistic methods, Dabney trusted and esteemed these men. Such men were the reason that Dabney had invested his life at Union Seminary, to multiply his life in the lives of those who would leave Union to preach the gospel. Yet while Dabney focused his own attentions on personal relationships, he continually urged his brethren to see the possibilities of concerted actions. This was particularly the case after he became aware of the comparative poverty of Presbyterianism in the Southwest. Dabney complained that the "strong Synod at home is accompanied by this fatal tendency to forget and neglect the work in their weaker sisters." Rather than cooperating according to the abiding genius of the Presbyterian system—"the strength of the whole ought to sustain each of the parts"—the churches too often acted like independent Congregationalists. Thus, Dabney urged the stronger sections of the Southern Presbyterian church—particularly the churches in the eastern seaboard—to invest their money in the weaker sections of Texas and Arkansas, building up the churches for the greater progress of the Presbyterian church. If the church did not continue to grow and progress in creating a Southern Zion, it would not be able to avoid the entangling web of the dreaded Northerners. And if the Southern church was absorbed, where would the pure gospel be preserved?[47]

$$6$$

Public Theologian

Upon the conclusion of the Civil War, Dabney was particularly concerned to hold on to the "good" while making his way in the New South. In order to hold on to the good, he decided to wage a new war: an ideological battle to preserve Southern civilization from the "corruptions" of the North. Having unleashed his talent for close reasoning and pungent writing in his *Defence of Virginia* and *Life of Jackson* during the Civil War, Dabney came to see that the best way to fight Yankees was not on a military battlefield, but on an ideological one. After the war, Dabney passionately believed that the Southerners' present duty was to "resolve to abate nothing, to concede nothing of righteous conviction. Truckle to no falsehood and conceal no true principle; but ever assert the right with such means of endurance, self-sacrifice, and passive fortitude as the dispensation of Providence has left you." While the degradation of Reconstruction might tempt young Southerners to choose "the *expedient*," Dabney urged them to stand firm for "the *right*," which was nothing less than "that standard of judgment which we held before our disasters." In order to spell out "the right," Dabney took every opportunity to write essays for Southern journals after the war, most of which defended Southern honor, articulated Southern principles, and attacked Southern enemies.[1]

What made standing for antebellum principles so difficult, Dabney concluded, was the rising tide of modernism rushing into Northern society by way of England and Europe and beginning to seep into the South as well.[2] For Dabney, this modernism was rooted in what he called "the sensualistic philosophy," a radical empiricism associated with Auguste Comte, Herbert Spencer, and John Stuart Mill. Positivism was responsible for many of the ills of modern American life—from egalitarian movements, such as abolitionism and feminism, to governmental centralization and bureaucratization. The sensualistic philosophy also made itself felt in the "anti-Christian science," Northern corporate capitalism, and public education, Dabney thought. In order to meet this deadly foe, he articulated a distinctively antimodern public theology, emphasizing "Bible Republicanism," agrarian values, and conservative Calvinism. Far from being merely traditionalist or anti-intellectual, Dabney's antimodernism was one of the few Southern responses to the new intellectual trends and represented the beginning point of a Southern antimodern critique of modern American culture. Ironically, Dabney's response to modernism placed him much closer to Northeastern progressives, such as Henry Adams, who typified antimodernism at the close of the nineteenth century, than to New South Presbyterians, such as W. H. Ruffner and James Woodrow, who accommodated themselves to the new intellectual ethos with little concern. Although by the 1880s New South Presbyterians generally viewed Dabney's "prophetic" pronouncements against the modern worldview as little more than "Dabney crotchets," in the early twentieth century, with the flowering of modernization in the South, Dabney was retrieved by the Vanderbilt Agrarians and their camp followers as one of the few who had genuinely understood the signs of the times and stood boldly against the modern gods of "Speed" and "Mass."[3]

The Sensualistic Philosophy

Dabney was convinced that the problems found in American character and institutions could be traced back to a false philosophy. He observed that the "decadence of political, commercial, and domestic virtue" in America was due to the fact that "the philosophy of Comte,

Stuart Mill, and Darwin has been rapidly gaining ground." Positivism—or, as Dabney preferred, "the sensualistic philosophy"—was the root of American troubles. By identifying positivism in this way, Dabney intended to make clear the far-reaching effect of philosophical materialism—this was the "atheism" latent in Darwin's evolutionary theory, the motive force for Spencer and Mill's utilitarian ethics, and the basis for the egalitarianism of the French Revolution, abolitionism, and feminism. Positivism was the modern acid eating away at traditional belief in God and historic creeds, providing a rationale and a naturalistic worldview for those who would confess themselves to be "agnostic." And positivism was the ground by which popularizing atheists, such as Colonel Robert Ingersoll, gained a public reputation.[4]

In Dabney's parlance, the sensualistic philosophy was a radical empiricism that "resolves all the powers of the human spirit into the functions of the five senses." The sensualists were generally positivists, who divorced metaphysics from physics, who maintained that truth could be gained solely through a careful consideration of phenomena. Scientific laws could be established only through inductive data gained through sensation, without resort to metaphysical hypotheses. As a result, positivists regarded any resort to intuitive powers, primitive judgments, or a priori laws to be embracing metaphysics and outside the realm of true science. Likewise, laws of consciousness and psychology were deemed to be beyond the pale of scientific investigation. Pushed to its ultimate extreme, positivism appeared to be a rank form of materialism, stripping human beings of an immaterial essence that survived death. Of course, such a view would eliminate any being, such as the Christian God, who could not be empirically verified through the five senses; positivism also sought to eliminate the possibility of the supernatural, such as miracles, which could not be empirically verified.[5]

What made positivists so dangerous to divines such as Dabney was that they appeared to be Baconians of the purest order. Taking the empirical, inductive approach associated with Scottish commonsense realism as their base, positivists emphasized "the apparent certainty of the exact sciences [and] the diversity of view and uncertainty which have ever appeared to attend metaphysics." For a culture that had given itself heart and soul to "Lord Bacon," the inductive method, and the logic of common sense, the belief that only knowledge that can be verified by sensation and experimental proof should be considered genuine was powerful and, for many, convincing. Further, the potential nonsectarianism of such knowledge appealed to Americans. Rather than debate metaphysical issues, which were the province of theologians, positivists held out the possibility of science that focused only on verifiable and sensible results. In the positivist approach, the supernatural could be taken out of the equation; the results of empirical research in the realm of the natural would be the only admissible evidence. As a result, even when Americans did not embrace Comte, they often held to the general worldview promoted by the positivists, a worldview of science and vague unbelief.[6]

In response, Dabney challenged positivism on a variety of fronts. First, he exposed the "corollaries" of positivism—its stark materialism as well as its rigid fatalism. Because positivism restricted itself only to matter and its appearance to the senses, he believed that it denied "spirit and the actings of spirit" as legitimate phenomena. This led to a general atheism, for no one could verify through sensation and empirical investigation the existence of deity. In addition, this materialistic theory led to fatalism. Dabney saw positivism as teaching, through its reliance on the uniformity of laws,

> that all the events which befall us are directed by a physical fate; that there is no divine intelligence, nor goodness, nor righteousness, nor will concerned in them; that our hopes, our hearts, our beloved ones, our very existence, are all between the jaws of an irresistible and inexorable machine; that our free agency, in short, is illusory, and our free will is a cheat.

Moreover, positivism also led to utilitarian ethics and a pragmatic approach to knowledge. The only "truth" that existed was what worked; the only way to discover what worked was through empirical investigation; hence, the only truth was that discovered by positivism. The net result of these corollaries, Dabney held, was "a gulf without an immorality, without a God, without a faith, without a providence, without a hope." Positivism was the worst possible type of skeptical thought.[7]

Dabney also responded to positivism by reasserting the truths taught by the Scottish enlightenment. Humankind throughout the centuries had consistently affirmed "the rudimental instincts of man's reason and conscience"—that the mind operated based on some "innate norms" that regulated thought and action; that some truth was accessible to the mind; that the universe implied a creator and a supernatural creation; that humans had a conscious will; and that there was a higher being who also had a conscious will and who could intervene in human affairs. In addition, though they denied it, the positivists were forced to operate based on innate norms: "[They] must have accepted some laws of thought, as sufficiently established, in order to construct [their] own thoughts." In order to study the physical world, humans had to presuppose rules of logic as well as the uniformity of natural laws, the regularity of causation, and the trustworthiness of sensation. These beliefs, he observed, constituted a "practical metaphysics" that guided even those who claimed to discard metaphysics. The positivist approach involved itself in circular reasoning—it denied intuitive norms, and yet needed them in order to reason at all. This was proof positive that the older insistence upon the laws of consciousness, as taught by Scottish realism, was correct.[8]

Dabney's greatest hope for the defeat of the sensualist philosophy, however, was not in logical evidence provided by the Scottish philosophy. Rather, it was in the universal human need for spiritual truth. No matter how stridently positivists denied the reality of the spiritual side of human beings, humans had "persisted in asking whence [their] spiritual being came, and wither it was going." Rather than deny the spiritual, science ought to "obey the spirit of true science," which manifested "the great truth that man was never designed by God for mental independence of him; that man needs, in these transcendent questions, the guidance of the infinite understanding; that while a 'positive philosophy' may measure and compare his material possessions, the only 'exact science' of the spirit is that revealed to us by the Father of Spirits." Dabney was confident that while science might seek to move humankind away from its spiritual destiny, men and women would be forced by their own spirits to seek God.[9]

Cautions Against Anti-Christian Science

Dabney's confidence was betrayed somewhat by the rise of evolution, not only in society at large, but particularly within the Southern Presbyterian church. Dabney believed that the natural sciences tended toward naturalism, and thus were ready-made for the "positive philosophy." Determined to spell out further how modern science was indebted to "sensualistic philosophy," Dabney devoted two chapters to a review and refutation of evolutionary theory in his book *The Sensualistic Philosophy of the Nineteenth Century*. He summarized evolution as the attempt to inform the law of uniformity with the power of natural selection. Evolutionists believed that the series of cause and effect "contains within itself a natural power of differentiating its effects, at least, slightly." This core belief played itself out in five laws: the laws of multiplication of animals in geometrical proportion, of limited population, of heredity, of variation, and of equilibrium in nature—or, as it was more popularly known, the law of "survival of the fittest." In order for these laws to bring about differentiation in species, it was necessary to "postulate a time sufficiently vast" so that evolution from the lowest and simplest species to the highest and most complex might occur—whether in animal and plant life or, as in Charles Darwin's *Descent of Man*, in human life. Moral development or spiritual interest evolved "out of the instinctive animal functions of the brute." Evolution as a process operated unintelligently and "blindly"; when evolution was successful, it was "by chance." This led evolution proponents to claim that the theory "totally explodes the teleological argument" for God as Creator.[10]

Dabney believed that evolution did nothing of the sort. Clinging to the characteristics of the older doxological science—design, order, and divine benevolence—and believing that evolution was nothing but a system of atheism and materialism, Dabney attempted to refute the leading proponents of evolutionary theory. He attacked Herbert Spencer, whom he identified as "the Aristotle of Evolutionism," for forsaking Christian presuppositions, such as God, spirit, and substance, and replacing these with the unifying idea of force. Believing that all absolutes were unknowable, Spencer held that God was unknowable and unverifiable. Thus, God could be dismissed from scientific reasoning. That did not mean that there was not a single power that unified all scientific endeavor. Spencer claimed that instead of deity, "material force" was that single power. Dabney mocked, "*Force* is Mr. Spencer's God. There is but one cause in the universe, *force*; and there is but one kind of effect in the universe, *motion*." All of creation, according to Spencer, had come about "by the sole action of blind force."[11]

Spencer himself, however, did not escape from the very problems that he claimed marred Christian natural theology, Dabney argued. First, Spencer's a priori idea of force was unconditioned and thus absolutely unknowable in the same way that he claimed the Christian God was. How could Spencer know that his "Force-God" existed at all? If Spencer attempted to take refuge in his observation of force, that would not do, because he claimed that "perception is as merely relative, and as utterly incompetent to have any valid cognition of unconditioned reality, as any other supposed faculty." After he posited this absolutely unknowable Force-God, Spencer then derived space and matter, which were knowable only through consciousness and thus were known only relatively. "Out of these unknowables," Dabney exclaimed, "Mr. Spencer is now prepared to construct the known Universe." Spencer's next move was to adapt Darwin's ideas of development to his universe in order to explain how everything had come into existence. "The whole is only an unhealthy dream," Dabney mused. Spencer's system was "overtly anti-Christian" and a "system of practical atheism." Spencer left no hope of human immorality, thus providing justification for sinners to "imbrute" themselves. Hence, Spencer's system was not fit for the Christian mind.[12]

Dabney saved his hardest blows, however, for Darwin himself. While Darwin (by 1875) had not abandoned belief in a first cause, Dabney claimed that even his terminology smacked of divine design. Natural selection "involves in its very name, a sophistical idea." Selection implied free choice by a personal being; thus, "nature," whoever or whatever it was, exercised personality qualities. Survival of the fittest was another "absurdity," for fitness "also implies design!" Some personal being had made the survivor fit by way of adjustment. Even worse, evolutionary theory begged people to believe the claim that "a vast tract of time must have elapsed, while 'natural selection,' acting blindly, failing, perhaps, myriads of times where it succeeded once, and then only establishing the slightest differentiations, was evolving the wondrous animated universe out of the rudest germs." This, to Dabney, was sophistry.[13]

Dabney believed that Darwin's evolution was also bad science because he could find no evidence for survival of the fittest in nature. First, nature's tendency was not evolution, but devolution. Dabney observed, "Surrender any individual of a 'developed' variety, to the rude hand of nature, and its uniform tendency is to degradation." This was evidenced in the lack of fertility or the production of inferior breeds in animals that had been bred as hybrids. Second, current paleontology did not support Darwin's theory. Other scientists, such as Hugh Miller, had already demonstrated that "some of the fossils discovered by him in *strata* so old as to have been supposed too old for any organized life, were of quite well developed *vertebrata*." It was simply not the case that the older strata had simpler life-forms, which then evolved into more complex life-forms. Third, if evolution were true, then humankind ought to be the "strongest and greatest animal." But the notorious fact was that humans were not. Human beings were superior as the result of their minds, their intellectual capacities, not their size. Thus, Darwin's theory suffered from "the total absence of verification." Not only was verification for Darwin's suppositions not available, it was not possible. By pushing the evolutionary process so far back into human history, there was no record of any evolutionary process. Darwinism was nothing more than a fancy. "It is related to science," Dabney deadpanned, "just as Gulliver's voyage to Lilliput is to geography."[14]

Finally, Dabney took all the evolutionary theorists to task for their materialism. These men, he charged, believed that "all the wonders of consciousness, intellect, taste, conscience, volition, and religious faith, are to be explained as the animal outgrowth of gregarious instincts,

172

and habitudes cultivated through them." Such a conception was "monstrous" and "an outrage to the manhood of our race." The only explanation for such base theories concerning the human spirit was that a "foul, juggling fiend" had possessed these evolutionists that they "should grovel through so many gross sophistries, in order to dig [their] way out to this loathsome degradation." This was nothing less than "modern paganism" that chose "the beast for his parent" and cast "his God utterly away." Consciousness and the spiritual nature of humans were facts of human existence that could come only through special creation. Any other attempt to account for it failed.[15]

Dabney's attack on evolution in *Sensualistic Philosophy* summarized several arguments that he had been developing for some time. For example, Dabney preached a sermon entitled "A Caution Against Anti-Christian Science" for the 1871 Synod of Virginia. He warned that modern science affected "positivism," attempting to explain all of life by "the laws of material nature and of animal life." This materialism was essentially naturalistic and anti-theological, hence infidel and atheistic. In fact, he believed that "these physical sciences continually tend to exalt naturalism; their pride of success in tracing natural causes, tempts them to refer everything to them, and thus to substitute them for a spiritual, personal God."[16]

As a result, Dabney felt called to sound a caution against what he deemed a "vain deceitful philosophy." This anti-Christian science was aggressively encroaching on biblical teaching, demanding that the Bible be trimmed to match the prevailing scientific opinion. Science no longer demanded that theology accede to the possibility of a pre-Adamite earth, but now science "required" theologians to admit that the six days of creation were geological ages, that the flood was local and not universal, that human beings had existed for at least 20,000 years, that there were multiple species having multiple origins, that the nebular hypothesis was the mode of creation, and that humankind had descended from the lowest type of animal life. All this resulted in scientists' adopting a "hostile and depreciatory" tone toward biblical revelation. Scientists also resented the intrusion of theologians into their discipline. They refused to use the Scriptures as the standard for their speculations; rather, they claimed that "the Scriptures really set-

tle nothing by their own testimony." Scientists held that they could
not presuppose the inspiration and infallibility of the Scriptures; thus,
their attitude was that "the Bible is fallible, but science infallible."
Hence, Dabney argued that though he could not charge "infidelity
upon all physicists, [yet] the tendency of much of so-called modern
science is skeptical."[17]

Dabney urged his auditors to stand upon biblical authority in resist-
ing modern science's claims and to recognize that the "assured results
of modern science" were hardly certain. "Modern physical science,"
he preached, "is not to be allowed to boast entire immunity from error,
or certainty of results, any more than the physical science of the scholastic ages." Though many claimed to be doing their science using the
Baconian method, in fact these were far from practicing the "experimental method." Hasty generalizations and hypotheses still misled
human thinking. These hypotheses appeared to be in a state of constant flux and change. There was nothing solid in scientific thought.
Some of these hypotheses, it was true, satisfied all the observed facts
known to the public, but they did not provide a mutually exclusive
argument that would destroy the biblical view. The Bible stood on the
defensive in any conflict with science; the burden of proof rested on
science, not theology.[18]

While Dabney expected to confront evolution in the physical sciences, he did not expect to have to defend the biblical account of creation within his own church communion. Yet in the mid-1870s Dabney became embroiled in a controversy with James Woodrow over the
relationship between Scripture and science. Woodrow, the Perkins Professor of Natural Science in Connexion with Revelation at Columbia
Seminary, had monitored Dabney's writings on science and religion
for several years, starting with Dabney's anonymous essay, "Geology
and the Bible," published in the *Southern Presbyterian Review* in 1863.
Ten years later, Woodrow believed that he had to respond. Deeming
Dabney's writings on science to be "assaults" and "an unremitting
warfare against Physical Science," Woodrow held that Dabney's views
were not only incorrect but "dangerous, because certain to lead to the
rejection of the Sacred Scriptures so far as he is here regarded as their
true interpreter." Woodrow was particularly upset by Dabney's iden-

tification of modern science with "sensualistic philosophy." While admitting that some scientists might pursue their work out of pride or depravity, Woodrow argued that most scientists were in fact believers. Science was not essentially atheistic; "the dangerous tendency is not at all in the study, but wholly in the student," he claimed. And yet, Woodrow later argued that scientists did not operate based on presuppositions, which was Dabney's argument, but rather cherished neutrality and the inductive method. The scientist "does not undertake to determine beforehand what the conclusion shall be, and then ransack nature for seeming facts to defend his opinion; he does not dictate to God what his works shall teach." Natural science was "neither Christian nor anti-Christian, neither theistic nor atheistic, any more than the multiplication table." Instead, most scientists only sought the truth and accepted whatever the facts of nature were. By exercising modesty and caution, the true scientist knew the limit of what science could and could not determine.[19]

Woodrow's true scientist insisted only on the facts that had been established through painstaking, Baconian methods. The issues that Dabney claimed encroached on biblical truth were not established facts, but hypotheses. Even worse, these theories and hypotheses were not even current, but in many cases over sixty years old. The only explanation for Dabney's errors had to be "his want of acquaintance with" current science. Woodrow mocked, "Ancient weapons are of no avail in modern warfare; and the medieval armor of the most gallant knight is no protection against a conical ball projected from the chassepot or needle-gun." Dabney did not appear to know that the extent of Noah's flood was not an issue for science but for biblical interpretation; that no conclusion had been drawn on the problem of human antiquity; that "science does not teach the plural origin of the human family"; and that the nebular hypothesis and development hypothesis were merely hypotheses, not established facts of science. The only true "encroachment" that scientists made on biblical revelation was in the claim that creation had existed longer than "ten or fourteen days" before human beings. At this point, Woodrow defended the argument for the earth's antiquity by claiming that "as soon as the earth is shown to be older than Adam by ten days, and this is perceived to be not contradictory of Scripture teachings, it becomes a matter of no consequence as regards the interpretation of the Bible how much more than ten days the time may have been." Furthermore, Woodrow thought the Bible was silent on the mode of creation. The Bible does not say whether God created "a finished world of sea and land" or whether God used "nebulous matter which he endowed with properties such that it would pass through successive changes until it reached the condition in which we now see it." Because the Bible was silent on the matter, because "it informs us that he created the world, but it does not tell us *how* he created it," the nebular or development hypotheses were not atheistic at all.[20]

In fact, Woodrow held that natural science assisted theology by illustrating "the wisdom and power and greatness of God as nothing else can" and by illuminating in new ways passages already understood as well as "gaining clearer insight into that meaning where it is obscure." The believer took the truths that science brought forth in order to worship God "with new emotions of admiration and reverence towards his Father whose thoughts he sees expressed in his works." At the same time, the unbeliever might "pervert the truths discovered by natural science." Yet that distortion did not signal a problem with science itself, but with the human heart. Woodrow claimed that the results of science were "not in the slightest degree affected by the religious views or character of its students." Christians and non-Christians working side by side in a lab often came to the same conclusions; "in every branch of science the same results are reached, whatever the religious views of the investigators." He was confident that "no line could be drawn which would separate Christians from infidels" in the actual doing of scientific work, but only in the uses made of that work. The Christian used science to glorify God, while the unbeliever used it for his own nefarious ends.[21]

The key point on which Woodrow and Dabney disagreed was whether the admission of an almighty, creative power at any point in the creative process ruled out naturalistic explanations of origins. Dabney had iterated on several occasions that "if, therefore, there is any authentic testimony that God did, from the first, create such an earth, no sound inference drawn from natural analogies is of any force to rebut that testimony." For the Christian, there was in fact an authentic testimony about creation—the biblical account itself. Genesis 1 was an authoritative account by the only eyewitness (God) about the mode of creation. Hence, the biblical accounts "must be absolutely authoritative in all their parts, without waiting on or deferring to any conclusion of human science whatsoever." Anything less than absolute biblical authority would bring doubt upon the central message of the Christian Scriptures—the death, burial, and resurrection of Jesus. Theology, the system of truth contained in the infallible Scripture, "is entitled to preliminary presumption." Science, in a subordinate position, may illustrate biblical truth, but it may not substitute for or stand above biblical truth.[22]

Woodrow also recognized the fundamental divide between Dabney and himself: "Dr. Dabney insist[s] that the *'absence* of the supernatural' must be proved before the law of uniformity may be applied; we [are] insisting that the *presence* of the supernatural must be proved before we are debarred from applying it." Without a consistent and unvarying application of uniformitarianism, Woodrow believed that skepticism was the only possible result. The law of uniformity "involves the very possibility of natural science, and indeed every kind of knowledge." Without a complete admission of the principle of "like causes produce like effects," Woodrow believed that Dabney must yield himself "to the hopeless skepticism which must flow from his waiting to prove the absence of the supernatural." Later, Woodrow claimed that "if scientific reasoning were restrained by such a mere puzzle [as Dabney suggested], the result would be universal skepticism." Woodrow later took his argument to its natural conclusion, admitting that he embraced evolution. In an 1884 address, he claimed that there existed "the probable absence of contradiction between the Scripture account of creation and the doctrine of Evolution, except in the case of man so far as regards his soul." Whereas Dabney believed that God did state how God had created, Woodrow denied that God had explicitly indicated the mode of creation. Dabney held onto the priority of the biblical material in regulating issues related to science; Woodrow believed that the apparent silence of the Bible on matters of science made most scientific theories admissible.[23]

Dabney's response to evolution was not anti-science or anti-intellectual, as some historians have claimed.[24] It was, however, antimodern. Rather than bowing to the conventions of modern rationalism, Dabney reasserted the priority of biblical revelation, a transcendental word from God, over modern scientific pretentiousness. That did not mean, however, that Dabney had little interest in science. Far from it— he prided himself on his contemporary knowledge of scientific development, and evidenced a close reading of the luminaries of what he deemed "anti-Christian science": Lyell, Huxley, Darwin, and Spencer. Rather, Dabney belonged to a cadre of amateur scientists who resisted attempts to reconcile science and religion in ways that favored science. These "Scriptural Geologists" were determined to read science through the lens of Scripture and, in many ways, prefigured contemporary "Creation Science" advocates. To allow science to dictate scriptural interpretation was rationalism and was sure to lead to error. Dabney believed that this was Woodrow's fatal flaw. In the midst of the evolution controversy in the PCUS, caused by Woodrow's 1884 evolution address, Dabney wrote to G. B. Strickler, "The positions taken by Woodrow in his attack on me in 1873 were rationalistic. The church ought to have seen it then, and to have taken the alarm. I did my duty and exposed those positions; but most seemed to think it was but one of the 'Dabney crotchets'; nobody took the alarm." Against the rationalism evident in modern science as informed by the positivist philosophy, Dabney urged the truth of the biblical revelation.[25]

Antibiblical Theories of Rights

Dabney was convinced that if the sensualistic philosophy won the day, civilization in America would be completely destroyed. All one had to do in order to see this end was to compare the fruits of the positivist philosophy against those from what Dabney deemed to be the biblical worldview: "On the one side we have such characters as the Jacobins and *sans-culottes* of Paris in her two reigns of terror, and those original 'Positivists,' the Bushmen of Africa, and the blacks of Australia; on the other, we have nearly all that has been good and true and pure in Christendom and without it." Yet Dabney did not have to go to Paris, Africa, or Australia to see the damage that radical empiricism could wreak. He believed that in America generally, and in the Northern states particularly, the effects of positivism could be seen through the embrace of "anti-biblical theories of rights" that denied God's sovereignty, providence, and moral law.[26]

The Northern "radical social theory" held that society was constituted by individuals "naturally absolute and sovereign as its integers" through a social contract. Each person's natural liberty was "the freedom to do whatever he wishes"; civil liberty consisted of "his natural prerogative not surrendered to the social contract." Every person under the social contract has the same rights and responsibilities, and to withhold those rights from some class would be a "natural iniquity." As a result, all distinctions of caste or hierarchy were "essentially and inevitably wicked and oppressive." Voting rights, under this logic, should be equally available to all adults. Hence, the logic of the Northern theory led to both abolitionism and feminism. Abolitionists argued from this starting point that "slavery in all its forms must be essentially unrighteous" because the slave system consisted in a select few holding "property in the involuntary labor of adult human beings, and control over their persons." Likewise, early feminists claimed that "women must be allowed access to every male avocation, including government, and war if she wishes it, to suffrage, to every political office, to as absolute freedom from her husband in the marriage relation as she enjoyed before her union to him, and to absolute control of her own property and earnings as that claimed by the single gentleman, as against her own husband."[27]

These late-nineteenth-century feminists also used this same logic to promote "women preachers," a trend that Dabney opposed as early as 1879. Dabney believed that the female desire for the pulpit arose from the spirit of the age. He accused those who claimed that female piety justified female preaching of using an argument that was "merely utilitarian and unbelieving." God ordained that female piety affected a more important sphere than the church—the home. "God has assigned to her a private sphere sufficiently important and honorable to justify the whole expenditure of angelic endowments—the formation of the character of children. This is the noblest and most momentous work done on earth." Next, in response to the claim that some women were called by God to preach, Dabney argued that this was a misunderstanding of the biblical doctrine of vocation. Simply because someone believed that the Holy Spirit called her to preach did not mean it was so. For God to call a person to a task that he had elsewhere prohibited her to do would be a contradiction of God's own Word. The Spirit never acted contrary to the Word, but always in accordance with it. The Word proclaimed that men alone were fit for ministerial office; hence, God the Spirit would not call a woman to that office. Further, when the apostle Paul taught the equality of males and females, it was in reference to the "privilege of redemption . . . of access to Christ and participation in his blessings," not to church office. Finally, simply because God may bless the preaching of women did not argue that women should be ordained to preach. Rather, "it is one of God's clearest and most blessed prerogatives to bring good out of evil." God's grace did not mitigate the fact that women who preached God's Word were disobedient.[28]

These leveling doctrines that supported feminism and abolitionism ultimately portended disaster, Dabney believed. By uprooting the hierarchical order preserved in families, anarchy was sure to result. "When God's ordinance of the family is thus uprooted, and all the appointed influences of education thus inverted; when America has had a generation of women who were *politicians*, instead of *mothers*, how fundamental must be the destruction of society, and how distant and difficult must be the remedy!" In addition, those who denied that God established an ordered society and distributed ability, wealth, and privilege unequally were utopian revolutionaries. Simply because all human beings were equal before the sight of God and born "of one blood" did not argue for "mechanical equality." Such was the doctrine of the "Jacobins" and the "Red Republicans" of the French Revolutions of 1787 and 1848. Rather, the rights of individuals differed as their "powers, knowledge, virtue, and natural relations to each other" differed. Therefore, an equitable government would "confer very different degrees of power, and very different degrees of restraint, upon different classes of members." Thus, an organic society that was just and equitable would preserve moral equality but also insist on civil inequality.[29]

Dabney's answer to the "rationalistic" egalitarian logic was a reestablishment of the Christian household led by white male masters, the central feature of what he called "Bible Republicanism." He argued that "the integers of which the commonwealth aggregate is made up, are not single human beings, but single families, authoritatively represented in the father and master." While the father served as master over the household and the mother served in her sphere, children were akin to slaves, minors under the tutelage of the master. In many ways, the household operated as a little commonwealth. For women and children, their situation was similar to slaves within the household: "The family is his State. The master is his magistrate and legislator . . . He is a member of municipal society only through his master, who represents him. The commonwealth knows him only as a life-long minor under the master's tutelage."[30]

Moreover, Dabney's household was an institute within which the most important principles of public life were learned, such as authority and subordination. "Every human being," he claimed, was "born under authority (parental and civic) instead of being born 'free' in the licentious sense." Parental authority over the household was wide-ranging and complete. Dabney observed, "Parental authority is the most remarkable and absolute one delegated by God to man over his fellowman. Consider: it authorizes the parent to govern the child for a fourth of his life as a slave." Subordination, "the natural state of man," was learned within the household as well. Every human being existed within a hierarchy, as taught by the household: there was an "equitable distribution of different duties and rights among the classes naturally differing in condition, and subordination of some to others, and of all to the law."[31]

As the cornerstone of Bible Republicanism, households trained white women to serve as the "matrons" of society, second in command to the white master and yet under his rule as well. In a series of articles published in the *Central Presbyterian* in 1867, Dabney paid homage to "the matron of Old Virginia" and provided a model of Southern womanhood for the Reconstruction period. While Northern women held up models of the strong-minded woman and agitated for women's rights, the ideal Southern woman assumed her sphere—"the fireside, the nursery, and the sanctuary of home"—and reveled in her aspiration—"to fulfill the duties of gentle mates to more rugged natures." The Southern matron drew her influence from her upbringing in the Bible and her home education, not the "Yankee" progressives' "college for females." These sources prepared her to be part of the ruling class—to care for children, slaves, and the poor as well as to entertain her social equals. Dabney believed that this type of Southern womanhood was the need of the hour. In 1868 he claimed that "never before was the welfare of a people so dependent on their mothers, wives, and sisters, as now and here. I freely declare that under God my chief hope for my prostrate country is in their women." Women as keepers of the home would nerve their men to stand firm for the principles for which they fought in the Civil War.[32]

Dabney was convinced that his Bible Republicanism was scripturally sound because it was advocated by Job and the apostle Paul as well as by George Washington and John Adams. The Bible indicated "God's preference for the representative republic as distinguished from the leveling democracy" and made "the household represented by the parent and master the integral unit of the social fabric, assigning to each order, higher or lower, its rule or subordination under the distributive equity of the law." To deny these biblical truths was to come perilously close to surrendering "the inspiration of the Scriptures to these assaults of a social science so-called." Dabney called on Southern Presbyterians to reject the modernistic rationalism driving the egalitarian political doctrines and to stand firm for Bible Republicanism. For he believed that there was only "one safe position for the sacramental host: to stand on the whole Scripture, and refuse to concede a single point."[33]

Secularized Education

Dabney's Bible Republicanism—with its emphasis on hierarchy, subordination, and inequality—had something to say not only to household relations, but also to public education. In the 1870s, Dabney stood firmly against any theory of education, whether public or parochial, that claimed the right to usurp the control of a child's education away from the household head. Prior to the Civil War, Virginia schools were essentially local and private. Rejecting Jefferson's program for universal education, state leaders stood fast against most school reforms. Virginia did allow part of the state literary fund to be used to fund "pauper schools" in 1810; and in the 1840s, as a result of the activity of William Henry Ruffner, a Presbyterian minister from Lexington, Virginia, the legislature allowed a free-school law that gave rise to a few short-lived schools. The state exercised no oversight over education, preferring to allow local associations of concerned parents and philanthropists to govern their schools. Reconstruction, however, brought about changes in Virginia's education system. Radical Republicans forced through a new state constitution in 1869, which mandated the creation of a universal public-school system for the state by 1876. Conservative anti-Reconstruction politicians were able to recapture political office in 1870, but they were unable to escape the constitutional mandate for state public education. In order to comply with the new constitutional requirement, they sought to hire an ill-paid superintendent of public instruction. In 1870, out of a dozen candidates, the Virginia General Assembly elected Ruffner to the office.

Ruffner's plan advocated a centralized system of public schools with a state board of education to exercise oversight over all schools in the state. The board, in turn, would appoint all county superintendents and district trustees, who were responsible for recruiting teachers, establishing schools, and mediating local problems. In order to fund the schools, the school law provided for a property assessment of ten percent and incorporated interest from the old literary fund. Counties were authorized to collect additional property and poll taxes, at the discretion of the local citizens. In order to make the plan palatable, the school law contained provision for segregated schools but mandated that blacks be educated as well as whites. The schools were not compulsory, and they were to be free for all from the ages of five to twenty-one.

Dabney, as well as other religious and political conservatives, withstood Ruffner's progressive plan. His argument against public education focused chiefly on the issue of state control in place of parental oversight, centralization instead of localism. Believing Ruffner's public-school system to be nothing short of "Radicalism," Dabney claimed that the plan embraced "the pagan, Spartan theory, which makes the State the parent." This theory denied that God had ordered society in such a way that parents determined "the social grade and the culture of children on their reaching adult age." Dabney argued that God equipped parents with the affection and power necessary to accomplish all that was necessary to prepare their own children for life in society. Further, Ruffner's system failed to recognize that children themselves must have a native desire to be educated. One can teach a child how to read, but only that child can want to "utilize a knowledge of letters." School officials did not have the power to overcome a child's intransigence; only parents did. All of this argued that "parents are the real architects of their children's destiny, and the State cannot help it."[34]

A centralized public-education system would be abused by those who sought to control it for nefarious ends. Public schools would inevitably be "wielded by the demagogues . . . in the interests of their faction." Not only would politicians manipulate the system, but Northern textbook producers would shape the "ethics and politics for the children of a whole State." Thus, the public-school system would "poison the minds of our own children against the principles which we honor" and "infect them with the errors which we detest." Not only would Southern children be exposed to Northern "lies," but public schools would provide the masses with only a "smattering" of education. This would leave them open to all sorts of socialistic and revolutionary theories. The members of the laboring class were "incompetent to navigate" the ocean of information and knowledge to which they would be exposed. Thus, "every manufactory is converted into a debating club, where the operatives intoxicate their minds with the most licentious vagaries of opinions upon every fundamental subject of politics and religion." This was exactly the state of affairs that "prepared the way for the 'International Society,' and the horrors of the

Paris *Commune*." The partially educated were "an easy prey to the most destructive heresies, social and religious."[35]

Rather than embracing the "heretical" and "utopian" notions of universal public education, with its leveling impulse and destructive results, society should recognize that God had ordained a hierarchy of superiors and inferiors. "God has made a social sub-soil to the top-soil, a social foundation in the dust, for the superstructure," Dabney averred. Everyone aware of social science knew that "influence descends." Rather than attempting to influence society from the bottom up, Virginians needed to recognize that "the most philanthropic mode for elevating the lower classes of society is to provide for the rise of the superior class." Such was "nature's process," which elevated "the whole mass by lifting it from above so that all the parts rise together." Such was also the principle behind the creation of the University of Virginia; only the state's superior sons were taught there, and yet, by "giving them a higher standard of acquirement," the entire state profited: "It has made thorough culture respectable, and diffused honest aspirations" to all.[36]

Dabney also objected to public education on religious grounds. The state was pledged not to establish religion. Yet any form of Bible-reading and prayer would establish a generic Protestantism at public expense. This would violate the consciences of Roman Catholics and Jews, who would rightly protest against being taxed to support Protestant public schools. To solve the problem, he suggested that one could force the majority religion on all who attend the public schools; one could provide vouchers for religious dissenters to attend private parochial schools; or one could attempt to limit public schools' education "in every case to secular learning," leaving religious instruction to parents at home. None of these solutions was adequate. It was wrong to violate non-Protestants' liberty of conscience; establishment of vouchers for religious schools would be a religious establishment; and nonreligious education was unthinkable and unworkable. The state did not have the right to educate because all education must lead to moral action; it was "impossible to separate the ethical and intellectual functions." In order to instruct in ethics, one had to adopt theological language and sources. The state could not teach the Bible in its

tax-financed schools, and thus "the State is unfit to assume the education function." State education might attempt to stand in a non-
Christian position and not to engage in moral training; in reality, however, there was no "neutrality"—"any training which attempts to be
non-Christian is therefore anti-Christian."[37]

In addition, it was wrong to mix Christian children with others
who came from families who cared little for religion. If Ruffner's plans
were carried out, "there must be a mixture of the children of the decent
and the children of the vile in the same society during the most plas-
tic age." The Christian parent, who desired "to choose the moral influences for his own beloved offspring," would be forced by the state
education system to "thrust" his children in with "all the moral lep-
ers among the children of a given district." The negative peer influence would teach the children of Christian parents far more than their
parents could possibly counteract. Teachers could not be counted on
to prevent wicked influence, either. Besides, God did not require parents to employ "our innocent and inexperienced children as the missionaries" to unconverted public-school students.[38]

Finally, Dabney objected to public education for fears of racial
mixing. While Ruffner's system provided for "separate but equal"
schools, Dabney warned that the leveling policy of public education
sprang from the same philosophy that "claims to make the blacks
equal, socially and politically, to the most respectable whites." Segregated schools were inconsistent with claims of racial equality, he
charged. School leaders knew this and were waiting for the time when
"all the staunch old Confederates like me have died out"; then they
would integrate the schools. At that time, Southern leaders would point
out, rightly, that Southern blacks were far better than the "degraded
and vicious" immigrants who were gaining admittance to Northern
public schools. In actuality, racial integration was unthinkable; this
pointed to a significant fault in Ruffner's system. It sought to level
social distinction between whites and blacks, rich and poor, and North
and South. To Dabney, who sought to maintain an ordered society,
progressive state-run education that usurped the parental prerogative
to educate and that leveled social and racial distinctions was ultimately
disordering, infidel, and dangerous.[39]

186

Christian Economy

Dabney's defense of the household also produced a stinging critique of modern corporate capitalism and presented an alternative vision of "Christian economy." Merging his theological vision of the household with the Jeffersonian myth of the superiority of agrarian society, Dabney's economics revivified a system similar to the antebellum system of agriculture that used the manual labor of blacks and poor whites to achieve the best division of labor and the highest possible efficiency. The household farm produced "more economically" because all the members of the household took a part in production. "On the well organized Southern farm," Dabney envisioned, "the plough, the axe, the scythe, the hoe, the team offered constant and remunerative work to the strong men; while the less valuable labor of the boys and girls, and the elderly, was equally as effective in the lighter task." The household farm permitted "the essential advantage of combination of labor" but also prevented the overaccumulation of property or radical increase of scale. Instead, most farms in Dabney's vision were "moderate holdings": "The smallest were not too small to employ most of the profitable appliances; the largest were not so large as to be cumbersome."[40]

Dabney further defended agriculture against the interests and slanders of industrial "robber-barons." He fervently denied that "the labor of the artisan and of commerce is skilled labor, while rustic labor is unskilled." The truth was that "the prairie farmer has developed higher intellectual skill and more varied resources, in place of the petty-fogging arts of the trader." Yet the farm community was being rapidly depleted as its best young men were drifting to factory jobs in the towns. As a result, the cities were becoming "human hives in which these drones are found in needless numbers, consuming, but producing no honey." Unproductive consumption, disease, pollution, political corruption, and unrest—all were the result of the depression of American farming interests and the slow death of Southern agriculture. Unless the concerns of the household farmer were addressed, social convulsion would ensue.[41]

Dabney placed the blame for the decline of family agriculture directly on corporate capitalism as developed in the North and advocated by many in the New South. He charged that incorporation was a medieval concept that could not be transferred to nineteenth-century economics without leading to "the overthrow of liberty." Corporations armed "favored individuals with powers of *aggression* against their fellows," he conjectured. These special privileges were not sought for protection from government tyranny; rather, incorporation was sought in order to gain "the power of a monopolist" in the marketplace. The government protected the corporations by passing legislation that was "invidious class-legislation, anti-republican in tendency, however republican in seeming, and favorable to oligarchy in business, and ultimately in the state." Bloated by its own profits and protected by government, the corporation was prey to corruption and wasteful inefficiencies that led to the degradation of morals and the squandering of public wealth. Thus, Dabney saw a bitter irony: the age that had fought a civil war for "republican equality" was committed to a form of capitalism that developed "a new oligarchy, a hundred-fold more ruthless and insatiable . . . than the landed aristocracy which the spirit of the age has swept away."[42]

Moreover, Dabney believed that modern capitalism produced a society that was ready to explode at any moment. Because Northern laborers were cut off from the paternalistic care of their employers, they resorted to labor unions, communes, and strikes in order to receive justice. Strikers established the rule of the mob, inevitably leading to violence aimed at both strike-breakers and employers. Such disorder horrified Dabney, and yet it was the necessary result of free labor: "No existing commonwealth organized exclusively upon the hireling labor theory has yet found a full remedy for this deplorable tendency." The Northern system of labor drew workers away from the country into the cities, which, in turn, broke up Northern households and was "injurious to public wealth." The labor force packed into cities, which were "great ulcers upon the body politic" and failed to produce public virtue or beneficial industry. The greatest condemnation that Dabney could utter of this Northern capitalistic system, was that it was "a form of slavery far more ruthless than domestic bondage."[43]

Ultimately, however, Dabney was realistic enough not to advocate a blind return to the past economically. He reluctantly recognized that the South needed Northern investment in order to revive its shattered postbellum economy. Though he defended the "former economic system of the southern states" to the end of his life, Dabney admitted that "justice" to the rising "New South" generation required that the older generation leave them to seek their own path. Still, he urged young Southerners to remember certain unchangeable principles that formed his theological response to the economic realities of the New South—in particular, the principle that God was the true owner of all property and wealth; humans simply used property as stewards. Dabney taught that God's Word outlined three appropriate purposes for wealth: personal sustenance, family need, and insurance against the future. Wealth was certainly not to be used in "superfluities" or on luxuries, which only produced a worldly conformity, led others to covet, and ruined one's own character. Such unproductive consumption was a "waste and perversion of a trust that should have been sacred to noble and blessed ends." Instead, excess wealth was to be used for evangelism and other ministries, for "every ignorant, degraded man who is enlightened and sanctified becomes at once a useful producer of material wealth, for he is rendered an industrious citizen. And every heathen community that is evangelized becomes a recipient and a producer of the wealth of peaceful commerce."[44]

Even though he admitted that Northern investment was necessary, Dabney warned that it could be disastrous as well. The great potential evil was that the North would *"Yankeeize the South."* By cooperating with the North, the New South men were in danger of making an idol out of wealth: "They exclaim: Let us develop! Develop! Develop! Let us have, like our conquerors, great cities, great capitalists, great factories and commerce and great populations." Such an idolatry would be "deadly"—for Northern culture was already decaying "like the tawdry pyrotechnics of some popular feast, burning out its own splendors into ashes, darkness, and a villainous stench of brimstone." In order to preserve the South from Northern idolatry and decay, young Southerners had to carefully balance their need for Northern investment and their Southern conviction that "the only sure wealth of the State is in cultured, heroic men, who intelligently know *their duty* and are calmly prepared to sacrifice all else, including life, to maintain the right." The way to maintain that balance, according to Dabney, was to preserve the principles of the "lost cause" and to adopt a public theology that affirmed both "an unchangeable God" and a God-ordained social hierarchy against the modernist-inspired, materialistic, egalitarian worldview. In this way, the South could erect a genuinely "new order" that would be "tolerable for honest men."[45]

"Hold Fast That Which Is Good"

Ironically, this cultural war that Dabney fought against positivism and its modernizing results placed him close to the Northeastern antimodernists that historian Jackson Lears observed in *No Place of Grace*. For example, Dabney's strong adherence to an older faith placed him closer to antimodernists, who were discovering ancient religions such as Buddhism or rediscovering Catholicism, than to New South Presbyterians, who downplayed their creeds in order to influence Southern culture. The older faiths—such as Buddhism or Catholicism or Protestant scholasticism—were thought to provide transcendence in a world of immanence, a "God of thunder" in an age of feminization. In a gilded age that made the seemingly impossible possible through unprecedented technological manipulation, antimodernists sought a refuge in otherworldly faiths, which proclaimed a transcendent deity who was shrouded in mystery. Though most scholars have failed to recognize the possibility that Old School Calvinism—as maintained at Princeton Seminary or defended by Dabney—could be as antimodern as Buddhism or Anglo-Catholicism, for Dabney it appeared that the older faith in a transcendent, sovereign deity both put him out of step with the prevailing modernist spirit of the age and provided resources to challenge the modern age of the Spirit.[46]

In addition, Dabney's critique of "soulless corporations" mirrored that of Northern antimodernists, who also feared the rise of corporate capitalism as destructive of republican virtue. These blue-blood elites from Boston and New York worried that the *nouveau riches* would fail to suppress the teeming immigrant populations, crowded

190

in cities and ripe for labor cataclysm. According to Northern elites, a renewal of republican morality coupled with paternalistic social control—typified in Prohibition legislation—was required in order to temper the potential disaster that lurked in Gilded Age economics. Moreover, as Lears demonstrated, these antimoderns also embraced an arts-and-crafts ideology that longed for a bucolic "simple life," which drew from Jeffersonian myths about the purity of the agrarian life. In this agrarian lifestyle, the household could be privatized, protected from the corruption lurking in market forces and rationalized economics. Only by returning to natural rhythms of life could the potential societal volcano brought about by modernization be defused. Dabney's public theology was in sympathy with many of the concerns of these Yankee antimoderns. From his rural hamlet of Farmville, Virginia, Dabney, as has already been noted, worried that the cities were becoming "human hives in which these drones are found in needless numbers, consuming, but producing no honey." He warned that unless the unproductive consumption, disease, pollution, political corruption, and unrest of the urban proletariat were addressed, social convulsion would result, throwing up "lava streams of anarchy and revolution, which will rend the whole superstructure and burn up the luxurious vineyards and gardens which bedeck its upper surface."[47]

Above all, Dabney's identification of "positivism" as the root of modern social ills paralleled Northeastern antimodern sentiments. Yankee antimodernists feared positivism, as Lears observed, because it placed human beings in the grip of deterministic laws outside of the loving care of God the Father almighty. Modern life felt as though it were "weightless" and unreal because humans were in the grip of impersonal forces beyond themselves. Hence, antimodernists embraced spiritualism and Eastern mysticism in an attempt to break free from materialism and determinism, and to connect with the transcendent. Though they did not deny the "scientific worldview" for which positivism stood, Northeastern antimodernists vainly attempted to wiggle free from the necessary conclusions of the positivist worldview. Dabney's opposition to positivism had similar antimodern purposes. He stridently denied that natural, mechanistic laws determined the fates of humankind. Instead, he consistently appealed to the human spirit, confident that all human beings seek a transcendent being outside of themselves. Rather than being bound to natural forces, human striving signaled that God had made humankind for himself and that God had revealed himself to his creation. Dabney was confident that the materialism of the modern worldview would ultimately prove self-destructive. And if modernism would not cave in on its own, Dabney's public theology would wage war and defeat it on the cultural battlefield. At times that might mean vilifying "Yankees" in order to preserve Southern order, but Dabney felt he had no other choice. As he saw it, nothing less than the future of biblical civilization and Christianity itself was at stake.[48]

7

Passing

s Dabney fought his cultural war against modernization mediated by "Yankees," convinced of the rightness of his cause, he recognized that he was losing influence and passing from the leadership position that he had held within the Southern Presbyterian church in the decades directly after the Civil War. It is almost as though in recognizing his passing, Dabney raised his voice ever louder, determined to make his fellow Southerners and Presbyterians pay attention to him. Yet he also admitted the futility of his actions. In 1879, toward the end of an article hammering the Southern church's participation in the Pan-Presbyterian Alliance, in a moment of brutal honesty, he whimpered, "Have I not written? There stands my 'Defence of Virginia and the South,' whose arguments, founded on Scripture and facts, are as impregnable as the everlasting hills. But who reads it? The self-satisfied insolence of the pharisaic slanderers makes them disdain it—they never condescend to hear of it. *I have no audience.*" As noted, in the debate over fraternal relations with the Northern church in the 1880s, Dabney was savagely attacked by Richard McIlwaine, an exchange that would have been hard to imagine a decade or two before when Dabney was at the height of his influence. And more famously, in 1894, Dabney observed to a young confidante, "I am the Cassandra of Yankeedom, predestined to prophesy truth and never to be believed by her country until too late."[1]

In actuality, Dabney's passing influence within his church had begun much earlier, within the institution that he allegedly dominated. The long-standing rivalry between Dabney and his brother-in-law and colleague, B. M. Smith, reached an impasse during the Reconstruction period. Smith's own biographer noted, "There was between them a mutual feeling of respect, admiration and affection. Yet their views of church and public policy at some points were quite antithetical, and strong-minded men as they both were, they never hesitated to oppose each other. Consequently, sharp words were often exchanged between them in private and public debate." During this period, the antithetical positions represented by Smith and Dabney led to their corresponding fortunes—Smith's more moderate positions gained for him a prominence that he had not known before, while Dabney's own influence slowly ebbed away within the small, tight-knit community of Hampden-Sydney, where the seminary was located. Though the documentary evidence is slight, due in part to Smith's own sanitized papers and Dabney's unwillingness to blame Smith directly, there are enough hints to put together a case that suggests a growing rift between the two men, one that had been slowly developing ever since they became related by marriage in 1848. This rift in turn led to the remarkable chain of events culminating in Dabney's "exile" from Virginia to Texas—at that time, a geographical, ecclesiastical, and intellectual marginality—and final passing to his eternal rest.[2]

Exiled from Virginia

B. M. Smith and Dabney held drastically different views on several public issues that brought them into conflict. For example, Smith and Dabney ardently disagreed over the propriety of public schools. Smith was a lifelong defender of public education in Virginia and had promoted it as early as the 1840s. When public education became a reality in Virginia in the 1870s, Smith was a prominent ally of William Henry Ruffner, who, not coincidentally, was one of Dabney's chief enemies during the period. Smith also presented a paper to the Educational Association of Virginia in 1870 that was critical of many of Dabney's positions on public schools. When Ruffner's plan for state schools was established, Smith became superintendent of public instruction for Prince Edward County from 1870 to 1881. Not only did the two men disagree on public education, but they also had a public disagreement over the relationship between Hampden-Sydney College and the Synod of Virginia. Smith had advocated the church's control and oversight of the college, while Dabney had strongly opposed this position as violating the spiritual nature of the church.[3]

Dabney and Smith also disagreed on the relationship between the conquered South and the victorious North. While Dabney was fearful that the South would be "Yankee-ized," Smith was promoting a reunion of feeling and ecclesiastical relations with the North. Confiding to Cyrus McCormick, Smith claimed that "the Virginia clergy have always been moderate, conservative men—and the influences now are all that way. But I am utterly opposed to all sectionalism. I go for a national church." Such a moderate spirit helped Smith in his fundraising efforts for the seminary. During Reconstruction, while the seminary was struggling to pay salaries and recover its lost endowment, Smith acted as its agent during long tours in the North, particularly in Baltimore and New York. Chief among the gifts that he secured was a $30,000 bequest from McCormick to endow a professorship: Smith's own chair of Oriental literature. Smith also used his influence in the North to secure a $30,000 gift from Henry Young of New York to endow the professorship of New Testament exegesis as well as a donation from the Brown family that was used to construct a new library building.[4]

Smith's ability as a fund-raiser made him the "savior" of the seminary and increased his reputation among the directors. By contrast, Dabney began to observe "the almost total decline of my weight and influence with my own board." One of his failures was his inability to convince the directors of the seminary and Hampden-Sydney College to buy up the property around the two institutions in order to create a "white man's town." Fearful that the "genteel country" people were moving to urban centers and new towns and were being replaced by African Americans, creating "an amoral negro town of the most sordid quality," Dabney urged the two boards to adopt a land speculation scheme with the institutions as the leading members. Participants in the program would make a pledge "not to sell an inch of these lands to any negro or pauperized white man" and "to concur in the sale of building lots on the parts most adjacent to the institutions, each proprietor fixing his own price." If the lands could not be sold, then the land improvement company would buy the lands so that they would not be "sold to negroes or untrustworthy whites." The object, Dabney stressed, was not to gain ownership of all the lands, but merely "control of all the adjacent lands in danger of occupancy by this rag town of negroes." The scheme was strenuously opposed by his brother-in-law, Smith, whom Dabney later remembered to have jibed, "Do not listen to Dr. Dabney; he is wild; he is such a Calhounist and is so deeply mortified at being whipped by the Yankees that he is a monomaniac on everything touching the Yankee and negro, etc." With Smith's opposition, Dabney's project failed to generate the necessary support.[5]

Shortly after this design failed, Dabney attempted to push his memorial on theological education through the Southern Presbyterian General Assembly. Though the trustees at Columbia Seminary considered the memorial, the Union Seminary board "refused by an express note to hear or read it at all and condemned and rejected it without knowing what was in it." Dabney was present at the meeting when it was rejected. He remembered that afterward, trustee John L. Kirkpatrick "then came up to me, holding my manuscript off daintily, as though he had some little reptile by the tail, and said with the supercilious civility which he knew how to affect: 'Dr. Dabney, I feel some embarrassment to know what disposition to make of this document.' I answered very quietly, reaching out my hand, 'I will relieve you, sir, of that embarrassment,' and took it." The public embarrassment that Dabney felt by this rejection, coupled with Smith's ascending star, was palpable. "I gradually and silently ceased to counsel," Dabney admitted in his autobiographical reflections. "The general guidance of the seminary passed away into other hands, within the faculty and without, who directed or misdirected them without my interposing."[6]

Dabney's observation that the guidance of the seminary was moving into other hands was appropriate, not only in reference to Smith's new influence, but also in pointing up the changing character of the board of trustees. In the 1870s, Union Seminary's board experienced a massive changeover. Of the sixty different trustees who guided the seminary during Dabney's thirty-year tenure, half came to their positions after the Civil War. More importantly, only five trustees during the period were Dabney students with any possible ties of loyalty to the theologian. In addition, of the trustees who were at Union Seminary in 1883 when Dabney resigned, only one (William Brown, editor of the *Central Presbyterian*) was on the board before the Civil War, when Dabney was the chief fund-raiser and leading man in the seminary. By and large, the trustees in the era during and after Reconstruction were New South men, hailing from prominent towns and working in large urban pastorates. As those instructed to care for Union Seminary, they were more interested in presenting a reconciling and more moderate front to the public than they were in promoting Lost Cause ideals and racial separation. Dabney's concerns were largely lost on the more urban and progressive trustees.[7]

Sometimes, though, even Dabney's colleagues failed to understand his perspective, causing great tension among them and embarrassment for Dabney. One of his colleagues, Henry Alexander, requested that Dabney support him in petitioning the board of trustees for a delay of the beginning of the academic year because of the unhealthiness of the Hampden-Sydney area, which, they both believed, led to "malarial" conditions. Dabney agreed to do so; he had long held that "these August openings were to cost me my health and probably my life" and, for that reason, "had not dared to keep my family in Prince Edward" during the summer months. But when Alexander and Dabney argued that the opening of the school year should be postponed to September, Smith and Thomas Peck both blasted Dabney in tones that were personal. Smith, Dabney remembered, "asserted that there never had been and could not be any malaria on the Hill, ridiculed our position, and assured the Board in substance that our apprehensions were the mere products of a cowardly imagination." As bad as that was, Peck was worse: "Turning pointedly to me, and fixing his eyes on my face, with his sternest austerity, he added about this: that the statements about possible malaria on the Hill were so certainly notoriously false that his only difficulty was to imagine how a person claiming to be cognizant of the facts could utter such statements without

197

an intention to deceive." Dabney did not make a reply, and the matter was dropped. Still, it seems odd that such an apparently inconsequential issue could elicit such a response, unless these pieces and hints are placed together. Only then is it apparent that the faculty was experiencing serious tensions and that Dabney's influence at Union Seminary was continuing to decrease.[8]

This impression was confirmed in Dabney's mind when he gave his famous speech on the New South for the 1882 commencement at Hampden-Sydney College. Not only did Dabney have to clear his speech topic with the college's president, but he also was given an unenviable time slot "with a tired and listless audience." When the time came for him to speak, B. M. Smith "rose in his place far forward and stalked down the aisle, with an air of ostentatious protestation." And though Dabney's speech was successful, with several "grave trustees" taking his hand and wringing it "while the tears were running down their cheeks," he did not even have the final word. The following day, Moses Hoge, Dabney's longtime friend who had become estranged because of their opposite paths within the Southern Presbyterian church, used his own speech to turn the hearts of the people away from the glories of the Old South, which Dabney had promoted, to the possibilities of the New South. While Dabney did not respond either to the slight of Smith or to the correction of Hoge, he could not help but feel that the bonds of affections that had tied his heart to Prince Edward County and to Union Seminary were snapping one by one.[9]

During these years, Dabney increasingly felt alone and isolated. His beloved church was moving in a direction that he reprobated to such a degree that he was fearful for his future position in the seminary if reunion with the Northern Presbyterian church were ever to be effected. "I knew that when it became a Yankee institution, under Yankee church government," he mused, "the rebel and traitor Dabney would not be retained there as professor, but would be kicked out ignominiously at the approach of old age." When he took a trip to Europe in 1880, his isolation struck him particularly hard. Writing to Hoge, Dabney lamented:

Few men of sixty years ever came to England with fewer acquaintances. Having lived all my life away from cities, where one meets foreigners, and notabilities, and being only known, so far as known at all, as an advocate of the losing and unpopular side of a cause fast becoming antiquated, I had the slimmest possible clues of social connection with anybody of Europe. Of these few, most failed me.

As a result, "I have made my journey in solitude: keeping my eyes and ears open, and holding very small communication with anyone." The loneliness that Dabney felt was palpable. Still, he was not ashamed of his stands or his heritage: "The old Virginians are by all odds the brightest, purest, and most graceful people I have met anywhere. Superior to their English progenitors," he asserted.[10]

Even with all of these negative feelings, Dabney intended to spend the rest of his career at Union Seminary. In 1882, however, his health intervened in a drastic way. Before this time, he had generally used his health as an excuse for withdrawing from unpleasant circumstances, whether he was truly desperately ill or not. Among examples already noted, he used "a spell of bronchitis" to resign his increasingly strained co-pastorate with Smith at College Church in 1874. Dabney's sickness of 1882, however, was a complete and total breakdown in health, one that knocked him out of operation for over three months. Typified by Dabney as a "severe ague" that led to high fever, congestion, and nasal discharge, he was treated with "enormous doses of quinine and condurango." Ironically, in light of his colleagues' claims a few years earlier, these were symptoms of and treatments for malaria, a parasitic disease that was not eliminated in the United States until the 1940s and 1950s. During his intense illness, Dabney had an apparent near-death experience:

> As I lay on my bed, in this easy, calm and rational state I heard, for a considerable time, hymn after hymn of soft and sweet sacred music, coming apparently from the direction of Mrs. Sarah Bocock's. There was some kind of soft instrument, accompanied by sweet female voices. I could never remember the tunes, though I had a faint impression that one was a very sweet hymn, new to me, which I had heard in Westminster Abbey, in London, in 1880. I called my wife to enjoy

the sweet music with me, and asked her if it might be some one of the girls of the neighborhood singing thus for my enjoyment. She declared that she heard nothing . . . After a time the music ceased, leaving me much pleased and refreshed. Such are the dry facts. What is the explanation? May it be that I had come so near death, the veil which separates us from the spirit world was a little lifted, so that I heard the sweet faint echoes of the heavenly choirs? Or, can it be that this strange music was the deceitful result of some morbid cerebral action in my own brain, now relaxing from its tension? I assert no opinion. I know the facts.[11]

After briefly recovering, Dabney was felled by a second protracted illness, which coupled pleurisy and pneumonia. In the midst of this intense and bitter illness, he noted that the board of trustees, in their annual meeting, "took no note of the danger through which I was passing, made no offer of succor." Clearly disappointed with the inattentiveness and insensitivity of his board, and nursing the many slights that he had endured over the past decade, Dabney had resigned himself to "die at his post" at Union Seminary, unappreciated and unloved.[12]

In this physical and mental condition, shortly after the completion of the 1882–83 school year, Dabney received a "strange providence." He had been elected professor of moral and mental philosophy at the new University of Texas at Austin. Though he claimed that his election was without his knowledge, in actuality, Dabney's son Charles had made it known in his own educational circles that his father was available for hire. Through the agency of R. K. Smoot, minister at First Presbyterian Church, Austin, Texas, Dabney was elected to the philosophy chair at the newly forming university. Dabney was uncertain what to do with this offer. He had rejected so many similar offers from Princeton Seminary, Hampden-Sydney College, Fifth Avenue Presbyterian Church in New York, and the University of Virginia. His longtime friend and doctor, Joseph Eggleston, urged him to go to Texas, where he would have a better chance for health in a "warmer, drier, and non-malarial residence." Dabney investigated the opportunity, apparently being well enough to travel to Texas himself to scout out the situation. He decided to accept the offer. It is unclear whether he intended, by accepting the offer, to preserve his health (as he afterward maintained) or to attempt one final time to wrest some type of note of appreciation from the trustees. If he intended the latter, he was disappointed. At the July 1883 trustees meeting at Richmond, Dabney tendered his resignation, accompanied by a letter from Eggleston, suggesting that his health necessitated this change. To Dabney's consternation, the board "simply accepted it immediately, suggesting no dissuasion or alternative, such as a furlough to rest or a year's residence in the South." This was the final straw: "only one decision was possible for a sensible and self-respecting man," namely, withdrawal from a place where Dabney evidently was not wanted, even though he had maintained his "loyalty to the seminary almost to the verge of indirect suicide and had met with no kind response whatever." Although Dabney wanted his move to Texas to sound like an act motivated by the preservation of his manly honor, in a few short years it felt like an exile from the only state in which he had ever lived and from the land that he passionately loved. As he wrote to his dear friend Eggleston in 1890, "Sometimes I feel it hard, that I have to spend the rest of my days in a sort of banishment from those who suit me best."[13]

Exiled to Texas

Dabney's first years in Texas were quite successful and pleasing. He was able to purchase a lot near the university and build a little house for his needs. In his lecture room, Dabney essentially recast moral philosophy lectures that he had delivered as early as 1857 while serving as temporary president of Hampden-Sydney College. In those years, he believed that his class "was reasonably large in numbers, poor in quality." But this was not too surprising for Dabney, who believed that "no school of philosophy could in this sense [of numbers] be popular in a community so crude as Texas in intelligence and culture." That first year of teaching, Dabney organized two classes, a junior and senior class. The junior class took Dabney's course in psychology and logic; the senior class took his history of philosophy course, which was "a critical review of psychology, practical ethics, natural theology, and political economy." In his second year teaching in Austin, Dabney added a postgraduate course of mental and moral philosophy and political economy.[14]

By subsequent accounts, Dabney was no easy teacher, a fact that he recognized himself. Not only did Dabney lecture, but he expected his students to have mastered his assigned textbooks, sometimes memorizing large sections of the text. As a result, in later years, when Dabney shared the teaching in the department with a younger professor, students would say, "Since I must take one course somewhere in philosophy, I take the junior for two reasons. It is more natural to study the beginning of a thing before the latter half; and I am told the junior is made easy for us, and the old Doctor makes the senior hard." Or older students would tell the newer ones:

> Fellows are you making up your options for your B.A. course? Yes, well then we tell you, if you want to have a "soft snap," you keep far away from old Dr. Dabney's courses, for he is one of those old fashioned teachers who believes in work and wants to carry his students in his lectures down to the bottom of things; and besides, when he marks them will not give any fellow a particle of a grade above what he earns.

Yet Dabney enjoyed his time teaching in the university, and for the first several years of his tenure, he was generally respected.[15]

There was some fear among Texas Presbyterians that with Dabney at the university, the denominational college in Sherman, Texas, would suffer. Also, some questions arose whether a Presbyterian minister should be involved with an institution that was committed to providing nonsectarian education. In order to answer such concerns, Dabney wrote a lengthy article for the *Southwestern Presbyterian* that was published in early 1884. Dabney claimed that simply because the University of Texas was a state institution did not mean that it was a "godless or anti-Christian one." Rather, the university shared the same basis as the state of Texas, that is, a theistic one. The state bill of rights demanded that elected officials "acknowledge the existence of a Supreme Being." In the same way, the state university was grounded on a theistic basis, and was required to respect all Christian denominations and render to all "common service." And because the university was grounded on a theistic basis, Dabney felt perfectly comfortable teaching there. The professors held as their official duty that "we can assert no particular ecclesiastical or theological system in teaching literature and science." Unofficially, the professors "claim their personal rights as heads of families and members of Christian society, to support the several forms of evangelical Christianity which they personally believe in." This, in turn, gave the professors a wide, though unofficial, spiritual influence for good. Hence, friends of Christianity as well as defenders of the separation of church and state had nothing to worry about with the university or Dabney's involvement with it.[16]

Likewise, Dabney claimed that those who supported denominational colleges ought not to worry about the university. Rather, "they ought to regard themselves as mutually consistent, and as interested in each other's welfare, because they are all parts of one great system of education." Ultimately, Dabney hoped that the University of Texas would more approximate the German university ideal of teaching only "post-graduates." That would result in the denominational colleges' being particularly necessary for educating young men—these schools would train the students in a basic college course, after which the student would go for postgraduate training at the university. Denominational colleges were also necessary because it was uncertain whether the university would continue to be generally theistic. Dabney warned that "anti-Christian influences may assume such ascendancy in the State, some day, that its rulers may insist on making the public education agnostic. But every Christian knows that such an education is virtually anti-Christian." If such an influence were to come to bear without the denominational colleges in good operation, "Christian truth would experience a disastrous overthrow before this accomplished godless learning backed up by the resources of the State." Finally, Dabney held that denominational colleges were vitally important for "rearing of candidates for the ministry." Because university professors were mainly "laymen" who "have achieved their fame in secular careers," students naturally followed their models into the world and away from ministerial service. At denominational colleges, the religious influences and examples would be more influential on young men and would produce ministerial candidates. As a result, Texas Presbyterians ought to continue to support the Presbyterian College of Texas, as vitally important for the future of the church in that state.[17]

Dabney's argument, however, appeared strangely inconsistent with his arguments against public education made in the 1870s. Against Ruffner, he had argued that state-funded education *had* to be agnostic because the state itself was agnostic. In Texas, however, Dabney claimed that because the state's constitution made reference to a supreme being, state-sponsored education would be permissible. It is hard to understand how such a vague religious requirement could be the difference between Virginia's public schools and the Texas state university. Moreover, when Ruffner proposed a broadly ethical Christianity as the foundation of Virginia's public schools, Dabney had mocked the possibility because education itself was a religious function that required discussion of key doctrinal issues such as sin and redemption. Yet Dabney in Texas appeared to be content with a higher educational system that was based on a broadly ethical, natural religion in which doctrinal or sectarian concerns were willingly set aside. Importantly, during their debate, Ruffner had rhetorically asked, "And how will you get along with your theory as respects colleges and Universities? Can you send a son to our State University?" Ruffner believed that Dabney could not with any sort of consistency do so. That Dabney still did not recognize the inconsistency at the time he wrote the article in 1884 was obvious.[18]

Although Dabney was involved with the university in its formative stages, he was also deeply concerned about the paucity of Presbyterian ministers in the state. Many of the Texas presbyteries struggled to find supplies for their vacant pulpits, and those candidates whom they did produce would go east to seminary, never to return. Six months after he arrived in Austin, after a weeknight prayer meeting, Dabney proposed a plan for a theological school to his fellow minister R. K. Smoot. Dabney's plan was to combine portions of the free education that the University of Texas offered to all qualified citizens with a special course of study that Dabney and Smoot would teach. Smoot willingly partnered with Dabney in the affair, doing "a large amount of gratuitous labor as teacher and as managing correspondent for eleven years." The two men offered their plan to the Presbytery of Central Texas, which commissioned Dabney and Smoot as teachers in this school, and committed themselves to raise the $600 necessary to employ an assistant for the two men.[19]

Almost from the beginning, though, the enterprise was plagued with difficulty. Dabney complained that Smoot "devised and wrote the charter without ever consulting me, the real founder of the school, and made himself a member and treasurer of the board, leaving me out." This charter, Dabney held, made the school "obnoxious" to a large portion of the presbytery and synod. Further, Smoot's reputation with his fellow ministers began to decline, a situation that would bottom out in the years shortly after Dabney's death. This resulted in the presbytery's failure to supply any money to the theological school; Dabney himself supplied the salary of the assistants. Also, the Presbyterian college at Sherman was characterized by a "dog in the manger enmity . . . which wished to engross everything at Sherman, while able to do nothing itself and unwilling that we should do anything." In particular, some Texas Presbyterians believed that the seminary should be located with the denominational college in Sherman, rather than in Austin. Still, Dabney nurtured the little school—he used his influence in the mid-Atlantic states to raise funds, eventually building the endowment to approximately $4,000; he helped to purchase a lot on Nunces Street and in 1889 built a facility that housed a lecture room and a library; and he donated five hundred books to the library, "the cream of my private library." He also succeeded in hiring two key assistants, William Red and Thomas Cary Johnson, who taught Old Testament Hebrew and New Testament Greek. By 1890, the school had thirteen students, nearly as many as Union Seminary had in 1853 when Dabney first started teaching there.[20]

Not only was Dabney pleased with the seminary's possibilities for carrying on his theological legacy, but starting in 1885, he also engaged, with his dear friend C. R. Vaughan, in an effort to preserve his thought in a set of collected writings. Vaughan was the one who had pitched the idea to the Presbyterian Committee of Publications in Richmond, and who bore the main editorial weight. But Dabney was also quite involved in suggesting articles to go into the volumes and in defending his selections. In particular, he was mystified at the committee's objection to including his pamphlet on "The Ecclesiastical Equality of Negroes" in his collected writings. "It was once fully sanctioned by the synod, published by Brown and Baird, almost committee work," he observed. "It advocates precisely the plan the Assembly occupies. I suppose our people are getting tired of standing up and preparing for amalgamation." Dabney and Vaughan devoted many, many letters of correspondence to the *Discussions*, attempting to put together the volumes and chart strategies for getting questionable essays approved. They were successful in getting the first three volumes through the pipeline; those volumes bore the committee's impress as they appeared from 1890 to 1892. The fourth volume, which contained "secular" documents, was a difficult sell, and both Dabney and Vaughan knew it. Dabney replied to one of Vaughan's notes:

> You say that after vol. III is out (probably October 15) your wrestle will begin about vol. IV. I surmise there will be a wrestle with Hazen [secretary of the committee]. He will probably demur at the inadequacy of our subscription list and the slowness of sales . . . In some respects, I crave the appearance of this 4th vol. more than the other three, because it will present a livelier picture of those good times and principles when we were still living men.

In the end, the committee rejected the fourth volume and Dabney was forced to publish it several years later under his own auspices. This rejection furthered Dabney's sense of alienation from his church: "The tone of his letter shows what I surmised before, that he has soured upon the whole publication of my works. I don't wonder. He finds out what I knew before, that southern Presbyterians don't want to read books written by their own friends who have sacrificed everything for the principles they professed to hold."[21]

Unfortunately, though the move to Austin helped Dabney's respiratory problems, it could do nothing for other health problems that plagued him. He eventually developed a large foreign mineral deposit in his bladder that required surgery in 1885. The surgery was botched so miserably and his bladder bruised so severely that his prostate gland became swollen and the entire bladder closed. For a long period afterward, Dabney would have to use a catheter. The following year, Dabney underwent surgery in an attempt to slow or cure an aggressive case of glaucoma. At first it was believed that the glaucoma would be cured, but in the end the prognosis came that Dabney would experience blindness. By 1890, not only was Dabney blind, but he experienced an intense prostatic ailment, which brought him to death's door. His death was widely reported in Presbyterian weeklies, but Dabney rallied through the ministrations of his doctors as well as of his oldest son, Charles, then president of the University of Tennessee. Yet, Dabney moved from one health problem to another. In order to manage his pain, the doctors had prescribed large doses of opium, and Dabney developed an opium addiction. Through his strength of will, Dabney demanded that he be weaned from the narcotic and was eventually free from opium use. It was amazing that Dabney was able to keep up all his varied activities in the midst of these reverses in health.[22]

Exiled from Texas

The beginning of the end of Dabney's active career had much to do with the health problems that he experienced in 1890. During his sickness, Dabney had entrusted his teaching at the theological school to Thomas Cary Johnson. Apparently, Smoot was furious; according to Dabney, "he expected me to die and to be made himself teacher of theology." Smoot's response was to maneuver Johnson out of the school and eventually out of Texas altogether. As Smoot attempted to grab more power in the school during Dabney's illness, he "alienated all the best students." After Dabney's health recovered sufficiently, Smoot himself experienced a difficult illness that nearly destroyed the school. By 1894, Dabney observed that "I have a suspicion that [Smoot] thinks of withdrawing . . . He may put the health pretext to the front, but I think the real cause is different; he has practically ruined the enterprise when we had 13 students and it was most promising, by his mismanagement, and he knows it. This will make him wish to get out of it." Smoot did indeed withdraw finally from the theological school in the early part of 1895, during the same months that Dabney experienced another bout of poor health, forcing the school to close. Though Smoot appeared willing to allow the seminary to die, Dabney continued to be solicitous for it, writing to the synod committee chairman who was responsible for candidates, urging him to do something for theological education in Texas. In the end, Dabney was rightly proud of his efforts—he claimed that Austin Theological School had produced twenty-seven licentiates with twenty laboring within synodical bounds "in spite of the follies and neglects of the synod and the presbytery itself." He was further confident that the seminary would not finally die: "It may be removed, but the reasons for such a school are so urgent that it must inevitably be reopened somewhere, and the property and library will be again utilized."[23]

More painful was Dabney's forced severing of ties with the University of Texas. Again, it appeared that his dismissal from the university was indirectly connected with his 1890 illness. At the time, Dabney wrestled with whether he should resign his position because of his blindness. He, in fact, decided to resign, but the trustees rejected his resignation. Instead, the regents moved to cut his teaching load in half and hire an adjunct. As a result, he remained at the university, and this appeared early on to be the right choice. The following school year, Dabney's supporters commissioned his portrait and presented it to the university during commencement activities in June 1891. Flattering speeches about Dabney's contribution to the university were made at that time, and Dabney finally felt appreciated. Even though the university would not hire Johnson as his adjunct, choosing instead a young man with a Ph.D. from Germany who was committed to "Germanized idealism," Dabney still believed that things were going well. But Dabney's adjunct, Walter Lefevre, almost immediately clashed with his senior over departmental policy. Lefevre lightened up the junior classes, assigning most of Dabney's texts as parallel readings. He also no longer required recitations, but followed the German model of lecture and discussion. This made the younger man's classes much more popular than Dabney's, to the chagrin of the senior professor.[24]

Lefevre did not stop there. In the fall of 1892, the members of the faculty committee made their report on curricular changes that sought to clarify the differences between required and elective courses. After the report was read, Lefevre sought to move a paper that he had written as a substitute for the faculty committee's report, even though he was not a member of the committee. His paper attempted to expand the elective system to an "extreme," making only one course in every department required. Dabney immediately saw that the upshot of Lefevre's paper was that "in philosophy, it should be his junior class which should be requisite, and my two senior classes which should be optional, thus ensuring himself large classes and for me small ones." By the following year, the regents noticed the declining popularity of Dabney's classes, believed that it was due to his health, and, at their meeting early in 1894, agreed in secret session to ask for his resignation. Dabney later believed that this decision had been promoted by Lefevre himself as part of his plan to "become sole professor of philosophy."[25]

The regents leaked their decision privately to Dabney through Major T. M. Harwood, mistakenly believing that his pride would compel him to take the hint and resign on his own. But the regents' plan went awry in several ways. First, Lefevre himself died quite unexpectedly. Second, Dabney was furious, believing that he had a lifetime contract with the university and that he should be the one to decide when he would no longer teach. As a result, he refused to resign, hoping to continue and force the regents to demand his resignation. Still, he knew what the end of the matter would be as early as March; writing to his son Charles, Dabney confessed:

> Mama is going to be very much distressed at the breaking up of our home we had here. It is the best fixed home we shall ever have in this world. We cannot continue to live here for very positive reasons. There will be nothing for me to do here. We will not have income enough to live . . . I do not know what will become of us nor of my property here: there is a great slaughter of business and nothing can be sold.

By May, the end had come—while making his report to the regents at the end of the school year, Dabney dismissed the reasons that the board had suggested for seeking his removal and offered to help hire a new assistant. The regents rejected this proposal and officially asked for his resignation. And while Dabney tried taking his case to the public, in the end it was worthless. He had been exiled from his life's second work.[26]

With his positions at the two Austin schools cut off, Dabney floundered, looking for work to do. In 1896, he wrote to Charles: "As to our own future years, Ma and I feel very forlorn, homeless, and embarrassed . . . Some, at least, partial employment I crave exceedingly. Without it an old man rusts out quick in mind and body and sinks into a dejection, tending to discontent and dotage." What Dabney particularly longed for was the opportunity "to go to some city representing social advantages and an occasional call for services pulpit and literary where I would be of some use and keep off dotage." He wrote unceasingly for the Presbyterian papers, attempted to put his moral philosophy lectures into a publishable form, and dictated his autobiographical reflections to his wife in order to set the record straight for posterity. Still, within Presbyterian circles, Dabney felt neglected. "The treatment I receive from the ruling spirits among some in my own Presbyterian church for whom I have worked so hard," he complained, "is little less doggish than I experienced from those Regents [at the University of Texas]." But Dabney neglected the signs of his own personal revival in the esteem of his fellow Presbyterians. For example, he was elected a commissioner to the 1895 General Assembly, which met in Dallas. When he did not attend because of a painful illness, his former students were so disappointed that they wrote him a letter "expressing our affectionate regard for you, our deep and abiding interest in you, and our sincere sympathy with you in the affliction which has kept you from meeting with us at this time." And at the Synod of Texas annual meeting for 1895, the synod directed Samuel King to convey the synod's care for Dabney during his illness.[27]

Because of his poor health, Dabney and his wife were also forced to leave their Austin home and move in with their son Samuel in Victoria, Texas, in August 1895. That was not a smooth transition. Apparently, Dabney's daughter-in-law resented the old theologian's presence in her home and "begrudged" any time that Samuel spent with his parents. As a result, Dabney confided to his oldest son that "we must keep house again or we will die quick. Your general remarks against two

210

masters in one house are just. In our case, they are imperative." Eventually, as a result of the tensions in Samuel's household caused by the old couple, Dabney and his wife built a new cottage, near their son's home. From there, he would prepare to go home, to Virginia and heaven, which for Dabney were mighty similar.[28]

Homecoming

Though his body was in Texas, Dabney's heart and mind were in Virginia. During his final years, Dabney charged his sons "not to leave my bones in Texas soil. I want them put by my boys at Hampden-Sydney College." Indeed, for Dabney, existence in Texas was as close to perdition as he desired to come. "I feel a great repugnance to a residence anywhere in Texas. It is a cursed low down state, its politics loathsome, its social morals repulsive," he griped. "It will lift a great burden from my spirits, could I leave the state, never to return." By contrast, Dabney's great desire was to return to Virginia, a place that presented idyllic images to his mind. "Had I my eyes, this question would be soon settled. I would go to Red Hill [in Virginia], and live in my own noble house there, 'the world forgetting by the world forgot,' spending the winter in some southern city."[29]

However, Dabney's mental vision of his beloved homeland was in danger of being disturbed by the agitation to move Union Seminary from Prince Edward County to Richmond. As early as 1893, Dabney had caught wind of plans to move the seminary. Writing to W. W. Moore, professor of Old Testament at Union Seminary, who was weighing a call to Louisville Seminary because of his frustration with the isolated location of Union, Dabney confidently predicted, "The seminary will never be removed now to a city. The fixed investments are too heavy, and the local attachments too strong. Neither will the seminary die by staying where it is. These Presbyterian things are mighty tough, they have as many lives as an old cat, and stand a quantity of killing." Dabney knew what he was about in writing to Moore, the prime mover in the plan to relocate Union at Richmond. And Moore had great fear about the amount of damage that Dabney could do to his plan to move the seminary. That fear led Moore to minimize Dabney's role in the life of the seminary in a history that the younger professor produced for Presbyterian papers. Dabney complained that Moore's history went "just about as far as it was possible without actually falsifying dates to efface me and my work." According to Moore, Dabney came to the faculty, was promoted, and resigned, "ending a blank thirty years" at Union Seminary. By minimizing Dabney's role, Moore was setting the stage for shutting out Union's most famous professor from the debate on whether or not the seminary should move to Richmond.[30]

Dabney would not be shunted to the side so easily. For one thing, he began to agitate with his few remaining Virginia allies. He wrote to his former doctor, Joseph Eggleston, urging him to examine Dabney's deed of gift of his land and house to the seminary. "If there is either a certainty or a good fighting chance for me to claim the forfeiture of this land in case of the removal of the seminary," Dabney strategized, "I give you authorization to say in case of its removal, my heirs will certainly reclaim the land." Dabney wrote similar letters to both Johnson and Vaughan, urging them to use his bequest "as a big stick along with other big sticks to fight the removal." He also wrote a long, vitriolic letter to the *Central Presbyterian*, protesting the move. He claimed that the seminary's relocation to Richmond would destroy Hampden-Sydney—both the community and the college itself. He insinuated that the move would illegitimately profit some of the leading lights of the board of trustees, particularly Lewis Ginter, whose Ginter Park would serve as home to the new seminary. He further feared the effect of training ministers in an urban setting, where they would become "clerical dudes" who could not relate to country Presbyterians. And finally, Dabney warned that the new buildings would be cost-prohibitive and ugly to boot. Contemporary architectural "humbuggery" would cause the new seminary to be "tricked off with some leaky Queen Anne turrets and tawdry ornaments devised by some pretender to architecture according to some Tuckahoe modification of the modernized bastard Byzantine style." Dabney's hopes were finally dashed; in October 1895, the Synod of Virginia passed the resolution necessary to move the seminary to Richmond, by a vote of 100 to 67. If Dabney planned to return to his native soil in death, it would be without his beloved seminary near his cemetery plot.[31]

Though Dabney lost the battle to keep Union Seminary at Hampden-Sydney, his last few years did see a renewed appreciation for the old master. He was invited to deliver lectures on moral philosophy at the new Louisville Seminary in the winter of 1894. These lectures were a triumph of sorts, a rebuke to those University of Texas regents who believed he was through as a teacher. One observer noted that Dabney moved through various branches of philosophy "with the steady step of one familiar with the ground, and with the calm, self-possessed spirit of one conscious of his ability to meet and refute every opposing error." In 1897, Dabney was elected as a commissioner from the West Texas Presbytery to the General Assembly at Charlotte, North Carolina. His appearance at the Assembly was in connection with the Southern church's celebration of the 250th anniversary of the Westminster Standards. Many younger ministers met the old theologian for the very first time. A young Walter Lingle, recently appointed as an assistant instructor of Greek and Hebrew at Union Seminary, was requested by J. B. Shearer to take the blind Dabney on a tour of Davidson College. Though Lingle wondered how he was to take a blind man on a campus tour, Dabney soon took over. "He directed me to lead him to the axis of the campus," Lingle remembered. "Then he asked me to tell about the buildings in front of him, the buildings on the right, and then the buildings on the left. He asked me the most detailed questions about each building and its use." After that, Dabney began to quiz Lingle about Hampden-Sydney and Union Seminary, "all about the faculties, the students, the buildings, and the village." In the end, "I felt like a squeezed lemon, and began to understand how he had acquired such a vast storehouse of knowledge of many subjects." Others, who were his former students, were convinced that this would be the last time they would see their revered mentor. When his paper was read at the Westminster Standards anniversary celebration, one observer pointed out that, though the paper was delivered in the middle of the program, it "was listened to with most profound attention . . . [and] while this was one of Dr. Dabney's latest public services to the church, it was one of his greatest." One of the most moving times was when Dabney offered a prayer during the Westminster Standards commemoration. The *Southwestern Presbyterian* reported that his

prayer "was so full and fitting, and carried us in such humble grati-
tude to the splendid past of Presbyterianism, and in such hopefulness
and trust to the future, and so voiced the present feelings and longings
of the great audience, that we cannot help noting it." It was a glorious week for a leader about ready to take leave from his people, one
who was not forgotten by his own, after all.[32]

After the Assembly, Dabney spent his last summer vacation in the
mountains of western North Carolina, around Asheville, with Charles
and his family. In the fall, he delivered a course of lectures on "The
Penal Character of the Atonement of Christ Discussed in the Light of
Recent Popular Heresies" at both Davidson College and Columbia
Seminary. These lectures, later published as *Christ Our Penal Substitute*, were warmly received at both institutions. Though they defended
Old School doctrines that were rapidly passing from fashion in portions of the Southern church, some of his hearers still preferred to listen to the doctrines of the old paths. One correspondent to a Presbyterian paper noted, "Though his natural sight has become darkened,
his mental vision is as bright and keen as ever, and if the voice may
have lost some of its old-time strength and fire, certainly his power of
expression and of acute analysis, his logical force and ability to argue
his thesis to an incontrovertible conclusion, abide with him as in the
days of yore." With the praises of a new generation in his ears, a generation that he was convinced had ignored him, Dabney returned to
his cottage in Victoria, Texas.[33]

A few days after the start of the new year of 1898, Dabney arranged
his papers and dictated a brief essay on his favorite teacher, Francis
Sampson, to be published in the *Union Seminary Magazine*. That
evening, chest pains forced him to bed and he slipped into a semicon-
scious state. His wife roused him once, receiving the comments that
he felt "a little easier. But the blessed rest is here . . . Be quiet." After
four hours of suffering, around 11:00 PM on January 3, 1898, Robert
Lewis Dabney passed away; his exile was over. Four days later, Dabney's body was returned to his beloved Virginia soil. In the little plot
that belonged to Union Seminary, where his three infant sons were
buried, a few hundred yards from the house that he had built and the
seminary building where he had lectured for thirty years, a couple of

blocks from College Church where he had preached semiregularly for seventeen years, Dabney's body was placed in its resting spot, clad in a Confederate uniform, awaiting the resurrection. Over the grave was placed a marker that read:

> Robert Lewis Dabney, Minister of the Gospel, Professor of Theology in Union Seminary, and of Philosophy in the University of Texas, Major in the Confederate Army, and Chief of Staff to Stonewall Jackson. "Prove all things, hold fast that which is good." In unshaken loyalty of devotion to his friends, his country, and his religion, firm in misfortune, ever active in earnest endeavor, he labored all his life for what he loved with a faith in good causes, that was ever one with his faith in God.

The voice of Southern Presbyterianism's preeminent postbellum theologian was silenced, but his legacy would continue on.[34]

8

Perspective

This biography began with the observation that Dabney was a much more complicated character than is generally admitted by friends and foes alike. After seven chapters that overviewed and interpreted Dabney's life, thought, and context, the narrow categories by which Dabney is typically assessed—either "prophet" or propagandist, patriarch or misogynist, Southern (or Calvinist) defender or racist—may still remain. In order to present a fuller perspective, this final chapter will consider Dabney with a wider lens and attempt to make the case that Dabney was far from unusual or aberrant, but was in fact a representative postbellum Southerner, one who stood both for the Southern conservative tradition and for conservative Presbyterianism. To do so, we must compare Dabney to others who either represented far different cultural and intellectual perspectives or shared his own blend of classical republicanism, Southern intransigence, and Presbyterian theology. In addition, gaining a more accurate perspective on Dabney requires that his continuing influence and legacy be assessed. Not only was Dabney an important figure for a minority within his own Southern Presbyterian church in the decades after his death, but his reputation and thought also continue to be significant for contemporary conservative Presbyterians. Finally, how Dabney should be remembered by historians and by those who are sympathetic to his intellectual and theological concerns will be appraised. By moving in these directions, this chapter seeks to provide a more full-orbed assessment of Dabney's continuing significance.

Representative

In the mental landscape of Robert Lewis Dabney, his commitment to Southern ideals of honor and manhood, mastery and gentility, was a major factor throughout his life and made him representative of many Southerners, both before and after the war. For example, there are significant parallels between Dabney and James Henley Thornwell. On the eve of the Civil War, Thornwell also used the language and logic of Southern honor and manhood to explain why the South had to secede. Writing in the *Southern Presbyterian Review* on "the state of the country," Thornwell held that the effect of Lincoln's election on an abolitionist platform essentially meant that "the North becomes the United States, and the South a subject province," nothing better than slaves of the Northern states. "Now, we say that this is a state of things not to be borne," Thornwell proclaimed. "A free people can never consent to their own degradation." Rather, the North must treat the South "with equal respect, and give them an equal chance. Upon no other footing can the South, with honor, remain in the Union." As noted in chapter 4, this same tone of affronted honor that characterized Thornwell's defense of Southern secession was found in Dabney's April 1861 letter to Samuel I. Prime.[1]

Likewise, Dabney's reasons for the war were articulated in a similar fashion by the more famous Thornwell. "The real cause of the intense excitement of the South," Thornwell observed, "is the profound conviction that the Constitution, in its relations to slavery, has been virtually repealed; that the Government has assumed a new and dangerous attitude upon this subject; that we have, in short, new terms of union submitted to our acceptance or rejection." Thornwell went on to claim that Lincoln's election revolutionized the federal government, moving it from a position of "absolute indifference or neutrality" on the slave issue to a stance of hostility and abolition. Though Thornwell's defense of slavery in his opening address to the Presbyterian Church in the Confederate States of America was mild, particularly compared to what Dabney envisioned, he still defended the institution. Thornwell offered a "biblical" presentation of the matter of slavery, claiming that "we venture to assert that if men had drawn their conclusions upon this subject only from the Bible, it would no more have entered into any human head to denounce Slavery as a sin, than to denounce monarchy, aristocracy, or poverty." Thornwell, like Dabney, also defended slavery by setting it within a broader defense of caste distinctions and hierarchy within society, and assailed the egalitarian logic of abolitionists that would "equally repudiate all social, civil, and political inequalities." This difference with their Northern brethren more than justified the separation of Southern Presbyterians into their own denomination so that they might not be precluded "from a wide and commanding field of usefulness" in the South. Honor and mastery were not issues that characterized Dabney alone; rather, they were part of the Southern mind of which he was an exemplar.[2]

In addition, Dabney's intellectual world was dominated by patterns that hailed from a synthesis of intellectual values that characterized American theology in the antebellum period: the rationality of the Scottish moral philosophy, the evangelical Calvinism of Old School Presbyterianism, and the classical republicanism of the early American republic. He was not unusual in holding to this synthesis, nor was he in his tenacious opposition to modern intellectual trends. Thornwell, again, provides a good point of comparison. As historian Theodore Dwight Bozeman pointed out several years ago, Thornwell and many other Old School theologians were indebted "to the traditions of British Anglican and Presbyterian rational 'orthodoxy' which took shape during the eighteenth century period of 'Enlightenment,' and upon which the scientific revolution had exerted a striking impact." Like Dabney, Thornwell was committed to reason and natural theology, interested in searching out "first principles," fairly confident that theology could be done via the "inductive method," and certain that the truths of physical and moral science jibed with biblical revelation. While Thornwell may have been more friendly to William Hamilton's adaptations of Thomas Reid's and Dugald Stewart's thought than Dabney was, his commitments to the prevailing intellectual method were strong enough for his leading disciple to claim that Thornwell "emphatically belonged to that class of thinkers who advocate what is known as the Philosophy of Common Sense, in contradistinction from the class whom he designates as Sensationalists." Thornwell's theological vision merged commonsense philosophy with Old School theology and classical republicanism (most evident in his defense of slavery and hierarchy) in a manner that Dabney would have recognized as similar to his own. While there were differences in emphases between the two theologians, perhaps because of Thornwell's preference for John Calvin and Dabney's for Francis Turretin, their theologies were related enough for one contemporary theologian to claim that they represented a single Southern Presbyterian approach to theology. By considering Dabney, historians gain a window on an intellectual stance that was on the losing side in the wars of intellectual history and thus generally ignored.[3]

Further, Dabney was representative as a white Southern male in expressing his intransigence toward the North, particularly during and immediately after Reconstruction. Dabney's most consistent ally in opposing any form of reunion with the North, whether political or religious, was B. M. Palmer, pastor of First Presbyterian Church, New Orleans. In 1870, when the Northern Presbyterian church sent its delegation to the Louisville General Assembly (moderated by Dabney) to seek fraternal relations with the Southern church, it was Palmer who chaired the committee on foreign correspondence that recommended against the Northerners' offer. Palmer's committee pointed out that the issues separating the two communions were "entirely of a public nature and involve great and fundamental principles." Palmer indicted the Northern church with forsaking the spiritual nature of the church, surrendering "all the great testimonies of the Church for the fundamental doctrines of grace" in the reunion of the Old and New School wings, and wrongly charging the Southern church with the sins of heresy and blasphemy. Palmer, like Dabney, never swayed from his opposition to relations with the Northern church. As late as 1887, Palmer wrote to Dabney, attempting to form a coalition that would pull out of the Southern church if it sought "fusion" with its Northern brethren. Concerned that the centennial celebration of the first

Presbyterian General Assembly would serve as a platform for progressives on both sides to call for a "committee of adjustment" that would lead to reunion, Palmer asked,

> Would this be a proper or wise course to pursue, in case things should drift so far as the appointment of a committee of adjustment; to call together immediately those members of the Assembly opposed to the measure, and put forth at once a platform of principles declaring our purpose to continue the existence of the Southern church, however large or imposing the number of those who may finally withdraw from it?

Both Dabney and Palmer maintained an intense opposition to friendly relations with the Northern church that led them to contemplate preserving a "pure" Southern church through separation if reunion became a reality.[4]

Dabney's intense Southern partisanship was part of a "Lost Cause ideology" that developed in the years after the war. As demonstrated by historians Charles Reagan Wilson and Gaines M. Foster, Dabney participated in the creation of a separate Southern identity in the postwar years. Dabney's *Life of Jackson* and *Defence of Virginia* both became required reading for members of the United Confederate Veterans, and Dabney provided several essays for various pro-South publications, such as D. H. Hill's *The Land We Love* and *The New Eclectic*, and A. T. Bledsoe's *Southern Review*. In one essay, Dabney defended Southern intransigence by holding that "the times demand 'good haters.' " There were those in the South who believed that "no 'hard names' must be called, no matter how 'hard' the deeds which are characterized"; Northerners ought to be forgiven all their crimes against the South. But the great men throughout history "were exceedingly prone to 'call a spade a spade,' " and Southerners ought to call Yankee crimes what they were.[5]

A few months earlier, Dabney had attacked the London *Spectator*, which claimed that the Southern cause was a "Lost Cause." Dabney petulantly declared that

Southerners do not "remember their late struggle by the name of the Lost Cause." We have heard of but one writer among them who adopts that term; and the rest dissent very energetically against the mistake of taking him as the exponent of either their ideas or history. To believe theirs a "Lost Cause" is, in their eyes, to despair of mankind; for they now regard it, just as much as ever, as the cause of constitutional freedom for all the families of men.

While Dabney dissented from the view that his was a Lost Cause, yet he demonstrated an intense Southern pride that sought to insulate his section from the rest of the country and that bore a great deal of similarity to the feeling of others who wrote for postbellum Southern journals. The difference between Dabney and others was that, while Dabney did imagine that Southern business and politicians would take the lead in creating a sense of Southern "otherness," his greatest hope was that the Southern Presbyterian church would serve as the bulwark of Southern purity.[6]

In fact, Dabney had developed an entire rationale for *not* reconciling with the North. In an essay written shortly after the end of the war, he analyzed the nature of anger, dividing it into two parts: simple resentment and moral reprobation. Simple resentment was an involuntary, temporary, intuitive response to wrong done; but moral reprobation was the rational response toward sinful acts committed against oneself or another. Further, moral reprobation demanded justice: that those who committed the sinful acts be punished for their crimes. Thus, the sentiment of moral reprobation could not be "morally wrong"; to feel satisfaction when moral reprobates received justice was not "immoral"; and to long for justice for those who aroused moral reprobation—one's enemies—was just and righteous. Christians, however, were never to take retribution into their own hands, but rather "the godly man always prefers to remit the penal settlement to a perfect God, and arrests his own forcible agency as soon as the purposes of mere self-defence are secured." In order to be reconciled to one's enemy, then, the Christian must demand reparation for "personal loss and natural evil inflicted"; he must trust that God will lead the sinner to salvation, which would remove the individual's guilt; and the one who committed the act must repent in order to reverse "moral defilement or depravity of character." Thus, the Christian's duty toward his enemy was not to love his enemy and forgive him no matter what. Instead, it was to demand *justice*—reparation, repentance, and moral reform. Once justice was received, then the Christian was ready "to forgive the element of personal *damnum* to his enemy, and to perform the offices of benevolence to his person, in spite of his obnoxious character." The application to the recently completed war was obvious—in order to effect a true reunion, whether in the state or in the church, the North had to pay reparations to the South, to repent for its war crimes, and to reform its government and society back to antebellum mores. Unless the North complied, the South's obligation was "to resist wrong within the lawful limits" and "to evade the power of the oppressor when resistance" was no longer feasible.[7]

Yet Dabney knew that he could not hold out forever. Like other Southern conservatives, he typified an Old Republican or Bourbon response to the rising New South. One historian grouped Dabney with a small group of anti-bourgeois reactionaries within the Democratic Party, who rebelled against "the New Departure" of the New South proponents. While New South men sought to modernize the South by accepting black suffrage, promoting social welfare, internal improvements, and public schools, and invidiously comparing slavery to black free labor as a superior system of economic relations, Dabney and other "Southern Bourbons" promoted "an Old South creed for the New South era": "moral rectitude, natural social and racial hierarchies, plantation economy, and a religious reverence for the Confederate past." This creed led Southern conservatives such as Dabney to promote localism, decentralized government, liberty, and free trade. Dabney viewed himself as a follower of Old Republicans, such as John Randolph of Roanoke, or of old Southern Democrats, such as John C. Calhoun. He was even approached about writing a biography of Randolph, but suggested that C. R. Vaughan write this "really valuable and charming book." Though others, both within church and general society, engaged in "dangerous billing and cooing with the Yankees," Dabney was determined to take a conservative stance against the egalitarian politics, free-labor economics, and sentimental ecclesiology that was destroying Southern society.[8]

This led Dabney to view his brand of conservatism as different from that promoted by well-known Northern conservatives. He warned fellow Southerners about the failures of Northern conservatives, making these men unworthy of trust. Northern conservatives, such as Charles Hodge, with whom Dabney had a lengthy correspondence in 1860–61, had "failed" to turn the North toward peace before the Civil War. As a result, Dabney wondered whether Northern conservatives could be trusted, whether they were truly impotent, or whether their overtures were "like the deceitful caresses with which the driver soothes a restless horse, while the harness is fastened on his neck." Ultimately, Dabney believed that Northern conservatives were weak men, plagued by caution and indecision. In the religious world, Dabney charged that "the only element of conservatism which [Northern ministers] call into action . . . is caution, a caution which prevents their jeopardizing their own quiet and prosperity by coming to the front and meeting the insolent aggression of the new opinions. They dissent, but practically acquiesce." Likewise, in the political world, Northern conservatives were impotent: "American conservatism is merely the shadow that follows Radicalism as it moves forward toward perdition. It remains behind it, but never retards it, and always advances near its leader." The result was that what Northern conservatives protested at one point was eventually incorporated into "conservatism" later on. Thus, Dabney mocked, "The only practical purpose which [conservatism] now serves in American politics is to give enough exercise to Radicalism to keep it 'in wind,' and to prevent its becoming pursy and lazy from having nothing to whip." Unlike Northern conservatives, their Southern counterparts stayed true to their principles, even when their age passed them by as important public figures.[9]

This conservatism led later budding cultural modernists, such as the Vanderbilt Agrarians and their successors, to latch on to Dabney as one who understood the signs of the times. John Donald Wade, one of the contributors to the agrarian manifesto *I'll Take My Stand* (1930), believed Dabney was one of the few who remained true to Southern conservative principles after the Civil War. Few listened to Dabney,

Wade observed: "People would not heed to him. As a minister, in his pulpit, he was harkened to. Outside his pulpit, though he showed never so plainly that the forces he denounced were deadly hostile to his pulpit and sought in the end to destroy it and all pulpits, he could gain no hearing." In addition, later conservative Richard M. Weaver praised Dabney's defense of Southern conservative values, claiming that "no one can fail to be impressed by the wide and solid scholarship of the better Southern churchmen of this period, and Dabney was perhaps foremost of them all." While other Vanderbilt intellectuals, such as John Crowe Ransom and Allen Tate, probably never heard of Dabney, and one in particular (Donald Davidson) would have appreciated Dabney's racial views while repudiating his apparent "fundamentalism," still there were deep continuities between the Southern conservative tradition represented by Dabney and the views of the twentieth-century intellectuals who followed in his train.[10]

Even Dabney's commitment to professionalism and denomination-building was representative of many religious elites in the nineteenth century. As historian Beth Barton Schweiger demonstrated for Virginia Baptists and Methodists in the same era in which Dabney lived, religious denominations in the nineteenth-century South moved from small, local affairs to large, bureaucratic institutions, requiring the professionalized knowledge provided at seminaries and demanding efficient denominational mission activities. Dabney lived this transition: growing up in a small rural congregation in Louisa County, receiving the best education available for that day, and moving through a series of calls to a position of prominence and importance among Southern Presbyterians in the key chair in one of the church's seminaries. Even as Dabney participated in the burgeoning literary industry of Presbyterian journals and newspapers, he was part of a larger trend of mobility and professional demarcation that granted ministers increased prestige within their enlarging denominations even while it decreased their importance within society at large.[11]

After these comparisons, it should be clearer to us that Dabney was hardly unique. Rather, he was a representative Southerner, Presbyterian, and professional minister, one who embodied the hopes and aspirations of many of his peers. Though he bore a great deal of intellectual similarity to Thornwell, because Dabney lived on the Reconstruction side of the Civil War (unlike Thornwell, who died in 1862), Dabney's intellectual development took a more dogmatic and pessimistic turn. He represented the philosophical and theological position of conservative Southern Presbyterians who clung to the Old School tradition too often associated merely with Princeton Seminary. In fact, Dabney distrusted Northern political and religious conservatives, and he never sought a rapprochement with them after the Civil War. Rather, he stood with other Southern Bourbons, who reprobated the way their New South brethren were flirting with Northern business by dismantling hierarchical aspects of Southern society in order to gain "Yankee" investment. And Dabney warred against New South Presbyterians, who sought friendly relations with Northern Presbyterians in exchange for a wider influence and importance in their own section. Dabney's commitment to his own personal honor, exemplified by loyalty to his principles, would not allow him to be degraded by moving away from positions he had held before the war. In this as well, he represented a significant portion of the Southern population for whom the word "Yankee" was a profanity. By understanding Dabney's mind, we gain a sense of the mind of an entire generation that felt alienated by the "coercive" war fought in order to preserve the Union.

Legacy

Not only was Dabney a representative Southern Presbyterian and conservative, but his legacy extended throughout the South. Perhaps Dabney's prime influence was in maintaining the continued vitality of the Old School tradition in the South. Though Dabney did not train nearly as many students as did Princeton's Charles and A. A. Hodge, many of Dabney's students generally maintained his no-nonsense Calvinism and commonsense philosophy. As historian Ernest Trice Thompson rightly observed, Dabney's theological position "had been that of the church in the Reconstruction period" and continued to exert influence through the Robert Lewis Dabney Chair of Theology at Union Seminary for fifty years. His successors in that chair—Thomas E. Peck, C. R. Vaughan, G. B. Strickler, and Thomas Cary Johnson—

continued Dabney's blend of Scots rationalism and Old School confessionalism. Dabney's moderate approach made his systematic theology textbook accessible for both Presbyterians and Baptists in the postbellum period. Not coincidentally, the decision by Union Seminary professor John Newton Thomas to stop using Dabney's theology as a textbook in 1940 was marked by students as both the end of an era and a signal that progressive theology was being fully embraced at the seminary.[12]

As progressive thought began to make prominent and important inroads into Southern Presbyterian life in the 1920s and 1930s, Dabney's positions received renewed attention through his younger disciples. Thomas Cary Johnson, in his little book *God's Answer to Evolution*, credited Dabney with influencing his views as he staked out a position similar to Dabney's own public theology of science. In the first lines of the book, Johnson confidently claimed that "the Christian has nothing to fear from physical science, nothing to fear from a true psychology, nothing to fear from a true philosophy, nothing to fear from a searching but sane higher criticism of the Christian Scriptures." What Christians should be concerned about was the instance in which

> the teacher of pure physical science . . . turns himself into a science-theologian when, for example, he treats evolution not as a working hypothesis in the realm of the physical, and not as a mere theory but as a fact, and an all-inclusive, all-explaining fact, when he turns this hypothesis into a metaphysical dogma, in his thought, and begins to develop a philosophy and a theology on this and related dogmas, no one of which has been either solidly proved, or apprehended by the faculty of rational intuition.

Such an individual, Johnson warned, heads into a "false 'theology' and a false 'philosophy,' " becoming "a blind guide of the blind." Also in this period, W. M. McPheeters, another longtime Dabney admirer, was the main protagonist in the charges against Hay Watson Smith, an Arkansas Presbyterian minister who publicly deviated from the theology of the Westminster Standards. Against Smith's claim that the

Westminster Standards were seventeenth-century documents that had no weight for contemporary Presbyterians, McPheeters invoked Dabney's cultural authority:

> Dr. Smith further forgets that, while the Westminster Confession and Catechisms were formulated in the seventeenth century, they were adopted by the Presbyterian Church in the United States, in 1861, and that they were adopted by men like James Henley Thornwell and Robert L. Dabney who had quite as intelligent an understanding of them as if they had drawn them up with their own pens.

Dabney could barely have defended the issue of confessional subscription in the Smith case better than McPheeters did. Indeed, the student would have made the master proud.[13]

Dabney's legacy also extended to his role in the continued separation of the Presbyterian Church in the United States (PCUS) from the Northern Presbyterian Church in the United States of America. Dabney's activity on behalf of ecclesiastical separation delayed "the reconciliation of the two great branches of the Presbyterian Church for nearly a generation." The arguments that Dabney articulated were used over and over again by Southern Presbyterian conservatives for generations—questions concerning Northern orthodoxy, disputes over confessional subscription, defenses of the spirituality of the church, and fears of racial mixing. Dabney became a symbol of lost orthodoxy—both doctrinal and social—for conservative dissenters within the Southern Presbyterian church. As conservatives sought to indict progressive denominational elites for leading the church to the theological and political left, Dabney's thought, along with James Henley Thornwell's, was rediscovered. Unfortunately, conservative Southern Presbyterians also protested Civil Rights "agitation," parroting Dabney's claim that integration would lead to racial intermarriage. One example of this occurred in 1957, when the conservative *Southern Presbyterian Journal* issued a statement that charged those who sought racial integration with fostering "the amalgamation of the races," which could only do "great harm to the finding of the ultimate Christian solution. Interracial social relations, rather than being the ideal to which the church should work, are actually compounding the problems they seek to solve." While the statement did not directly reference Dabney, it had obvious parallels to his own thought. And while conservatives were able to frustrate progressive designs within the PCUS for decades, they also were eventually forced to secede, creating the Presbyterian Church in America (PCA) in 1973 in order to preserve biblical authority, confessional subscription, the spirituality of the church, and conservative social mores. Freed of "fundamentalist" influence, the PCUS rejoined Northern mainline Presbyterians in 1983 to form the Presbyterian Church (USA).[14]

Not only was Dabney important for those who fought progressive thought in the Southern Presbyterian church, but he continues to exert influence within the PCA. One example of this was the debate over an overture to the 2002 PCA General Assembly. Overture 20 on racial reconciliation submitted by Nashville Presbytery was approved by the General Assembly by a wide margin and committed the church to "confess our involvement" with the "heinous sins attendant with unbiblical forms of servitude—including oppression, racism, exploitation, manstealing, and chattel slavery." The overture produced a great deal of discussion on the church's official news Web site, and during the discussion, Dabney became a contested and debated figure. One writer, after quoting from Dabney's essay against including African Americans in public education and his speech on "the ecclesiastical equality of Negroes," observed, "When I've mentioned these [statements] to friends, they've responded with, 'Well, you just have to understand Dr. Dabney.' OK. Maybe I don't quite understand Dr. Dabney. But, I do understand that he had a view of black people that did not express the equality expressed in Galatians 3:28." Another writer, on the opposite side, claimed that the adopted overture essentially meant "that I, my ancestors, the Confederate States of America itself, many great Southern theologians like Dabney, Thornwell, Palmer, Girardeau, men like Robert E. Lee, Stonewall Jackson, George Washington, Patrick Henry, et al are all guilty of 'heinous sin' and 'stand in opposition to the gospel.' " A third writer, an African-American minister in the church, referring indirectly to Dabney, pointed out that "from reading some of their [the founders of the PCUS] thoughts on people of

African descent, it's pretty clear that I, an African-American, should-n't be ordained into any office within God's church." The entire exchange, which included several other voices, served as one example that Dabney remained a contested figure within the church, a found-ing father to be either admired or explained away. Those who admired Dabney desired to hold on to the denomination's Southern Presbyter-ian roots, while those who rejected Dabney did so in an effort to posi-tion the church in more inclusive terms.[15]

Dabney's legacy might also be evaluated by comparing his views to broader currents in Southern fundamentalism. Dabney's insistence on continued separation from the Northern church because of fears of theological and cultural corruption paralleled later fundamental-ists' rationale for separatism. This "pursuit of purity" that both Dab-ney and fundamentalists shared was based on a tight matrix of polit-ical, cultural, and theological conservatism. Politically and culturally, fundamentalists such as Dabney warred against state (Northern) inter-ference in racial relations. Demanding that the state allow Southern-ers to handle their own racial affairs, fundamentalists urged a politi-cal conservatism that emphasized limited governmental powers. For example, the leaders of Bob Jones University (BJU) both defended seg-regation publicly and sided with far-right defenders of the status quo. In 1960, the founder of the school, Dr. Bob Jones, Sr., published a pam-phlet entitled *Is Segregation Scriptural?* in which he made the "con-nection between integration, modernist religion, and the coming one-world church led by the Antichrist." This connection between social, religious, and political liberalism not only motivated the university's rationale for its ban of interracial dating (which it finally discarded in 2000) but also demonstrated a stream of thought that led back to men such as Dabney. In addition, in the 1960s, BJU started Americanism Conferences, designed to marry conservative religion and right-wing politics. Among the annual conference speakers were radical-right leaders Billy Joe Hargis and Dan Smoot. Moreover, in 1964, the school awarded an honorary degree to Alabama Governor George Wallace for his defense of the South against Civil Rights "agitators." Of course, when an issue of "theological importance"—such as evolution or Pro-hibition—was on the table, many fundamentalists willingly set aside their fears of government interference to urge federal intervention in order to secure their desired end, a truly "Christian" America. Theologically, fundamentalists stood for a "hard evangelicalism," with biblical inspiration, inerrancy, and authority at the head of the theological creed. When the state attacked the Bible, whether in political pronouncements or by way of educational policy, fundamentalists rose to the battle for "the biblical worldview" against all comers. And like Dabney, fundamentalists scorned other religious conservatives—particularly those who remained in the mainline denominations rather than separate and those who advocated a "new evangelicalism" in the 1940s—as weak men who would ultimately forsake the biblical stand for modernism or state socialism. Both Dabney and later fundamentalists urged a hard stand for "the whole Scripture."[16]

Remembrance

If this was Dabney's legacy, then the question can be rightly raised whether he is worth remembering at all, save as an interesting historical artifact from the nineteenth-century South. One way of providing an answer is to compare Dabney with another late-nineteenth-century figure from a drastically different cultural background and situation—Abraham Kuyper, the multitalented Dutch theologian, educator, and politician. After all, it is widely taken for granted that Kuyper continues to serve as an important conversation partner for contemporary Reformed thought. One example of this was the depth of scholarly attention paid to Kuyper in 1998, the centennial anniversary of his Princeton Seminary Stone Lectures, entitled "Lectures on Calvinism." The outpouring of "Kuyperiana"—conferences, books, and journals all probing his thought for contemporary application—made James Skillen's question at the end of one conference collection appear incredibly rhetorical: the question "Why Kuyper Now?" did not need to be answered, for most Reformed and even non-Reformed academics confessed that Kuyper's thought provided "Christian insight and motive for action in today's world."[17]

This attention accorded to Kuyper stood in stark contrast to the general neglect by contemporary evangelicals of Southern theologians such as Dabney. And yet this state of affairs is somewhat puzzling. If the neglect of Dabney and other Southerners is due to their political incorrectness, the recent work on Kuyper makes it plain that he also had his patriarchal, racially insensitive moments. If the exaltation of Kuyper is due to his polyglot career, the same admiration should be extended to Dabney for his own wide range of interests and activities. In fact, a comparison between the two men is enlightening, and not only because Dabney and Kuyper were Reformed kin and near contemporaries, though separated by an ocean. Rather, a comparison is possible and interesting because Dabney and Kuyper had substantive similarities in the area of public theology. Both were profoundly conservative, viewing the egalitarianism unleashed by the 1789 French Revolution to be the disastrous spirit of modernism, blurring distinctions between classes, races, and sexes. Modernism was both ideology and praxis, both poisonous philosophical underpinning and dangerous practical outworking. The leveling spirit of modernism had to be opposed by Christians through a consistent antimodern stance—where the culture said there was no God, Christians had to assert God's sovereignty over all life and God's divine order expressed in various sovereign spheres, such as church, state, and family. As a result, both Kuyper and Dabney withstood "anti-biblical theories of rights" while championing God's moral order.[18]

As was true for Dabney, Kuyper understood that modernism was a worldview, a philosophical perspective that portended destructive consequences for church and society. According to Kuyper, the modern worldview sought "to build a world of its own from the data of the natural man, and to construct man himself from the data of nature." The modern philosophy was false because it denied God's existence and God's creational and providential order in the world. In God's place, modern philosophers substituted humankind and the sensory data gathered by humans. Hence, modernism was at its basis anti-Christian and engaged in "moral combat" with Christianity. For Kuyper, the modern worldview was represented by "pantheism," a broad term that included most of nineteenth-century philosophy. Pantheism did away with transcendent deity and imbued the progress of the period with divine attributes. In doing so, pantheism denied both

232

beginning and ending points to human history; matter was involved in eternal process. Hence, the pantheism of the modern age was materialistic, bereft of any hope for the human spirit. While academic pantheistic philosophy was in general disrepute because of Nietzsche's rise, Kuyper believed that the general ethos of modern culture was characterized by belief in a process-God that was leading humankind to higher stages of development. Because the modern ethos was pantheistic, the evolutionary theory, which represented "one of the most fertile ideas of pantheism, that of never-ceasing process," was perfectly fitted for the temper of the age. Darwin's argument, Kuyper observed, was not "a compelling, tightly argued proposition"; rather, it was "a hypothesis supported by a highly deficient process of induction whose general acclaim is rooted not in incontestable facts, still less in complete proof, but in a general cultural mood." By virtue of the fact that modern men and women wanted "to rid [themselves] of God," Darwin's "purely atheistic" theory was widely trumpeted.[19]

But modernism was not simply abstract philosophical theory confined to European universities or Northern salons. Kuyper, as well as Dabney, was concerned that many had adopted the materialist position without being fully conscious of doing so. Both held that the most important conduit for modernism was not academic philosophy, but the social attitudes and political economy associated with the French Revolution. Kuyper heaped scorn upon the French Revolution, claiming that "the principle of that Revolution remains thoroughly anti-Christian." It was rooted in "the odious shibboleth, 'No God, no Master,' " and sought nothing less than "the liberation of man as an emancipation from all Divine Authority." The French Revolution introduced "a change of system, of political organization, of general human theory." The Revolution "broke down" the social bonds of "an organically integrated society" and "left nothing but the monotonous, self-seeking individual asserting his own self-sufficiency." Above all, Kuyper claimed that "the Scriptures were unraveled and the Word of God shamefully repudiated [by the Revolution] in order to pay homage to the majesty of Reason." The spirit of the modern age—independence from God and exaltation of humankind—was the spirit of the French Revolution.[20]

Because the modern worldview exalted human beings to the place of God, broke the socially organic bonds that held society together, and promoted a radically egalitarian view of natural rights, modernism led to the blurring of traditional distinctions of gender, class, and race. Both theologians stood opposed to the manner in which modernism sought to redraw the spheres that had "traditionally" separated women and men. Kuyper, for example, worried that "an attempt is being made to transform the two sexes, masculine and feminine, into a neutral hybrid of the two." Moreover, women were invading spheres traditionally reserved for men—particularly university education and politics. In order to shore up the wall between the sexes, he sought to reestablish marriage, which he fretted was being transformed into "free love," as the proper female calling and sphere. In order to uphold marriage, Kuyper "dichotomize[d] the cultural mandate by gender." As feminist scholar Mary Stewart van Leeuwen demonstrated, Kuyper held that God urged women to be fruitful and multiply, while men were to subdue the earth. One fine example of this type of Christian womanhood, according to Kuyper, was the Boers: "The Boers consider fecundity a blessing of the Almighty, and the wife-mother rejoices without a shadow of *feminisme* in her unquestioned predominance in family life and social arrangements. Free from all desire of luxury, Boer women are almost exclusively devoted to their husbands and their children." In addition, he strongly opposed the movement for women's suffrage in the Netherlands, which he identified with the French Revolution's emphasis on radical individualism and egalitarianism. Kuyper warned that if women forsook their "biblical" callings for the public sphere, their natures would become "masculinized" and "the essential power of the woman over the man" would diminish. He blamed nineteenth-century feminism for participating in the blurring of the boundaries separating women and men, another example of the evil effects of the French Revolution.[21]

Like Dabney, Kuyper also opposed the way in which modernism blurred distinctions between classes. As van Leeuwen observed, Kuyper took it "for granted that middle-class households will have servants, and that lower-class families will prepare some of their children for their service." These class distinctions were rooted in the divine will.

Kuyper held that "God himself has divided unequally the wealth of his creation . . . Among people there is no equality and there can be none. Everything differs. People from people, station from station, and even in the same social station family to family." To be sure, he championed the "little people"; still, it is not clear that he believed that social mobility was the solution to the social problem. Moreover, while he worried about the injustice that the modern economy perpetrated against the poor and feared the potential for cataclysmic upheaval if the poor attempted to annihilate distinctions between wealth and poverty through revolution, he still affirmed a providentially ordered society where every citizen knew his or her place.[22]

While Kuyper did not share Dabney's race antipathy, he did wobble on racial issues. Although Kuyper held that "Calvinism condemns not merely all open slavery and systems of caste, but also all covert slavery of women and of the poor," he also believed that blacks were outside the organic method of human advancement, "the commingling of blood." While the descendants of two sons of Noah, Shem and Japheth, "have been the sole bearers of the development of the race," he believed that "no impulse for any higher life has ever gone forth from the third group," that is, the descendants of Ham. Kuyper also claimed that the inhabitants of Africa represented "a far lower form of existence" that failed to participate in the developing lifestream of humanity. As a result, he strongly defended the dealings of the Boers with their black African neighbors. When the Boers had instituted race-based slavery earlier in the nineteenth century, they "were compelled to take effective measures to safeguard their families." South African slavery was not as harsh as that in the American South; rather, the Boers "have treated their slaves as good children. They have habituated them to work and have softened their manners." In fact, the Boers "understood that the Hottentots and the Bantus were an inferior race and that to put them on an equal footing with whites, in their families, in society, and in politics would be simple folly." Equality for Africans would ultimately lead to "the danger of mixed liaisons," the "scourge" of amalgamation and miscegenation. Separating the races in South Africa would prevent the kind of disastrous race relations experienced in America, where black "racial passion" led them to seek "conquest over the white man." Kuyper concluded that "between blacks and whites there will never be lasting reconciliation." As Dutch sociologist D. Th. Kuiper noted, Kuyper's racial perspectives differed little from those of other "scholars and socio-political movements (liberal-conservative and Marxist movements included) during the last quarter of the nineteenth century and the first decades of the twentieth century." More to the point, Kuyper's fears of racial equality were fueled by the potential for social convulsion that would result from the "co-mingling" of "black and white" blood, a type of equality and fraternity promoted by that most modern of revolutions, the French Revolution.[23]

Both Kuyper and Dabney recognized that modernism had the potential to remake society completely in both the American South and the Netherlands. Springing from a principle that substituted human in place of divine authority, the modern worldview was attempting to de-Christianize the West, with disastrous results. In order to preserve the permanent things of Christian civilization, Dabney and Kuyper both articulated public theologies that stood for "ordered liberty." For both theologians, ordered liberty defined natural rights and civil liberties not in a framework offered by modernism's "anarchic individualism," but in terms of the "social bond individualism" taught by God through general and special revelation and providentially established in local institutions, especially the household.[24]

Kuyper shared Dabney's assurance that Scripture revealed truth for ordering public life. In castigating pantheism's blurring of distinctions in modern life, Kuyper turned from the human authority trumpeted by modernism to the divine authority found in the Bible. The Scriptures were "a cedar tree of spiritual authority" for modern life, he claimed. And the Scriptures demarcated "a life-sphere of our own on the foundation of palingenesia, and a life-view of our own thanks to the light that the Holy Spirit kindles on the candelabra of Scripture." What is more, as theologian John Bolt noted, Kuyper's "Christian-historical imagination" was "rooted in divine revelation"; as a result, he honored the past "by reappropriating its 'truth' through creative application to the present, with the visionary promise of future blessing." Most often, for Kuyper, Calvinism as a life system assumed the priority of Scripture in public theology. As a result, when he upheld the "absolute sovereignty of God" as the basis for civil liberty, he assumed that divine sovereignty was to be demonstrated by the self-revelation of God in Scripture.[25]

Kuyper held that ordered liberty was best established by recognizing God's sovereignty over social spheres and each sphere's delegated authority to develop its own organic life without interference from the state. Human beings had liberty within the order of the spheres to develop their associated life to the fullest. This provided a key difference between Kuyper's vision and that of the French Revolution: "In the French Revolution a civil liberty for every Christian to agree with the unbelieving majority; in Calvinism, a liberty of conscience, which enables every man to serve God according to his own conviction and the dictates of his own heart." While the liberal nation-states, modeled on the revolutionary political economy of the French, denied that authority came from God, but rather resided coercively in the nation-state, Kuyper's neo-Calvinist sphere sovereignty sought liberty of conscience from the intrusion of the state. To be sure, the principle of "sphere sovereignty" never received the definitive outworking by Kuyper that it later received by Herman Dooyeweerd.[26] Yet in much of Kuyper's discussion of sphere sovereignty, he made it clear that the household was a basic sphere, more so than the sphere of church or state, the chief mode of human relationship in the world. This was true because the household was the first order of creation; God created man and woman and charged them to multiply and to subdue the earth. From this original creation sphere, God ordained other cultural spheres, such as government, art, science, and church. For Kuyper, however, the household was foundational and supported these other spheres.[27]

As a result, Kuyper defended "houseman's suffrage" as the best means of representing the people against those who advocated either state sovereignty or popular sovereignty. As political philosopher Henk Woldring noted, Kuyper believed that "families make a nation a nation and they nourish the 'public spirit' of the people. [Kuyper] argues that the heads of households are representatives of the 'public spirit' of the people that is the vital and formative power of a nation." Families themselves represented the basic organic sovereign sphere of society; as a result, families participated in the sphere of the state through their household heads. "By that same Word of God," he observed, "the family is portrayed as the wonderful creation through which the rich fabric of our organic human life must spin itself out." Societal organization was rooted in the family, in the household. Though Kuyper recognized that universal popular suffrage was an irresistible eventuality, he advocated "houseman's suffrage" to the end of his life.[28]

Another example of the foundational nature of the household was the intense debates in which Kuyper participated over education. Like Dabney, Kuyper argued that state-controlled education was a secularized education in which the state overstepped its bounds and usurped the parents' role; it was "counter-church" and served as "a sectarian school of modernism." In order to challenge state-controlled education, he forged a Christian School Society that sought "the wholesale destruction of state-controlled education in favor of parentally guided education." Eventually, the movement for Christian schools outside of state control helped to establish the framework for Kuyper's Antirevolutionary Party. Yet it must be noted that he was not interested in church-controlled education either. At the establishment of Kuyper's Free University, he urged that "we must therefore resist tooth and nail any imposition upon learning by the church of Christ. At the real risk of suffering at its hands, the church must insist that learning never become a slave but maintain its due sovereignty upon its own ground and live by the grace of God." Kuyper's determination to maintain the boundaries between church and school evidenced itself during the church-merger discussions in the early 1890s. The context of the debate was whether the theology department of a university or a separate theological school was the proper place for ministerial training. Kuyper argued that because of the scientific nature of academic theology, it deserved a department within a Christian university where it was free from church control, yet where ministerial candidates could be adequately trained. The important point was the separation of spheres—the church had to do with worship, catechesis, and creeds; the university had to do with scientific learning. And the university was overseen by trustees and faculty, who acted *in loco parentis*.[29]

238

As is evident from Kuyper and Dabney's opposition to public schools, both theologians made important points for localism and against centralization in their public theologies. John Bolt demonstrated that when Kuyper developed the platform of his Anti-Revolutionary Party, he stood for decentralized power and the importance of localism, putting him fairly close to the Jeffersonian stream in American political economy. In article 10 of the platform, Kuyper held that "it is the desire [of the Antirevolutionary Party] that local and municipal autonomy be restored by means of decentralization, insofar as this does not conflict with the requirements of natural unity or violate the rights of individual persons." This article bore uncanny similarity to the tenth article of the United States Bill of Rights, which reserved powers not delegated to the federal government to the individual states. Both Kuyper and the American Constitution stood for localism in order to protect the rights of citizens against the coercive power of both the church and the state. As James W. Skillen recognized, Kuyper urged a principled pluralism, which rose from his belief that "human beings ought to submit directly to God's ordinances, which are given for the healthy development of a diverse creation order." Hence, in arenas under the domain of the household, such as education, neither the church nor the state could interfere. Rather, the "good order of creation" for education came "not through mediation by ecclesiastical authorities but by the directly sustaining, immediately experienced, common grace of God in every sphere of life."[30]

As this review should make plain, both Dabney and Kuyper presented a similar antimodern critique of the modern worldview and its social results, and both crafted public theologies that resembled each other in surprising ways. Like Kuyper, Dabney had emphasized a biblical world-and-life view that honored God's sovereign control over humankind and that upheld social structures, local control, and separation of church and state. Granted, Kuyper's public theology appeared much more sophisticated with the appropriation of the concepts of worldview, antithesis, and sphere sovereignty, not to mention the added stress on common grace. And Kuyper's public thought has generated far more admirers, disciples, and academic attention than Dabney's. Still, the two theologians' rejoinders to the modern worldview and the net result of these public theologies shared fundamental commonalties—the avowed biblical basis, the reliance on Calvinism, the basis in creation orders, the centrality of households, and the emphasis on localism.

Of course, there were differences between these two theologians as well. For example, Kuyper was a Romantic, while Dabney imbibed little in the way of German thought.[31] Kuyper was, for all intents and purposes, a Whig, a devotee of New England and Alexander Hamilton; Dabney was a Democrat, an ardent Southerner, a follower of Thomas Jefferson and, especially, John C. Calhoun.[32] Kuyper's name became associated with "neo-Calvinism," a modernization of the old faith; Dabney abhorred all those who innovated from the older Calvinist creed.[33] More substantially, though Kuyper attacked secular and liberal monisms, he appropriated one of his own (in the form of "the Calvinistic worldview") for his strategic purposes. Dabney, by contrast, despised monism, and clung to the American version of the Scottish philosophy to the end of his career.[34]

But the most consequential difference between Dabney and Kuyper was in their views on the goal of public theology. Kuyper's worldview approach, together with his doctrine of common grace, led irresistibly to a transformationist approach to culture. This was most famously expressed in his statement that "there is not a square inch in the whole domain of our human existence over which Christ, who is Sovereign over all, does not cry: 'Mine!' " The ultimate end in view for Kuyper was "re-Christianizing the Netherlands; the renewal of a Christian, national culture." Hence, while his thought attempted to set forward a principled pluralism, and while his ideas were always functional in nature, Kuyper's commitments contained the seeds of a theocratic— or, better, theonomic—temptation. If Christian duty emphasized "serving God in the world" and realizing "the potencies of God's common grace," whereby nature was transformed by grace, then Kuyper's Calvinistic life system would not be satisfied until there was "a Science which will not rest until it has thought out the entire cosmos; a Religion which cannot sit still until she has permeated every sphere of human life; and so also there must be an Art which, despising no single department of life, adopts, into her splendid world, the whole of human life, religion included." This expansive vision of Calvinism's import could turn theonomic, a demand that one privileged view of God's will must be established in every human sphere.[35]

By contrast to Kuyper's transformationist approach, Dabney's public theology was always a defensive maneuver, not a rationale for transforming social structures. The Bible did speak to public issues, but where the Bible was silent there was liberty. Dabney claimed that all human actions fell into one of three classes: actions that the Bible commanded; actions that the Bible prohibited; and "actions [that] Scripture leaves indifferent." In the first two areas, church courts were to follow the Scriptures and enjoin or prohibit what God did. "In the third case, they are to leave the actions of his people free to be determined by each one's own prudence and liberty, and this because God has left them free." The church could not bind Christian conscience if there was no biblical command. Many evangelical church leaders "overstepped" the "metes and bounds between the kingdoms of Christ and of Caesar," Dabney held, "because there have always been churchmen greedy of power, worldly-minded and dictatorial." God granted Christian liberty, which ought not to be thrown away by those who would "betray the cause entrusted to them." Ultimately, it was not the task of either individual Christians or Christianity in general to transform society, Dabney believed. Rather, the Christian's sole task was "to deliver the whole revealed will of God for man's salvation." Anything more confused the spheres of Christ and Caesar; anything less was unfaithfulness to the gospel.[36]

Ironically, though Dabney attempted to maintain a defensive posture while Kuyper had an offensive pose, their public theologies both ended up in essentially the same place. Though Kuyper himself used language of the antithesis, his later followers, particularly in the United States and Canada, more often emphasized the other two intellectual contributions of the Kuyperian vision: common grace and the ordering structures of sphere sovereignty. As common grace came to override Kuyper's emphasis on the difference that regeneration made—with its two kinds of people and two kinds of science—the secularization of the sacred not only became a possibility, but actually happened at places such as Free University of Amsterdam. As a result,

241

American neo-Calvinists continue to worry that their institutions committed to Kuyper's ideals could follow Free University's path, and such concern is warranted.[37] As historical work on late-nineteenth-century American Protestantism has demonstrated, when Protestants came to believe that the progressive "spirit of the age" was actually the work of the Holy Spirit, so that progress and divine immanence merged, there was no place from which to launch a critique against the capitulation of the church to the mores of an increasingly secular age. In a similar fashion, as modern Kuyperians attempted to transform culture by obeying God's law in every human sphere and by cooperating with God's common grace, the temptation became the identification of social "progress"—however defined from either the left or right—with God's activity. As the sacred was secularized, or as things common were identified with the continued unfolding of redemptive history, the public positions that some Kuyperians held looked suspiciously like moderate-to-liberal American politics granted divine sanction.[38]

Ultimately, Dabney ended up in a position similar to Kuyper's, although he arrived there in another way. For Dabney, the social order of the antebellum South was God-ordained. To deny that Southern patriarchy not only paralleled Abrahamic patriarchy but also replicated biblical norms concerning representative governments and the centrality of households was to "surrender the inspiration of the Scriptures to [the] assaults of a social science so-called." During and after the Civil War, Dabney participated in Southern mourning over the "Lost Cause," and though he recognized that a New South had to rise, he was by no means happy about it. Rather, he emerged as part of a coterie of Southern religious leaders who defended the Confederate cause, attacking those such as George Washington Cable who besmirched the memory of the Old South while fanning the fading flame of Southern separatism during the waning decades of the century. Hence, Dabney's public theology failed by sacralizing the secular. By assuming that God was a Southern gentleman, by embracing a form of culture-Protestantism, Dabney had no place from which to exercise his considerable critical abilities upon Southern culture and his own public theology.[39]

242

Yet Dabney and other Southern ministers like him have an ironic legacy. Though they embraced a form of culture-Protestantism that inured them from critiquing their own perspectives and culture, though they were hopelessly captive to their culture especially on matters related to race and gender, these ministers also occupied the position of standing against the rising tide of modernism. In the familiar language of H. Richard Niebuhr, while Dabney embraced a "Christ of culture," namely, the intellectual habits and culture of the antebellum South, this oddly placed him in the position of "Christ against culture," standing against the rising tide of modernism that was prevalent in the North and beginning to seep into the South. Like Kuyper and others, Dabney was a "modern antimodernist," the difference being that Dabney's modernity was an earlier version, leaning toward the modern forms of thought that typified the late eighteenth and early nineteenth centuries, as opposed to Kuyper's embrace of mid-nineteenth-century Romantic forms of thought and imagination. This observation coheres well with historian George M. Marsden's recent insistence that Niebuhr's categories "work if we emphasize that they are not mutually exclusive." Christian groups often express different aspects of Niebuhr's categories: "With respect to one culture activity they may typically express one motif, with respect to another they may characteristically adopt quite a different stance." Going beyond Marsden, it could be said that a cultural stance could function in multiple ways—hence, Dabney's "cultural captivity," his deep loyalty to antebellum social and intellectual mores, was quite antithetical to the rising modernism of the postbellum period. The upshot of this was that the characteristic of Dabney frequently noted—his "prophetic" insight that allowed him to incisively critique aspects of modern culture—was rooted in an equally modern worldview.[40]

Thus, the limitation of public theologies such as Dabney's and Kuyper's can be traced, strangely enough, to their failure to maintain the antithesis between church and world. Both theologians ought to have known better, for they each had resources that would have maintained the distinctions between the secular and the sacred. Dabney had the doctrine of the spirituality of the church, which restricted the church's work to Word, liturgy, polity, and mercy while leaving room for individual involvement in the public sphere; Kuyper's doctrine of the antithesis added together with his belief in the separation of church and state could have produced a spirituality of the church doctrine similar to that of the Southern Presbyterians. Further, both had other options at hand—Dabney could have used American Reconstruction as an opportunity to seek racial and social justice within the courts of the PCUS; Kuyper might have coupled more chastened attitudes toward the possibilities of cultural transformation with a nuanced view of the abiding brokenness of sovereign spheres, which would not be healed until the consummation of the age. Perhaps the limitations that these public theologies reveal point to a deeper difficulty with public theology in general. For public theology is a universalizing task, an attempt to apply theological norms to public issues in such a way as to provide a Christian, hence true and required, approach to these concerns. But factors other than theology, such as social location, ethnicity, and education, often appear more decisive in public actions. Maybe it claims too much to believe that the church's theology can provide norms for the world's politics, that theologians can somehow redeem the hallways of the United States Congress. In addition, by investing public concerns with theological language and authority, the stakes for the public square are raised manyfold. Part of the challenge of contemporary culture wars has been the way in which participants have made their positions carry religious freight with appropriate anathemas for those who disagree. By presenting one's public views and affiliations as religiously derived and required for Christian faithfulness, not only is there little wiggle room when things go differently than planned, but above all, there is no place for self-criticism, no opportunity to recognize the possibilities of self-deception, no chance to extend charity to fellow believers who see things differently—in a word, no *liberty*.[41]

This observation points back to the question that opened this section. Robert Lewis Dabney should be remembered today not only because he was a representative postbellum Southerner, or even because he was one of the most important Southern Presbyterians in the history of that branch of the Christian church, both of which are certainly true. Rather, Dabney should be remembered because the past is the parent of the present, because many of the public stances of evangelical Christians either fail to maintain the spiritual nature of the church or fail to provide room for humility and self-criticism, and because recognizing Dabney's failures can help point evangelicals in a different direction to "a more excellent way." While Dabney and other Southern Presbyterians undoubtedly sought to preserve the gospel in its purity, yet by investing their identities in a particular region, by identifying their public positions as God-ordained, and by allowing their thought to be shaped by the contours of their age, they were bereft of resources to arrest the tides of modernity that swept over the churches in the generations that followed. Instead, if they had recognized that the form of this present age is passing away and that God's kingdom is not to be identified with any nation in this present age but with the work of Christ's church, then leaders such as Dabney could have equipped believers to order their understanding of life in this world correctly—the Christian's highest priority is what he or she does on the Lord's Day in the worship of the church. That is where redemption ultimately happens in Word and sacrament; that is where Christ rules as King; and that is where the Christian pilgrim can find a foretaste of rest from all the jazz and noise and excitement of this weary world. In the eyes of the world, it may not be much. But to the Christian, that is the house of God and that the gate of heaven. If Dabney's example can teach Christians this lesson, then we can be grateful for every remembrance of him. And perhaps Dabney himself would be pleased—as a firm believer in the didactic use of history, he would urge us to "harken to the striking instruction of these instances" of his own life story, even if it meant that the result would be less than flattering to his reputation. After all, he continues to urge those who visit his Hampden-Sydney gravesite, "Prove all things; hold fast that which is good."[42]

245

Notes

Introduction

1. Thomas Cary Johnson, *Life and Letters of Robert Lewis Dabney* (1903; repr., Carlisle, Pa.: Banner of Truth, 1977), 513–14 (hereafter *LLD*).

2. Peyton H. Hoge, "Robert Lewis Dabney," *North Carolina Presbyterian*, 19 February 1890; Thomas Cary Johnson, "Robert Lewis Dabney—A Sketch," in *In Memoriam: Robert Lewis Dabney, 1820–1898*, ed. Charles W. Dabney et al. (Knoxville: University of Tennessee Press, 1899), 10; J. B. Shearer, "The Man and the Scholar," in *In Memoriam*, 19.

3. Moses D. Hoge, "Regnant Men," in *In Memoriam*, 28; J. H. Rice Jr., "A Lover of the South," in *In Memoriam*, 35; *LLD*, 569.

4. Ernest Trice Thompson, *Presbyterians in the South*, 3 vols. (Richmond, Va.: John Knox, 1963–73), 2:446, 3:470–71; Frank Bell Lewis, "Robert Lewis Dabney: Southern Presbyterian Apologist" (Ph.D. diss.: Duke University, 1946).

5. Charles Reagan Wilson, "Robert Lewis Dabney: Religion and the Southern Holocaust," *Virginia Magazine of History and Biography* 89 (1981): 80–89; Donald Mathews, "Crucifixion—Faith in the Christian South," in *Autobiographical Reflections on Southern Religious History*, ed. John B. Boles (Athens, Ga.: University of Georgia Press, 2001), 38 n.7; Mathews, "The Southern Rite of Human Sacrifice," *Journal of Southern Religion* 3 (2000), available from http://jsr.as.wvu.edu/mathews.htm, accessed 22 March 2001; John Thomas Cripps, "A Biography of R. L. Dabney," available from www.pointsouth.com/csanet/greatmen/dabney/dab-bio.htm, accessed 18 June 2002; and *Robert Lewis Dabney: The Prophet Speaks*, ed. Douglas W. Phillips (San Antonio: VisionForum, 1997), 8, 10.

6. S. F. Tenney, "Death of Rev. R. L. Dabney, D. D.," *Christian Observer*, 12 January 1898; *LLD*, 566; B. M. Palmer, "The Christian Warrior," in *In Memoriam*, 20; Thornton Sampson, "The Teacher and Friend," in *In Memoriam*, 38.

7. David H. Overy, "Robert Lewis Dabney: Apostle of the Old South" (Ph.D. diss.: University of Wisconsin, 1967), 242.

8. Dabney, "The Doctrinal Contents of the Confession—Its Fundamental and Regulative Ideas, and the Necessity and Value of Creeds," in *Memorial Volume of the Westminster Assembly, 1647–1897* (Richmond, Va.: Presbyterian Committee of Publications, 1897), 92, 95, 99, 101–2. See also Sean Michael Lucas, " 'He Cuts Up Edwardsism by the Roots': Robert Lewis Dabney and the Edwardsian Legacy in the Nineteenth-Century South," in *The Legacy of Jonathan Edwards: American Religion and the Evangelical Tradition*, ed. D. G. Hart, Sean Michael Lucas, and Stephen J. Nichols (Grand Rapids: Baker, 2003), 200–214.

9. Dabney to Moses D. Hoge, 9 January 1840, in *LLD*, 72; Dabney to Moses D. Hoge, 31 March (1840?), in *LLD*, 73; *LLD*, 61–62, 340–41, 447; Letter to James Woodrow, in Woodrow, "A Further Examination of Certain Recent Assaults on Physical Science," *Southern Presbyterian Review* 25 (1874): 262; the paper read at the Victoria Institute in 1886 was "Final Cause," (*Discussions*, 4 vols. [1890–97; repr., Harrisonburg, Va.: Sprinkle, 1982], 3:476–91).

10. Robert Lewis Dabney, *Life and Campaigns of Lieut.-Gen. Thomas J. Jackson* (1866; repr., Harrisonburg, Va.: Sprinkle, 1983), 101.

11. Overy, "Robert Lewis Dabney"; Dabney, "The New South," in *Discussions*, 4:21–23.

12. Calhoun to Mrs. Thomas G. Clemson, 28 April 1848, in Calhoun, *Correspondence Addressed to John C. Calhoun, 1837–1849*, ed. Chauncey S. Boucher and Robert P. Brooks, in *Annual Report of the American Historical Association (1899)* (Washington: American Historical Association, 1900), 2:752, quoted in Eugene D. Genovese, *The Southern Tradition: The Achievement and Limitations of an American Conservatism* (Cambridge: Harvard University Press, 1994), 48.

Chapter 1: Preparation

1. James H. Rice Jr., "A Lover of the South," in *In Memoriam: Robert Lewis Dabney*, ed. C. W. Dabney et al. (Knoxville: University of Tennessee Press, 1899), 35.

2. Dabney, "True Courage," in *Discussions*, 4 vols. (1890–97; repr., Harrisonburg, Va.: Sprinkle, 1982), 4:437.

3. Rice, "Lover of the South," 35.

4. Dabney to Moses D. Hoge, 25 February 1841, Hoge Family Papers, Presbyterian Historical Society, Montreat, N.C. (hereafter Montreat).

5. Charles W. Dabney, "The Origin of the Dabney Family in Virginia," *Virginia Magazine of History and Biography* 45 (1937): 121–43; Charles W. Dabney, "Colonel

Charles Dabney of the Revolution: His Service as Soldier and Citizen," *Virginia Magazine of History and Biography* 51 (1943): 186–99.

6. Thomas Cary Johnson, *Life and Letters of Robert Lewis Dabney* (1903; repr., Carlisle, Pa.: Banner of Truth, 1977), 6–10 (hereafter *LLD*); Dabney, "Colonel Charles Dabney of the Revolution"; on the maternal side, Dabney's mother, Elizabeth Price, traced her lineage back to the illustrious Randolphs of Virginia, one of the first families in the state. See *LLD*, 11–12.

7. *LLD*, 1, 14–19; Dabney to Charles William Dabney, 4 February 1845, in *LLD*, 91.

8. *LLD*, 37, 46–49, 72; Moses D. Hoge to Dabney, 7 January 1842, in *LLD*, 74.

9. *LLD*, 91–92; Dabney to Charles William Dabney, 4 February 1845, in *LLD*, 91; Dabney, "Reminiscences of John Randolph," *Union Seminary Magazine* 6 (1894): 14–21.

10. *LLD*, 27–28, 55, 61–62, 86–87; Dabney to his mother, 20 August 1836, in *LLD*, 31.

11. Dabney, "Notes on Political Economy," MS, Robert Lewis Dabney Papers, Alderman Library, University of Virginia, Charlottesville (hereafter UVA); *LLD*, 80, 561–63.

12. *LLD*, 42–43, 550, 567; Dabney, "Autobiography," MS, UVA. Dabney refers to his conversion in his *The Five Points of Calvinism* (Richmond, Va.: Presbyterian Committee of Publication, 1895), 18.

13. Dabney, "The State Free School System," in *Discussions*, 4:202, 206.

14. *LLD*, 24, 41–42, 120–21, 299; Dabney to G. Woodson Payne, 22 January 1840, in *LLD*, 67.

15. Robert Lewis Dabney, *A Defence of Virginia (And Through Her, of the South)* (1867; repr., Harrisonburg, Va.: Sprinkle, 1991), 229.

16. Dabney, "The Christian Soldier," in *Discussions*, 2:622; Robert Lewis Dabney, *Syllabus and Notes of the Course of Systematic and Polemic Theology*, 2d ed. (1878; repr., Carlisle, Pa.: Banner of Truth, 1977), 404–6.

17. *LLD*, 55; David H. Overy, "Robert Lewis Dabney: Apostle of the Old South" (Ph.D. diss.: University of Wisconsin, 1967), 23–24; Dabney to Charles William Dabney, 13 November 1840, in *LLD*, 57–59.

18. Dabney, "The Christian Soldier," 622; Dabney, "True Courage," 436–37.

19. Dabney to Moses D. Hoge, 25 February 1841, Hoge Family Papers, Montreat; Overy, "Robert Lewis Dabney," 11. There are some stark parallels between Dabney's fatherless upbringing and Charles Hodge's; compare with James Turner, "Charles Hodge in the Intellectual Weather of the Nineteenth Century," in *Charles Hodge Revisited: A Critical Appraisal of His Work*, ed. J. W. Stewart and J. H. Moorhead (Grand Rapids: Eerdmans, 2002), 43–44.

20. *LLD*, 44–49, 79; Overy, "Robert Lewis Dabney," 3, 10, 17, 29.

21. *LLD*, 42–43.

22. Dabney to Moses D. Hoge, 18 November 1841, Hoge Family Papers, Montreat.

23. *LLD*, 82, 85; Dabney to Charles William Dabney, 22 November 1844, in *LLD*, 84; *Centennial General Catalogue of the Trustees, Officers, Professors, and Alumni of Union Theological Seminary in Virginia, 1807–1907*, ed. Walter W. Moore and Tilden Scherer (Richmond, Va.: Whittet and Shepperson, 1907).

24. Dabney, "Union Seminary and Theological Education," *Watchman and Observer*, 15 July 1852; Dabney, "Standard of Ordination," in *Discussions*, 3:556; Dabney, "A Thoroughly Educated Ministry," in *Discussions*, 2:661–63.

25. *LLD*, 89–90, 102; Overy, "Robert Lewis Dabney," 39.

26. Dabney in his autobiographical reflections credited David Humphreys of Augusta County, Virginia, another seminary classmate; however, Johnson identifies William Richardson: compare Dabney, "Autobiography," MS, UVA with *LLD*, 104.

27. Launcelot Minor to Dabney, 4 May 1847, in *LLD*, 99; Committee of Tinkling Spring Presbyterian Church to Dabney, 19 April 1847, in *LLD*, 105–6; Dabney, "Autobiography," MS, UVA.

Chapter 2: Pastor

1. Dabney, "Autobiography," Robert Lewis Dabney Papers, Alderman Library, University of Virginia, Charlottesville (hereafter UVA).

2. Dabney to his mother, 16 July 1847, UVA.

3. Dabney, "Autobiography," MS, UVA; Dabney to his mother, 26 August 1847, UVA.

4. Dabney to Charles William Dabney, 17 January 1848, UVA.

5. Dabney to Charles William Dabney, 7 March 1848, UVA. In his autobiographical reflections, Dabney claims that the wedding day was March 28. Following those reflections, that is the date that Johnson gives, (Thomas Cary Johnson, *Life and Letters of Robert Lewis Dabney* [1903; repr., Carlisle, Pa.: Banner of Truth, 1977], 116; hereafter *LLD*). But this letter indicates that the plan was to marry on Thursday, March 30, 1848. Which is right? One solution could derive from the fact that Dabney's autobiographical reflections were recorded by his wife; surely she would have corrected him if he had been incorrect. Hence, I follow the March 28 date.

6. Dabney to Charles William Dabney, 17 January 1848, UVA; Dabney to his mother, 1 May 1848, UVA; Dabney to his mother, 9 January 1849, UVA.

7. Dabney to Charles William Dabney, 6 February 1849, UVA; Howard McKnight Wilson, *The Tinkling Spring, Headwater of Freedom: A Study of the Church and Her People* (Fishersville, Va.: The Tinkling Spring and Heritage Presbyterian Churches, 1954), 287. This building was one of four church buildings that Dabney designed. It is still in use by Tinkling Spring Presbyterian Church.

8. Dabney to his mother, 26 February 1849, UVA; Dabney to Charles William Dabney, 18 April 1849, UVA; Dabney to his mother (?), 30 July 1849, in *LLD*, 109.

9. Dabney to Charles William Dabney, 31 December 1849, UVA; Wilson, *The Tinkling Spring*, 289.

10. Dabney to Charles William Dabney, 20 February 1849, UVA; Dabney to his mother, 26 February 1849, UVA. Dabney was delightfully human and male; a year before, when Charles's first child was born, Dabney congratulated him by writing, "I was proposing to Lavinia to invent the most impudent message to send to sister Dele, that I could; but I believe I have nothing to send except my best wishes; and the prayer that her son may be ~~as well endowed~~ [Dabney struck this out lightly so as to be clearly read] as happy and prosperous in all his afterlife, as his Daddy is proud of him now" (Dabney to Charles William Dabney, 24 May 1848, UVA).

11. Dabney to his mother, 3 April 1850, UVA.

12. Dabney to Charles William Dabney, 4 December 1848, UVA; Dabney to Charles William Dabney, 31 December 1849, UVA; Dabney to Betty Dabney, 6 July 1850, UVA.

13. Dabney to his mother, 8 October 1849, UVA; Dabney to his mother, 15 November 1849, UVA; Dabney to Charles William Dabney, 4 August 1851, UVA; Dabney to Charles William Dabney, 4 September 1851, UVA; Dabney to Charles William Dabney, 7 January 1852, UVA.

14. Dabney to his mother, 9 January 1849, in *LLD*, 110; Dabney to his mother, 9 July 1849, UVA; Dabney to his mother, 29 July 1850, in *LLD*, 113; *LLD*, 111–14; *Session Minutes*, Tinkling Spring Presbyterian Church, Fisherville, Virginia, 1847–53 (microfilm), Montreat, N.C. (hereafter Montreat); Wilson, *The Tinkling Spring*, 290. Wilson reported that thirty-three new members were added for 1850; the disparity may be due to a couple of others who joined after the revival was over (p. 290).

15. Dabney, Sermon on Psalm 116:12, MS, Robert Lewis Dabney Papers, William Morton Library, Union Theological Seminary in Virginia, Richmond (hereafter UTSVA).

16. *Session Minutes*, Tinkling Spring Presbyterian Church, Fishersville, Virginia, 1847–53 (microfilm), Presbyterian Historical Society, Montreat. Dabney and the session also dealt with two other lengthy cases of church discipline during his ministry: Samuel Black, who was suspended for unrepentant intemperance, and the case of Benjamin Strait and David Bell, who were repentant under the charge of violent anger and fighting.

17. Dabney, "Autobiography," MS, UVA; Dabney to Betty Dabney, 4 March 1853, in *LLD*, 124; *LLD*, 123–24.

18. Henry M. Woods, *Robert Lewis Dabney, 1820–1898: Prince Among Theologians and Men* (Richmond, Va.: Presbyterian of the South, 1936), 8; *LLD*, 552–53; J. B. Shearer, "The Man and Scholar," in *In Memoriam: Robert Lewis Dabney, 1820–1898*, ed. Charles W. Dabney et al. (Knoxville: University of Tennessee, 1899), 18–19; L. S. Marye, "A Light Gone," in *In Memoriam*, 31.

19. There are 431 extant sermons in the Dabney Papers, UTSVA. My irreplaceable guide to these sermons was the index compiled by David F. Coffin Jr. ("Index: Robert Lewis Dabney Papers, 1834–1898" [unpublished document in author's possession, 2002]). I thank Dr. Coffin for permission to utilize this guide.

20. Dabney to C. R. Vaughan, 12 December 1885, Vaughan Papers, Montreat.

21. For example, several of the sermons included in Dabney's *Discussions* were initially preached before the time that Vaughan, the editor, noted. "The Bible Its Own Witness" (*Discussions*, 4 vols. [1890–97; repr., Harrisonburg, Va.: Sprinkle, 1982], 1:115–31) was preached first to Dabney's College Church congregation in March 1867 before being preached in the Union Seminary chapel; "The Believer Born of Almighty Grace" (*Discussions*, 1:482–95) was first preached at Tinkling Spring in May 1853 before the soldiers heard it in 1862; and "Parental Responsibilities" (*Discussions*, 1:676–93) was offered to Dabney's College Church congregation in March 1869 before the Synod of Virginia heard it in 1879. Even Dabney's most famous sermon, his valediction to Stonewall Jackson entitled "True Courage" (*Discussions*, 4:435–52), contained recycled material from his earlier sermon by that title preached to Hampden-Sydney students enlisting in the war in 1861.

22. Two examples of sermons preached to African Americans were sermons on Luke 19:10 and John 4:24, both MS, UTSVA. This paucity of sermons geared toward blacks did not reflect the practice of other Presbyterian ministers in the Deep South, such as Charles Colcock Jones and John L. Girardeau, who regularly preached to blacks on occasions separate from whites; see Erskine Clarke, *Wrestlin' Jacob: A Portrait of Religion in Antebellum Georgia and the Carolina Low Country* (1979; repr., Tuscaloosa, Ala.: University of Alabama Press, 2000).

23. Dabney, Sermon on Genesis 6:5, MS, UTSVA.

24. Dabney, Sermon on Romans 5:6 and John 6:44, MS, UTSVA. Other sermons that emphasized key doctrines in an evangelistic fashion were Romans 10:16 (on faith and repentance, preached first in 1853), Romans 9:16 (on God's sovereignty in grace, preached first in 1855), and Genesis 2:17 (on human depravity, preached first in 1859), all MS, UTSVA.

25. Dabney, Sermon on Genesis 27:38, MS, UTSVA.

26. Dabney, Sermon on 1 Kings 18:21, MS, UTSVA. Dabney eventually wrote this sermon out in full, intending it for a book of "Army Sermons" that was never published.

27. Dabney, Sermon on Matthew 6:25, MS, UTSVA; Dabney, Sermon on Matthew 16:26, MS, UTSVA. Other sermons dealt with money, including sermons on 2 Samuel 24:24 (first preached in 1851) and 1 Corinthians 7:31 (1848), both MS, UTSVA.

28. Dabney, Sermon on Luke 9:23, MS, UTSVA.

29. Dabney, Sermon on Matthew 15:21–28, MS, UTSVA.

30. Dabney, Sermon on Romans 8:16, MS, UTSVA.

31. Dabney, Sermon on Genesis 4:9 (1852), MS, UTSVA. A separate sermon that Dabney preached in 1850 on the same text made similar points. Temperance was a live issue for Dabney because Augusta County had a town, locally called "Whiskeyville," that was notorious for alcoholic manufacture." See also Sermon on Proverbs 23:29 (n.d.), MS, UTSVA.

32. Dabney, Sermon on Exodus 18:21, MS, UTSVA; Dabney, "The State Free School System," in *Discussions*, 4:202, 206.

33. Dabney, Sermon on Matthew 9:38, MS, UTSVA; Dabney, Sermon on 1 Samuel 1:27–28, MS, UTSVA. See also Sermon on Malachi 2:15 (1874), MS, UTSVA. The sermon on 1 Samuel 1 was one of Dabney's most effective recruiting sermons for Union Seminary. During his lengthy preaching tours from 1854 to 1860, Dabney preached this sermon at least twenty-five times. Interestingly, none of Dabney's three surviving sons became ministers.

34. Dabney, "The World White to Harvest: Reap, or It Perishes," in *Discussions*, 1:575–94; *LLD*, 167. Other sermons on missions included Sermon on Nehemiah 3:28–30 (1853) and Sermon on Psalm 2:8 (1860), both MS, UTSVA.

35. Dabney, Sermon on Matthew 6:19–21, MS, UTSVA; Dabney, Sermon on Genesis 43:27–30, 45:1–3, 46:29, MS, UTSVA. For other examples of funeral sermons, see sermons on 2 Samuel 12:23 (1850); Job 7:16 (1849); Job 10:2 (1852); Psalm 39:9 (1849); Proverbs 3:1–2 (1864); Jeremiah 10:23 (c. 1879); Luke 12:6–7 (1850); 1 Corinthians 7:28–31 (1850); 1 Corinthians 15:55–57 (1850); 2 Corinthians 4:17 (1851); Hebrews 12:10 (1850); James 4:14 (1849), all MSS, UTSVA.

36. *LLD*, 198; Samuel Chester Hall, *Memories of Four-Score Years* (Richmond, Va.: Presbyterian Committee of Publication, 1934), 82. Examples of Dabney's later sermons include sermons on Esther 5:3 (1880); Psalm 97:1 (1882); Psalm 111:10 (baccalaureate sermon for Hampden-Sydney College, 1876); Proverbs 11:2 (baccalaureate sermon for Davidson College, 1881); Matthew 5:43 (1880), all MS, UTSVA.

37. Dabney to Charles William Dabney, 30 April 1852, UVA.

38. In 1858, Dabney wrote a lengthy review of Breckinridge's systematic theology that accused the Kentucky theologian of plagiarism. Needless to say, that did not strengthen their relationship. See Dabney to Moses D. Hoge, 2 February 1858, UTSVA, and Dabney, "Breckinridge's Theology," in *Discussions*, 1:29–72.

39. Dabney, "The State and Claims of Union Theological Seminary," *Watchman and Observer*, 15 July 1852.

40. Moses D. Hoge to Dabney, 18 December 1852, UTSVA.

41. Dabney, "Autobiography," MS, UVA; Moses D. Hoge to Dabney, 28 May 1853, UTSVA; Dabney to Charles William Dabney, April 1853, quoted in Wilson, *The Tinkling Spring*, 294.

42. William S. White to Dabney, 4 April (?) 1853, in *LLD*, 134–35; *Minutes of the Lexington Presbytery*, 1853, 250–52, quoted in Wilson, *The Tinkling Spring*, 295.

Chapter 3: Professor

1. Dabney, "Autobiography," MS, Robert Lewis Dabney Papers, Alderman Library, University of Virginia, Charlottesville (hereafter UVA); Moses D. Hoge to Dabney, 18 December 1852, Robert Lewis Dabney Papers, William Morton Library, Union Theological Seminary in Virginia, Richmond (hereafter UTSVA).

2. Dabney to G. B. Strickler, 2 November 1883, in Thomas Cary Johnson, *Life and Letters of Robert Lewis Dabney* (1903; repr., Carlisle, Pa.: Banner of Truth, 1977), 141–42 (hereafter *LLD*); Dabney, "Lectures on Church History and Government," MS, Robert Lewis Dabney Collection, Presbyterian Historical Society, Montreat, N.C. (hereafter Montreat); C. R. Vaughan to Dabney, 10 March 1856, in *LLD*, 143; William H. Foote to Dabney, 11 January 1854, in *LLD*. For an insightful look at Dabney as a church historian, see James H. Smylie, "The Burden of Southern Church Historian: World Mission, Regional Captivity, Reconciliation," *Journal of Presbyterian History* 46 (1968): 274–307. I thank Wayne Sparkman for this reference.

3. Hodge's charge against Thornwell can be found in James Henley Thornwell, *The Collected Writings of James Henley Thornwell*, ed. B. M. Palmer, 4 vols. (1871–73; repr., Carlisle, Pa.: Banner of Truth, 1974), 4:228. For a thorough discussion of some of the issues, see A. Craig Troxell, "Charles Hodge on Church Boards: A Case Study in Ecclesiology," *Westminster Theological Journal* 58 (1996): 183–207.

4. Dabney, "Lectures on Church History and Government," MS, Dabney Collection, Montreat.

5. Dabney, "Theories of the Eldership," in *Discussions*, 4 vols. (1890–97; repr., Harrisonburg, Va.: Sprinkle, 1982), 2:119–57.

6. Moses D. Hoge to Dabney, 11 April 1855, UTSVA; Dabney to Moses D. Hoge, 12 April 1855, UTSVA.

7. Dabney, "A Thoroughly Educated Ministry," in *Discussions*, 2:665, 675–76.

8. Dabney, "Union Seminary and Theological Education," *Watchman and Observer*, 15 July 1852; Dabney, "The General Assembly of 1881," *Southern Presbyterian Review* 32 (1881): 560–61.

9. Dabney, "Decline of Ministerial Scholarship," *Presbyterian Quarterly* 11 (1897): 169; Dabney, "University of Texas and the Colleges," *Southwestern Presbyterian*, 14 February 1884; Dabney, "A Thoroughly Educated Ministry," 672; Dabney, "The Standard of Education," in *Discussions*, 3:560–62.

10. Dabney, "Memorial on Theological Education," in *Discussions*, 2:69–70.

11. *LLD*, 323; David H. Overy, "Robert Lewis Dabney: Apostle of the Old South" (Ph.D. diss.: University of Wisconsin, 1967), 259; Dabney, "Autobiography," MS, UVA; Overy mistakenly dated this memorial as 1877 instead of 1869; Dabney, "Decline of Ministerial Scholarship," 167, 171, 173; Dabney, "The Influence of the German University System on Theological Literature," in *Discussions*, 1:454–61.

12. Dabney, "Memorial on Theological Education," 72–75. Dabney opposed the introduction of science into the theological curriculum long before he was engaged in his debate with James Woodrow. For an example, see Dabney, "Union Seminary and Theological Education," *Watchman and Observer*, 15 July 1852.

13. Dabney, "Decline of Ministerial Scholarship," 173–74; Dabney, "Memorial on Theological Education," 67–69.

14. Dabney, "Relations of Our Theological Seminaries to Our System of Church Government," *Presbyterial Critic* 1 (1855): 7–10; Dabney, "Memorial on Theological Education," 59–66.

15. Dabney, "Decline of Ministerial Scholarship," 165; Dabney, "Standard of Ordination," in *Discussions*, 3:553–54.

16. Dabney, "Relations of Our Theological Seminaries to Our System of Church Government," 11–12.

17. Dabney, "Memorial on Theological Education," 49–56.

18. Dabney, "Union Seminary and Theological Education"; Dabney, "Relations of the Seminaries to the General Assembly," *Presbyterial Critic* 1 (1855): 60–61.

19. W. W. Moore to his mother, 16 August 1878, in J. Gray McAllister, *The Life and Letters of Walter W. Moore* (Richmond, Va.: Union Theological Seminary, 1939), 77; Peyton H. Hoge, "Robert Lewis Dabney," *North Carolina Presbyterian*, 19 February 1890; W. S. Lacy to Dabney, 21 February 1890, UTSVA.

20. Dabney, *Life and Campaigns of Lieut.-Gen. Thomas J. Jackson* (1866; repr. Harrisonburg, Va.: Sprinkle, 1986), 101; Dabney, *Syllabus and Notes of the Course of Systematic and Polemic Theology*, 2d ed. (1878; repr., Carlisle, Pa.: Banner of Truth, 1977), 86–90. For a convenient summary of Dabney's commitment to common sense, see "Inductive Logic Discussed," in *Discussions*, 3:377–78.

21. Dabney, "Inductive Logic Discussed," 371, 378–79; Dabney, "Geology and the Bible," in *Discussions*, 3:106–8, 115.

22. Dabney, *Syllabus and Notes*, 93–94; Dabney, "Inductive Logic Discussed," 366–67.

23. Dabney, *Syllabus and Notes*, 79; Dabney, *The Sensualistic Philosophy of the Nineteenth Century Considered*, 2d ed. (New York: Anson, 1887), 213–15, 218–19.

24. Dabney, *Syllabus and Notes*, 83–85.

25. Dabney, "Inductive Logic Discussed," 389–90, 394–402.

26. Ibid., 418–23.

27. Dabney, "Final Cause," in *Discussions*, 3:479, 483, 486–87, 486–91; Dabney, *Sensualistic Philosophy*, 109–12.

28. Dabney, "Broad Churchism," in *Discussions*, 2:447, 452; Dabney, "The Doctrinal Contents of the Confession—Its Fundamental and Regulative Ideas, and the Necessity and Value of Creeds," in *Memorial Volume of the Westminster Assembly, 1647–1897* (Richmond, Va.: Presbyterian Committee of Publications, 1897), 95.

29. S. F. Tenney, "Death of Rev. R. L. Dabney, D.D.," *Christian Observer*, 12 January 1898. Dabney observed in his autobiographical reflections that "if I ever had any special intellectual growth, I owed it to three things: first, the University of Virginia M.A. course; Dr. Sampson; and my subsequent mastering of Turretin's theology" (Dabney, "Autobiography," MS, UVA).

30. Dabney, *Syllabus and Notes*, 144, 287–91, 341–49; Dabney, "The Influence of the German University System on Theological Literature," 458–59. In a separate reflection, Dabney approved of Archibald Alexander's conviction that "the Reformed

Protestant theology reached its zenith in the seventeenth century" (Dabney, "Doctrinal Contents of the Confession," 92).

31. Hoge, "Robert Lewis Dabney"; in *LLD*, 169–70; Dabney, "Doctrinal Contents of the Confession," 93.

32. Dabney, "Refutation of W. Robertson Smith," in *Discussions*, 1:401–4, 413, 439.

33. Dabney, "The Bible Its Own Witness," in *Discussions*, 1:115–31.

34. Dabney, *Syllabus and Notes*, 276–79, 285–86; Dabney, *Jackson*, 98–105.

35. Dabney, *The Five Points of Calvinism* (Richmond, Va.: Presbyterian Committee of Publication, 1895), 6, 9–10; Dabney, *Christ Our Penal Substitute* (1898; repr., Harrisonburg, Va.: Sprinkle, 1985), 11. See also Dabney, *Syllabus and Notes*, 306–51; Dabney, "Doctrine of Original Sin," in *Discussions*, 1:143–68; Dabney, "Vindicatory Justice Essential to God," in *Discussions*, 1:466–81.

36. Dabney, *Christ Our Penal Substitute*, 14, 24; Dabney, *Syllabus and Notes*, 500–535. See also two letters that spell out nuances in Dabney's view of the atonement: Dabney to W. M. McPheeters, 10 November 1890 and 1 December 1890, W. M. McPheeters Papers, Montreat.

37. Dabney, *Christ Our Penal Substitute*, 15–17, 32, 93–98, 111–15.

38. Dabney, *Five Points of Calvinism*, 38–59, 70–71.

39. Dabney, *Syllabus and Notes*, 869, 874–79.

40. E. Brooks Holifield, *The Gentlemen Theologians: American Theology in Southern Culture, 1795–1860* (Durham, N.C.: Duke University Press, 1978), 154; "Historical facts of argument on Parochial schools," MS, UTSVA. See also Dabney, "The Last General Assembly," *Watchman and Observer*, 17 July 1851.

41. Dabney, "Autobiography," MS, UVA; Herbert Clarence Bradshaw, "Dr. Dabney and College Church," *The Record of Hampden-Sydney Alumni Association* (July 1850): 34–35.

42. Dabney to his wife, 19 May 1856, 23 May 1856, UVA; Dabney to his wife, 29 May 1856, in *LLD*, 165–66. Dabney also served as a commissioner to the 1852 General Assembly in St. Louis while he was pastor at Tinkling Spring.

43. Dabney to Charles William Dabney, 15 November 1855 and 12 December 1855, in *LLD*, 168–73.

44. Dabney to his wife, 29 May 1856 and 19 July 1858, UVA; Overy, "Robert Lewis Dabney," 241.

45. Thomas Cary Johnson, *The Life and Letters of Benjamin Morgan Palmer* (Richmond, Va.: Presbyterian Committee of Publication, 1906), 235; Charles Hodge to Dabney, 24 March 1860, in *LLD*, 200; Hodge to Dabney, 31 March 1860, in *LLD*, 202. Hodge obliquely makes reference to this larger Princeton purpose of union (Charles Hodge to Dabney, 24 March 1860, in *LLD*, 200).

46. Dabney to Charles Hodge, 10 April 1860, in *LLD*, 203; Dabney to A. T. McGill, 8 May 1860, in *LLD*, 207–8.

47. *Centennial General Catalogue of the Trustees, Officers, Professors, and Alumni of Union Theological Seminary in Virginia, 1807–1907*, ed. Walter W. Moore and Tilden Scherer (Richmond, Va.: Whittet and Shepperson, 1907); Edward Howell Roberts, *Biographical Catalogue of the Princeton Theological Seminary, 1815–1932* (Princeton, N.J.: Theological Seminary of Presbyterian Church, 1933).

48. Dabney, "Union Seminary and Theological Education"; Dabney, "Autobiography," MS, UVA.

Chapter 4: Patriot

1. Dabney, "The Christian's Best Motive for Patriotism," in *Discussions*, 4 vols. (1890–97; repr., Harrisonburg, Va.: Sprinkle, 1982), 2:401–6.

2. Ibid., 406–12.

3. Dabney to Charles William Dabney, 15 January 1851 and 23 December 1859, Robert Lewis Dabney Papers, Alderman Library, University of Virginia, Charlottesville (hereafter UVA); Dabney, "Autobiography," MS, UVA.

4. See Bertram Wyatt-Brown, *Southern Honor: Ethics and Behavior in the Old South* (New York: Oxford University Press, 1980).

5. Walter Scott, *Ivanhoe*, Modern Library Classics (New York: Random House, 2001), 318–19; G. Harrison Orians, "Walter Scott, Mark Twain, and the Civil War," *South Atlantic Quarterly* 40 (1941): 342–59.

6. See Bertram Wyatt-Brown, *The Shaping of Southern Culture: Honor, Grace, and War, 1760s–1880s* (Chapel Hill, N.C.: University of North Carolina Press, 2001).

7. Dabney to Charles Hodge, 23 January 1861, Robert Lewis Dabney Papers, William Morton Library, Union Theological Seminary in Virginia, Richmond (hereafter UTSVA); Dabney, "On the State of the Country," in *Discussions*, 2:421–29.

8. Dabney, "Christians, Pray for Your Country," in *Discussions*, 2:393–95 (emphasis his).

9. Dabney to Moses D. Hoge, 19 March 1858, UVA.

10. Dabney to Moses D. Hoge, 4 January 1861, in Thomas Cary Johnson, *Life and Letters of Robert Lewis Dabney* (1903; repr., Carlisle, Pa.: Banner of Truth, 1977), 221–22 (hereafter *LLD*); Dabney to his mother, 28 December 1860, in *LLD*, 215.

11. James Henley Thornwell to Dabney, 24 November 1860, in *LLD*, 223–24; Dabney, "A Pacific Appeal to Christians," in *Discussions*, 2:413–20.

12. Dabney to Charles Hodge, 23 January 1861, UTSVA; Charles Hodge to Dabney, 29 January 1861, UTSVA. The entire exchange was spread over five letters: Dabney to Charles Hodge, 12 December 1860, Hodge Collection, Montreat, N.C. (hereafter Montreat); Hodge to Dabney, 15 December 1860, UTSVA; the two letters mentioned above; and finally, Dabney to Hodge, 13 February 1861, Charles Hodge Collection, Presbyterian Historical Society, Montreat. A full discussion can be found in Sean Michael Lucas, " 'Hold Fast That Which Is Good': The Public Theology of

Robert Lewis Dabney" (Ph.D. diss.: Westminster Theological Seminary, 2002), 116–23.

13. *LLD*, 224–25, 563; Dabney, "On the State of the Country," 421–23.

14. Dabney, "On the State of the Country," 423–45.

15. Ibid., 426, 428–29.

16. Ibid., passim.

17. *LLD*, 231–32.

18. Dabney preached a sermon to these Hampden-Sydney Volunteers on 26 May 1861. Entitled "True Courage," this sermon was later recycled by Dabney in his more famous sermon on the death of Stonewall Jackson, with a new introduction and concluding applications. See Sermon on Luke 12:4–5, MS, UTSVA.

19. Dabney, "Autobiography," MS, UVA.

20. Dabney to Betty Dabney, 12 July 1861, in *LLD*, 238; Dabney to his mother, 19 July 1861, in *LLD*, 239; Dabney to Betty Dabney, 22 July 1861, in *LLD*, 241.

21. Dabney to Charles William Dabney, 31 October 1861, in *LLD*, 243; *Minutes of the Synod of Virginia, 1861* (Lynchburg, Va.: Johnson and Schaffter, 1861); Dabney, "Autobiography," MS, UVA.

22. Dabney, "Declaration of the PCCSNA," MS, UTSVA.

23. Ibid.

24. Ibid.

25. Ibid.

26. *LLD*, 249–55.

27. *LLD*, 254, 261–63; Dabney, "Autobiography," MS, UVA; David H. Overy, "Robert Lewis Dabney: Apostle of the Old South" (Ph.D. diss.: University of Wisconsin, 1967), 111.

28. Dabney, "Autobiography," MS, UVA; J. William Jones, *Christ in the Camp, or Religion in the Confederate Army* (1887; repr., Harrisonburg, Va.: Sprinkle, 1986), 252; Henry Kyd Douglas, *I Rode with Stonewall* (Chapel Hill, N.C.: University of North Carolina Press, 1940), 98, 101; *LLD*, 264.

29. Dabney, "Autobiography," MS, UVA.

30. Douglas, *I Rode with Stonewall*, 101; James I. Robertson Jr., *Stonewall Jackson: The Man, The Soldier, The Legend* (New York: Macmillan, 1997), 461, 467.

31. Jones, *Christ in the Camp*, 256, 529–34; "Chaplains in the Army of Northern Virginia: A List Compiled in 1864 and 1865 by Robert L. Dabney," ed. W. Harrison Daniel, *Virginia Magazine of History and Biography* 71 (1963): 327–40. Likewise, Herman Norton failed to list Dabney in his roster compiled from several archival sources (*Rebel Religion: The Story of Confederate Chaplains* [St. Louis: Bethany, 1961], 115–34).

After the war, Dabney intended to publish a collection of "Army Sermons," which he had preached during the Civil War. His ostensible purpose was to demonstrate that Southern preaching during the war was not "political," as some Northerners charged. This collection, however, was never published.

32. *LLD*, 272–73; Dabney, "Autobiography," MS, UVA; Dabney to T. J. Jackson, 5 March 1863, UVA; Haskell M. Monroe Jr., "The Presbyterian Church in the Confederate States of America" (Ph.D. diss.: Rice University, 1961), 287–93; James A. Lyon, "Slavery and the Duties Growing out of the Relation," *Southern Presbyterian Review* 16 (1863): 1–37.

33. Dabney to Charles William Dabney, 15 January 1851, UVA; Dabney to Charles William Dabney, 6 March 1851, UVA; *LLD*, 273–75; Dabney to Moses Hoge, 25 January 1863, Hoge Family Papers, Montreat; Dabney to T. J. Jackson, 5 March 1863, UVA; Theodrick Pryor to Dabney, 4 June 1873, UTSVA; Dabney, "Advertisement to the Reader," MS, UTSVA.

34. Dabney, *A Defence of Virginia (And Through Her, of the South) in Recent and Pending Contests Against the Sectional Party* (1867; repr., Harrisonburg, Va.: Sprinkle, 1991), 32, 42–43, 85–87.

35. Ibid., 61–64, 69.

36. Ibid., 21, 25, 94–95, 98, 116, 207.

37. Ibid., 101, 103, 106, 110–12, 116–24.

38. Ibid., 145–46, 149, 153–54, 176–85.

39. Ibid., 295–348; "Economic Effects of the Former Labor System of the Southern United States," in *Discussions*, 4:372, 378–79.

40. Dabney, *Defence of Virginia*, 128–30; Erskine Clarke, *Wrestlin' Jacob: A Portrait of Religion in Antebellum Georgia and the Carolina Low Country* (1979; repr., Tuscaloosa, Ala.: University of Alabama Press, 2000); Eugene D. Genovese, *A Consuming Fire: The Fall of the Confederacy in the Mind of the White Christian South* (Athens, Ga.: University of Georgia Press, 1998), 3–33.

41. Douglas F. Kelly, "Robert Lewis Dabney," in *Reformed Theology in America: A History of Its Modern Development*, ed. David F. Wells (Grand Rapids: Baker, 1997), 217.

42. Dabney, *Defence of Virginia*, 159–61.

43. For more contemporary biblical arguments against slavery, see Stephen R. Haynes, *Noah's Curse: The Biblical Justification of American Slavery* (New York: Oxford University Press, 2002).

44. Dabney to G. Woodson Payne, 22 January 1840, in *LLD*, 67–68.

45. Dabney to Charles William Dabney, 15 January 1851, UVA.

46. Dabney, *Defence of Virginia*, 213–41.

47. Ibid., 279–81, 293, 353; Dabney, "Capital and Labor," in *Discussions*, vol. 5 (Harrisonburg, Va.: Sprinkle, 1999), 391. The way in which Dabney merged racial prejudice and proslavery arguments problematizes contemporary defenses of "Southern slavery, as it was"; see, for an example, Steve Wilkins and Doug Wilson, *Southern Slavery, As It Was* (Moscow, Ida.: Canon Press, 1996). Wilkins and Wilson depend on Dabney's *Defence of Virginia* while claiming that "all forms of race hatred or racial vainglory are forms of rebellion against God" (p. 14). This judgment appears to contradict their earlier description of Dabney as "a godly man who fought for the South"

(p. 13) as well as to complicate their use of his proslavery arguments that were deeply motivated by racial prejudice.

48. *LLD*, 280–81; Douglas Southall Freeman, *The South to Posterity: An Introduction to the Writing of Confederate History* (New York: Charles Scribners, 1939), 40; Jubal Early, "Dabney's Life of Stonewall Jackson," *New Eclectic* 3 (1869): 726–28; Dabney, "Dr. Dabney's Reply to General Early," *New Eclectic* 4 (1869): 565–69; Dabney, "Stonewall Jackson," *Southern Historical Society Papers* 11 (1883): 125–35, 145–58.

49. *LLD*, 292.

50. Dabney, "True Courage," in *Discussions* 4:436.

51. Mary Anna Jackson to Dabney, 16 January 1865, in Overy, "Robert Lewis Dabney," 145; Jonathan M. Young, "Psychology of the South: Robert Lewis Dabney, the Race God, and Sacramental Purity" (M.A. thesis: University of North Carolina, 1993), 53; Robertson, *Stonewall Jackson*, 256, 496–97, 711–12, 851, 856, 861, 863, 867, 872, 876, 894.

52. Charles Reagan Wilson, "Robert Lewis Dabney: Religion and the Southern Holocaust," *Virginia Magazine of History and Biography* 89 (1981): 79–81; *LLD*, 292–93.

53. Dabney to Hugh Guthrie, 9 June 1864, in *LLD*, 284; Dabney to D. H. Hill, 1 December 1873, in Overy, "Robert Lewis Dabney," 161.

54. Samuel Hall Chester, *Memories of Four-Score Years* (Richmond, Va.: Presbyterian Committee of Publication, 1934), 77.

Chapter 5: Presbyterian Partisan

1. Charles Reagan Wilson, "Robert Lewis Dabney: Religion and the Southern Holocaust," *Virginia Magazine of History and Biography* 89 (1981): 79; Dabney to his mother, 15 February 1868, in Thomas Cary Johnson, *Life and Letters of Robert Lewis Dabney* (1903; repr., Carlisle, Pa.: Banner of Truth, 1977), 303 (hereafter *LLD*).

2. Dabney to Moses Hoge, 2 January 1867, in *LLD*, 303; Dabney to Moses Hoge, 16 August 1865, in *LLD*, 305, 307.

3. Dabney, "Fraternal Relations," in *Discussions*, 4 vols. (1890–97; repr., Harrisonburg, Va.: Sprinkle, 1982), 2:485.

4. Jack P. Maddex, "From Theocracy to Spirituality: The Southern Presbyterian Reversal on Church and State," *Journal of Presbyterian History* 54 (1976): 448.

5. Harold M. Parker Jr., "The Independent Presbyterian Church and Reunion in the South, 1813–1863," *Journal of Presbyterian History* 50 (1972): 89–110.

6. See Harold M. Parker Jr., *The United Synod of the South: The Southern New School Presbyterian Church* (Westport, Conn.: Greenwood, 1988).

7. Dabney, "Our Position," in *Discussions*, 2:177; Moses D. Hoge to Dabney, 7 July 1857, 14 July 1857, and 19 October 1857, Robert Lewis Dabney Papers,

William Morton Library, Union Theological Seminary in Virginia, Richmond (hereafter UTSVA); Dabney, "The Examination Rule," *Central Presbyterian*, 7 November 1857.

8. E. T. Thompson, *Presbyterians in the South*, 3 vols. (Richmond, Va.: John Knox, 1963–73), 2:120; *LLD*, 286; *Minutes*, General Assembly of the Presbyterian Church in the Confederate States (1863), 253–58.

9. John Miller, "Report of the Committees of Conference of the General Assembly and the United Synod of the Presbyterian Churches in the Confederate States of America, on the Subject of a Union Between the Two Bodies," *Southern Presbyterian Review* 16 (April 1864): 253–64.

10. B. M. Palmer, "The Proposed Plan of Union Between the General Assembly in the Confederate States of America and the United Synod of the South," *Southern Presbyterian Review* 16 (April 1864): 264–78.

11. Ibid., 278–307.

12. Dabney, "On Fusion with the United Synod," in *Discussions*, 2:298–301.

13. Ibid., 301–11.

14. *Minutes*, General Assembly of the Presbyterian Church in the Confederate States (1863), 271–72, 273, 276–77; *LLD*, 287.

15. *LLD*, 287–88.

16. John L. Girardeau, "Our Ecclesiastical Relations to Freedmen," *Southern Presbyterian Review* 18 (1867): 1–17.

17. J. B. Adger, "The General Assembly at Memphis," *Southern Presbyterian Review* 18 (1867): 146–65, substitute resolutions on 161–63; Thompson, *Presbyterians in the South*, 2:211–15.

18. *LLD*, 319–21.

19. Dabney, "Ecclesiastical Equality of Negroes," in *Discussions*, 2:199–200.

20. Ibid., 200–202.

21. Ibid., 202–4.

22. Ibid., 204–10.

23. Ibid., 210–12.

24. Ibid., 212–16.

25. Ibid., 216–17.

26. *LLD*, 321; *Minutes of the Synod of Virginia, 1867* (Lynchburg, Va.: Johnson and Schaffter, 1867), 40; Stuart Robinson to Dabney, 31 March 1868, UTSVA; B. M. Palmer to Dabney, 30 December 1872, UTSVA.

27. Just a few years before, Dabney had written that "while we believe that 'God made of one blood all the nations of men to dwell under the whole heavens,' we know that the African has become, according to a well-known law of natural history, by the manifold influences of the ages, a different, fixed *species* of the race, separated from the white man by traits bodily, mental and moral, almost as rigid and permanent as those of *genus*" (Dabney, *A Defence of Virginia (And Through Her, of the South) in Recent and Pending Contests Against the Sectional Party* [1867; repr., Har-

261

risonburg, Va.: Sprinkle, 1991], 353). Thus, Dabney claimed that blacks were so different from whites that they were practically a different class of creation. Needless to say, this view is breathtaking in its prejudice.

28. Compare with Stephen R. Haynes, *Noah's Cause: The Biblical Justification of American Slavery* (New York: Oxford University Press, 2002), 177–219.

29. Thompson, *Presbyterians in the South*, 2:137–40. The Pittsburgh Orders can be found in *The Presbyterian Historical Almanac and Annual Remembrancer of the Church for 1866*, ed. Joseph M. Wilson (Philadelphia: Joseph M. Wilson, 1866), 43–45.

30. "The New Church," *Southern Presbyterian Review* 22 (1870): 559–65.

31. Dabney to Moses D. Hoge, 2 January 1867, in *LLD*, 303; Dabney to his wife, 23 May 1870, UTSVA; *LLD*, 350–51.

32. *LLD*, 352.

33. Ibid., 355; Charles Hodge, "Delegation to the Southern General Assembly," *Biblical Repertory and Princeton Review* 40 (1870): 449.

34. Dabney, "Broad Churchism," in *Discussions*, 2:447–63.

35. Dabney, *Presbyterianism, with the Modern Improvements* (n.p.: n.d.), 11.

36. Dabney, "Fraternal Correspondence," in *Discussions*, 2:466, 468; Dabney, "Fraternal Relations," 472–75, 496; Dabney to Moses D. Hoge, 17 February 1877, Hoge Family Papers, Presbyterian Historical Society, Montreat, N.C. (hereafter Montreat).

37. Dabney, "Fraternal Relations," 480, 484–85, 492.

38. Dabney, "The Pan-Presbyterian Alliance," in *Discussions*, 2:528–42. See also Stuart Robinson, "Letter to the Editor," *Central Presbyterian*, 22 March 1876; Dabney, "Letter from the Rev. Dr. Dabney," *Central Presbyterian*, 19 April 1876; Dabney, "Pan-Presbyterian Alliance," 543–48; Dabney, "The Southern Church and the Presbyterian Alliance," in *Discussions*, 2:549–59.

39. Dabney, "Fraternal Relations," 495–96, 500–502.

40. This and the previous paragraph: Dabney, "The Atlanta Assembly and Fraternal Relations," in *Discussions*, 2:503–28.

41. Ibid., 522–26.

42. Dabney, "Letter from Dr. Dabney on Organic Union," *Central Presbyterian*, 4 May 1887; Richard McIlwaine, "Organic Union," *Central Presbyterian*, 18 May 1887; C. R. Vaughan, "Reply to Dr. McIlwaine," *Central Presbyterian*, 15 June 1887; Dabney, "Incurable Misconceptions," *Texas Presbyterian*, 13 July 1894.

43. Dabney, "Atlanta Assembly and Fraternal Relations," 524.

44. *LLD*, 167; Dabney, "Shall Campinas College Die?" *Central Presbyterian*, 21 February 1894; Dabney, "Building the Church's Walls," *Christian Observer*, 2 September 1896.

45. *Centennial General Catalogue of the Trustees, Officers, Professors, and Alumni of Union Theological Seminary in Virginia, 1807–1907*, ed. Walter W. Moore and Tilden Scherer (Richmond, Va.: Whittet and Shepperson, 1907), 81; *LLD*, 330,

358–60, 406–9, 457–58; Dabney, "Shall Campinas College Die?"; H. F. Williams, *In South America: Our Missions in Brazil* (Richmond, Va.: Presbyterian Committee of Publications, n.d.); Samuel R. Gammon, *The Evangelical Invasion of Brazil* (Richmond, Va.: Presbyterian Committee of Publications, 1910).

46. J. Gray McAllister and Grace Owings Guerrant, *Edward O. Guerrant: Apostle to the Southern Highlands* (Richmond, Va.: Richmond Press, 1950), 71; Dabney to E. O. Guerrant, 12 September 1877, in McAllister and Guerrant, *Edward O. Guerrant*, 81; Dabney to Guerrant, 6 June 1879 and 14 April 1881, UTSVA; Dabney to Guerrant, 5 August 1889 and 19 January 1897, in McAllister and Guerrant, *Edward O. Guerrant*, 105–6, 120.

47. Dabney, "Building the Church's Walls."

Chapter 6: Public Theologian

1. Dabney to Moses D. Hoge, 16 August 1865, in Thomas Cary Johnson, *Life and Letters of Robert Lewis Dabney* (1903; repr., Carlisle, Pa.: Banner of Truth, 1977), 305, 307 (hereafter *LLD*); Dabney to T. J. Jackson, 5 March 1863, Robert Lewis Dabney Papers, Alderman Library, University of Virginia, Charlottesville; Dabney, "The Duty of the Hour," in *Discussions*, 4 vols. (1890–97; repr., Harrisonburg, Va.: Sprinkle, 1982), 4:119; Dabney, "True Courage," in *Discussions*, 4:436.

2. Modernism, modernization, and antimodernism are notoriously difficult words and movements to define. For the purposes of this chapter, I understand "modernism" to be a philosophical movement that was essentially positivist, arising in the mid-nineteenth century in Europe and fleshing itself in the early twentieth century in literature and art. "Modernization" was the process of social and economic transformation that began early in the nineteenth century, but reached its (second) climax in America during the 1870s and 1880s. It was related to and drew from, but was not equivalent with, modernism. "Antimodernism," in the way that I am using it, stands for a general revulsion against and dissent from the modern worldview (expressed by modernism or positivism) and the modernization taking place in American life. These three working definitions are drawn from Daniel J. Singal, "Towards a Definition of American Modernism," in *Modernist Culture in America*, ed. Daniel J. Singal (Belmont, Calif.: Wadsworth, 1989), 1–27; Singal, *The War Within: From Victorian to Modernist Thought in the South, 1919–1945* (Chapel Hill, N.C.: University of North Carolina Press, 1982), 3–33; Richard D. Brown, "Modernization: A Victorian Climax," in *Victorian America*, ed. Daniel Walker Howe (Philadelphia: University of Pennsylvania Press, 1976), 29–44; and T. J. Jackson Lears, *No Place of Grace: Antimodernism and the Transformation of American Culture, 1880–1920* (Chicago: University of Chicago Press, 1981), especially 4–58.

3. Dabney to G. B. Strickler, 26 September 1884, in *LLD*, 345–46; Lears, *No Place of Grace*, 261–98; John Donald Wade, "Old Wine in a New Bottle," *Virginia Quarterly Review* 11 (1935): 240–43.

4. Dabney, "The Influence of False Philosophies upon Character and Conduct," in *Discussions*, 4:570–71; Dabney, "The Latest Infidelity," in *Discussions*, 4:506–39.

5. Dabney, *The Sensualistic Philosophy of the Nineteenth Century Considered*, 2d ed. (New York: Anson, 1887), 1.

6. Dabney, "Positivism in England," in *Discussions*, 3:24–25. Dabney reused most of this material in his *Sensualistic Philosophy* as well as his *Syllabus and Notes of the Course of Systematic and Polemic Theology*, 2d ed. (1878; repr., Carlisle, Pa.: Banner of Truth, 1977).

7. Dabney, "Positivism in England," 27–29, 32.

8. Ibid., 33, 37.

9. Ibid., 59.

10. Dabney, *Sensualistic Philosophy*, 109–12.

11. Ibid., 114–24, 166.

12. Ibid., 124–30.

13. Ibid., 172–74.

14. Ibid., 174–80.

15. Ibid., 180–86.

16. Dabney, "A Caution Against Anti-Christian Science," in *Discussions*, 3:116–18.

17. Ibid., 118–23.

18. Ibid., 123–27.

19. James Woodrow, "An Examination of Certain Recent Assaults on Physical Science," *Southern Presbyterian Review* 24 (1873): 328–33, 338, 346, 351–52.

20. Ibid., 339–45, 362.

21. Ibid., 353–55.

22. Dabney, "Geology and the Bible," in *Discussions*, 3:98–100, 106–8, 115.

23. James Woodrow, "A Further Examination of Certain Recent Assaults on Physical Science," *Southern Presbyterian Review* 25 (1874): 266, 271; Woodrow, *Evolution: An Address Delivered May 7th 1884* . . . (Columbia, S.C.: Presbyterian Publishing House, 1884), 14–15, 18.

24. See Ronald L. Numbers and Lester D. Stephens, "Darwinism in the American South," in *Disseminating Darwinism: The Role of Place, Race, Religion, and Gender*, ed. R. Numbers and J. Stenhouse (New York: Cambridge University Press, 1999), 124, 128.

25. Dabney to G. B. Strickler, 26 September 1884, in *LLD*, 345–46.

26. Dabney, *Sensualistic Philosophy*, 206.

27. Dabney, "Anti-Biblical Theories of Rights," in *Discussions*, 3:499–501.

28. Dabney, "The Public Preaching of Women," in *Discussions*, 2:96–118. Dabney also dealt with the same issue in "Let Women Keep Silence in the Church," *Christian Observer*, 7 October 1891, using similar arguments.

29. Dabney, *A Defence of Virginia (And Through Her, of the South)* (1867; repr., Harrisonburg, Va.: Sprinkle, 1991), 254–56, 266.

30. Dabney, *Defence of Virginia*, 229; Dabney, *Syllabus and Notes*, 398; Dabney, "A Mother's Crowning Glory," in *Discussions*, vol. 5 (Harrisonburg, Va.: Sprinkle, 1999), 375, 381; Dabney, *The Practical Philosophy: Being the Philosophy of the Feelings, of the Will, and of the Conscience, with the Ascertainment of Particular Rights and Duties* (1897; repr., Harrisonburg, Va.: Sprinkle, 1984), 338; Dabney, "Women's Rights Women," in *Discussions*, 4:495.

31. Dabney, "Women's Rights Women," 495; Dabney, *Syllabus and Notes*, 783.

32. Dabney, "A Mother's Crowning Glory," 373–84; *LLD*, 318; Dabney, "Duty of the Hour," in *Discussions*, 4:120–22.

33. Dabney, "Anti-Biblical Theories of Rights," 498–99, 503, 520.

34. Dabney, "State Free School System," in *Discussions*, 4:192, 194, 197; Dabney, "Negro and the Common School," in *Discussions*, 4:189.

35. Dabney, "State Free School System," 205, 210–14.

36. Ibid., 202, 206.

37. Ibid., 216–22.

38. Ibid., 207–8, 210.

39. Ibid., 208–9.

40. Dabney, "Economic Effects of the Former Labor System of the Southern States of the U.S.," in *Discussions*, 4:382–84; Dabney, "Principles of Christian Economy," in *Discussions*, 1:26.

41. Dabney, "The Depression of American Farming Interests," in *Discussions*, 4:323, 325–26.

42. Dabney, "Industrial Combinations," *Land We Love* 5 (May 1868): 27, 29, 31; Dabney, "The Philosophy Regulating Private Corporations," in *Discussions*, 3:332, 334–35, 337.

43. Dabney, "Labor Unions, the Strike, and the Commune," in *Discussions*, 4:294–320 (quotations on 304–5, 307); Dabney, "Depression of American Farming Interests," 326.

44. Dabney, "Economic Effects of the Former Labor System"; Dabney, *Practical Philosophy*, 448–95; Dabney, "The New South," in *Discussions*, 4:16, 19; Dabney, "Principles of Christian Economy," 2, 4–7, 23, 27.

45. Dabney, "The New South," 16, 17, 19, 22.

46. Lears, *No Place of Grace*, 217–60.

47. Ibid., 26–32, 60–96; Dabney, "Depression of American Farming Interests," 323, 325–26.

48. Lears, *No Place of Grace*, 22–25, 32–46; Dabney, "Positivism in England," 59.

Chapter 7: Passing

1. Dabney, "The Southern Church and the Presbyterian Alliance," in *Discussions*, 4 vols. (1890–97; repr., Harrisonburg, Va.: Sprinkle, 1982), 2:558 (emphasis mine); Dabney to Thomas Cary Johnson, 1 July 1894, Robert Lewis Dabney Papers, William

Morton Library, Union Theological Seminary in Virginia, Richmond (hereafter UTSVA).

2. Francis R. Flournoy, *Benjamin Mosby Smith, 1811–1893* (Richmond, Va.: Richmond Press, 1947), 69–70. Smith kept a copious and detailed diary for most of his life; the only volume missing was for the years 1870 to 1887. His biographer noted, "No entries were made in his diaries from 1870 to 1887, and almost all of his letters and papers of the time were destroyed" (p. 118).

3. These disagreements are highlighted in Flournoy, *Benjamin Mosby Smith*, 125–41.

4. B. M. Smith to Cyrus McCormick, 12 May 1866, in ibid., 86.

5. J. Gray McAllister, *The Life and Letters of Walter W. Moore* (Richmond, Va.: Union Theological Seminary, 1939), 79–80; Dabney, "Autobiography," MS, Robert Lewis Dabney Papers, Alderman Library, University of Virginia, Charlottesville (hereafter UVA); Dabney to Joseph D. Eggleston, 29 October 1894, UVA.

6. Dabney, "Autobiography," MS, UVA. Dabney's "Memorial" is discussed in chapter 3.

7. Information on trustees gathered from *Centennial General Catalogue of the Trustees, Officers, Professors, and Alumni of Union Theological Seminary in Virginia, 1807–1907*, ed. W. W. Moore and Tilden Scherer (Richmond, Va.: Whittet and Shepperson, 1907) and *Ministerial Directory of the Presbyterian Church, United States, 1861–1941*, ed. E. C. Scott (Austin: Von Boeckmann-Jones, 1942).

8. Dabney, "Autobiography," MS, UVA.

9. Ibid.; Peyton H. Hoge, *Moses Drury Hoge: Life and Letters* (Richmond, Va.: Presbyterian Committee of Publication, 1899), 403–5.

10. Dabney, "Autobiography," MS, UVA; Dabney to Moses D. Hoge, 7 August 1880, Hoge Family Papers, Presbyterian Historical Society, Montreat, N. C. (hereafter Montreat).

11. Dabney, "Autobiography," MS, UVA.

12. Ibid.; David H. Overy, "Robert Lewis Dabney: Apostle of the Old South" (Ph.D. diss.: University of Wisconsin, 1967), 261–62.

13. Dabney, "Autobiography," MS, UVA; Overy, "Robert Lewis Dabney," 262; Dabney to Joseph D. Eggleston, 13 September 1890, UVA. The trustees did issue a minute for their records, noting Dabney's contributions to the seminary, as did his West Hanover presbytery; both are in Thomas Cary Johnson, *Life and Letters of Robert Lewis Dabney* (1903; repr., Carlisle, Pa.: Banner of Truth, 1977), 439–41 (hereafter *LLD*).

14. Dabney, "Autobiography," MS, UVA.

15. *LLD*, 445–46; Dabney, "Autobiography," MS, UVA.

16. Dabney, "The University of Texas and the College," *Southwestern Presbyterian*, 14 February 1884.

17. Ibid.

18. W. H. Ruffner, *Public Free School System* (n.p.: n.d. [c. 1874]), 28.

19. Dabney, "Autobiography," MS, UVA.

20. Ibid.; Dabney to Thomas Cary Johnson, 9 March 1888, UTSVA.

21. Dabney to C. R. Vaughan, 12 December 1885, Vaughan Papers, Montreat; Dabney to C. R. Vaughan, 20 October 1892 and 29 October 1892, UVA. Much of the Dabney–Vaughan correspondence can be found at UTSVA.

22. Dabney to C. R. Vaughan, 1 May 1886, Vaughan Papers, Montreat; Peyton H. Hoge, "Robert Lewis Dabney," *North Carolina Presbyterian*, 19 February 1890; W. S. Lacy to Dabney, 21 February 1890, UTSVA; Overy, "Robert Lewis Dabney," 268–70; *LLD*, 484–85.

23. Dabney, "Autobiography," MS, UVA; Dabney to George Summey, 31 July 1894, in Thomas White Currie Jr., "A History of Austin Presbyterian Theological Seminary, Austin, Texas, 1884–1943" (Th.D. diss.: Union Theological Seminary, 1958), 31–32; Dabney to S. B. Campbell, 15 May 1895, UVA. Eventually, Austin Presbyterian Theological Seminary did open on the foundations of Dabney's little school.

24. Dabney to Charles W. Dabney, 29 April 1890, UTSVA; *LLD*, 460–62, 488; Dabney, "Autobiography," MS, UVA.

25. Dabney, "Autobiography," MS, UVA; Dabney to Thomas Cary Johnson, 1 July 1894, UTSVA.

26. Overy, "Robert Lewis Dabney," 295–96; Dabney to Charles W. Dabney, 23 March 1894, UVA.

27. Dabney to Charles W. Dabney, 23 March 1894, UVA; Dabney to Charles W. Dabney, 3 May 1896, UVA; Dabney's students to Dabney, 22 May 1895, in *LLD*, 504–5; Samuel King to Dabney, 4 November 1895, UVA.

28. Dabney to Charles W. Dabney, 23 March 1894, UVA; Dabney to Thomas Cary Johnson, 1 July 1894, UTSVA; Dabney to S. B. Campbell, 15 May 1895, UVA; Dabney to Charles W. Dabney, 3 May 1896, UVA.

29. Dabney to Charles W. Dabney, 3 May 1896, UVA.

30. Dabney to W. W. Moore, 14 May 1893, in McAllister, *Life and Letters of Walter W. Moore*, 230; Dabney to Thomas Cary Johnson, 1 September 1894, in Overy, "Robert Lewis Dabney," 308.

31. Dabney to Joseph D. Eggleston, 29 October 1894, UVA; Overy, "Robert Lewis Dabney," 309; Dabney, "Do Not Remove Union Seminary," *Central Presbyterian*, 18 September 1895.

32. T. D. Witherspoon, *Central Presbyterian*, 16 January 1895, quoted in *LLD*, 496; Walter L. Lingle, "Dr. Robert Lewis Dabney," *Christian Observer*, 29 October 1952; *LLD*, 514–15.

33. J. B. Shearer, *Central Presbyterian*, 20 October 1897, in *LLD*, 520.

34. Dabney, "Francis S. Sampson, D. D.," *Union Seminary Magazine* 9 (1898): 282–84; Overy, "Robert Lewis Dabney," 314–15; *LLD*, 524; Charles Reagan Wilson, "Robert Lewis Dabney: Religion and the Southern Holocaust," *Virginia Magazine of*

2222222

22222

History and Biography 89 (1981): 89. Ironically, this issue of the *Union Seminary Magazine* contained sketches of the new Richmond campus with its Queen Anne turrets.

Chapter 8: Perspective

1. James Henley Thornwell, "The State of the Country," *Southern Presbyterian Review* 13 (1860–61): 880.

2. Ibid., 866–67; Thornwell, "Address to All the Churches of Jesus Christ," in *The Collected Writings of James Henley Thornwell*, ed. J. B. Adger (1871–73; repr., Carlisle, Pa.: Banner of Truth, 1974), 4:455, 456, 458.

3. Theodore Dwight Bozeman, "Science, Nature and Society: A New Approach to James Henley Thornwell," *Journal of Presbyterian History* 50 (1972): 308; John L. Girardeau, in B. M. Palmer, *The Life and Letters of James Henley Thornwell* (1875; repr., Carlisle, Pa.: Banner of Truth, 1974), 541; Morton Smith, *Studies in Southern Presbyterian Theology* (Phillipsburg, N.J.: Presbyterian and Reformed, 1987).

4. Thomas Cary Johnson, *The Life and Letters of Benjamin Morgan Palmer* (Richmond, Va.: Presbyterian Committee of Publication, 1906), 318–20; B. M. Palmer to Dabney, 23 April 1887, Robert Lewis Dabney Papers, William Morton Library, Union Theological Seminary in Virginia, Richmond (hereafter UTSVA). Dabney and Palmer conferred over church affairs during the late 1880s; see, for example, Dabney to C. R. Vaughan, 1 May 1886, Vaughan Papers, Presbyterian Historical Society, Montreat, N.C. (hereafter Montreat).

5. Gaines M. Foster, *Ghosts of the Confederacy: Defeat, the Lost Cause, and the Emergence of the New South* (New York: Oxford University Press, 1987), 49–51, 117; Charles Reagan Wilson, *Baptized in Blood: The Religion of the Lost Cause, 1865–1920* (Athens, Ga.: University of Georgia Press, 1980); Dabney, "Laus Iracundiae," *New Eclectic* 5 (1869): 524–29.

6. Dabney, "The Partisanship of the 'Spectator,' " *New Eclectic* 3 (1868): 341.

7. Dabney, "The Christian's Duty Towards His Enemies," in *Discussions*, 4 vols. (1890–97; repr., Harrisonburg, Va.: Sprinkle, 1982), 1:706–21.

8. William Todd Groce, "Robert Lewis Dabney and the New South Critique" (M.A. thesis: University of Tennessee, Knoxville, 1988); Dabney to C. R. Vaughan, 20 October 1892, Robert Lewis Dabney Papers, Alderman Library, University of Virginia, Charlottesville (hereafter UVA); Dabney to R. H. Fleming, 15 March 1888, Dabney Collection, Montreat.

9. Dabney, "Declaration of the PCCSNA," MS, UVA; Dabney, *Life and Campaigns of Lieut.-Gen. Thomas J. Jackson* (1866; repr. Harrisonburg, Va.: Sprinkle, 1986), 154; Dabney, "Anti-Biblical Theories of Rights," in *Discussions*, 3:517, 520; Dabney, "Women's Rights Women," in *Discussions*, 4:496.

10. John Donald Wade, "Old Wine in a New Bottle," *Virginia Quarterly Review* 11 (1935): 240–41, 244–46; Richard M. Weaver, *The Southern Tradition at Bay: A History of Postbellum Thought* (New Rochelle, N.Y.: Arlington House, 1968), 140–43.

11. Beth Barton Schweiger, *The Gospel Working Up: Progress and the Pulpit in Nineteenth Century Virginia* (New York: Oxford University Press, 2000).

12. Ernest Trice Thompson, *Presbyterians in the South*, 3 vols. (Richmond, Va.: John Knox, 1963–73), 2:446, 3:470–71; Thomas Cary Johnson, *Life and Letters of Robert Lewis Dabney* (1903; repr., Carlisle, Pa.: Banner of Truth, 1977), 337; Dabney to John A. Broadus, 22 July 1879, John A. Broadus Papers, Archives, James P. Boyce Centennial Library, Southern Baptist Theological Seminary, Louisville, Kentucky.

13. Thomas Cary Johnson, *God's Answer to Evolution* (Richmond, Va.: Presbyterian Committee of Publication, 1924), 5; W. M. McPheeters, *A Reply to a Communication of Rev. Dr. Hay Watson Smith* (n.p., 1929), 15; McPheeters, *Facts Revealed by the Records in the So-called Investigations of the Rumors Abroad Concerning the Soundness in the Faith of Rev. Dr. Hay Watson Smith* (n.p., 1934). McPheeters expressed his admiration to Dabney in an 1896 letter, writing: "I meet many of your old pupils. There is but one mind among us in reference to yourself, namely that we were the most fortunate of pupils, and you the best of teachers" (McPheeters to Dabney, 7 February 1896, UTSVA).

14. Thompson, *Presbyterians in the South*, 2:226, 3:9; Joel L. Alvis, *Religion and Race: Southern Presbyterians, 1946–1983* (Tuscaloosa, Ala.: University of Alabama Press, 1994), 5–6; Rick Nutt, "The Tie That No Longer Binds: The Origins of the Presbyterian Church in America," in *The Confessional Mosaic: Presbyterians and Twentieth-Century Theology*, ed. M. J. Coalter, John M. Mulder, and Louis B. Weeks (Louisville: Westminster John Knox, 1990), 248–54; "Weaverville Group Supports Racial Segregation Attitudes," *Presbyterian Outlook*, 2 September 1957, 4.

15. Bill Lamkin, "Letter to the Editor: In Support of Overture 20—A Statement on Racism"; Bill Johnson, "An Open Letter to My Brothers That Voted for Overture 20"; Lance Lewis, "Letter to the Editor: An Answer to the Dilemma," all from www.christianity.com/pcanews, accessed on 4 April 2003. These letters did not have specific URLs, but were found by using the Web site's search function. I printed off paper copies and have them in my files.

16. Samuel S. Hill Jr., "Northern and Southern Varieties of American Evangelicalism in the Nineteenth Century," in *Evangelicalism: Comparative Studies of Popular Protestantism in North America, the British Isles, and Beyond, 1700–1990* (New York: Oxford University Press, 1994), 284; Hill, *Southern Churches in Crisis Revisited* (Tuscaloosa, Ala.: University of Alabama Press, 1999), xxxviii–xlv; Mark Taylor Dalhouse, *An Island in the Lake of Fire: Bob Jones University, Fundamentalism, and the Separatist Movement* (Athens, Ga.: University of Georgia Press, 1996), 105–6.

17. James Skillen, "Why Kuyper Now?" in *Religion, Pluralism, and Public Life: Abraham Kuyper's Legacy for the Twenty-first Century*, ed. Luis E. Lugo (Grand Rapids: Eerdmans, 2000), 372.

18. James Bratt and Ronald Wells characterized Kuyper as a "modern antimodernist" in "Piety and Progress: A History of Calvin College," in *Models for Christian*

Higher Education: Strategies for Success in the Twenty-first Century, ed. R. T. Hughes and W. B. Adrian (Grand Rapids: Eerdmans, 1997), 143.

19. Abraham Kuyper, *Lectures on Calvinism* (1931; repr., Grand Rapids: Eerdmans, 1994), 11, 18–22; Kuyper, "The Blurring of the Boundaries," in *Abraham Kuyper: A Centennial Reader*, ed. James D. Bratt (Grand Rapids: Eerdmans, 1998), 371–72, 377; Kuyper, "Modernism: A Fata Morgana in the Christian Domain," in *Abraham Kuyper: Centennial Reader*, 101.

20. Kuyper, "Blurring of the Boundaries," 369, 388; Kuyper, *Lectures on Calvinism*, 10–12; Kuyper, *The Problem of Poverty*, ed. James Skillen (Grand Rapids: Baker, 1991), 44; Kuyper, "Maranatha," in *Abraham Kuyper: Centennial Reader*, 212; Kuyper, "Uniformity: The Curse of Modern Life," in *Abraham Kuyper: Centennial Reader*, 24.

21. Kuyper, "Uniformity: The Curse of Modern Life," 28; Kuyper, "Blurring of the Boundaries," 382; Kuyper, *Lectures on Calvinism*, 27; Mary Stewart van Leeuwen, "The Carrot and the Stick: Kuyper on Gender, Family, and Class," in *Religion, Pluralism, and Public Life*, 59–84; Kuyper, "The South African Crisis," in *Abraham Kuyper: Centennial Reader*, 332.

22. Van Leeuwen, "Carrot and the Stick," 74–75; Kuyper, *When Thou Sittest in Thine House: Meditations on Home Life* (Grand Rapids: Eerdmans, 1929), 283, quoted in van Leeuwen, "Carrot and the Stick," 74; Kuyper, "Blurring of the Boundaries," 382; James D. Bratt, "Passionate about the Poor: The Social Attitudes of Abraham Kuyper," *Markets and Morality* 5 (Spring 2002): 35–45. See also Kuyper, "Manual Labor," in *Abraham Kuyper: Centennial Reader*, 231–54, which pictures a laboring class that does not ascend into the bourgeoisie.

23. Kuyper, *Lectures on Calvinism*, 27, 32, 34; Kuyper, "South African Crisis," 337, 339, 340; D. Th. Kuiper, "Theory and Practice in Dutch Calvinism on the Racial Issue in the Nineteenth Century," *Calvin Theological Journal* 21 (1986): 51–78. Compare with George Harinck, "Abraham Kuyper, South Africa, and Apartheid," *Princeton Seminary Bulletin*, n.s. 23 (2002): 183–87.

24. I am indebted to John Bolt for the phrase "ordered liberty": John Bolt, *A Free Church, A Holy Nation: Abraham Kuyper's American Public Theology* (Grand Rapids: Eerdmans, 2001), 162; the phrases "anarchic" and "social bond" individualism come from Richard M. Weaver, "Two Types of American Individualism," in *The Southern Essays of Richard M. Weaver*, ed. George M. Curtis III and James J. Thompson Jr. (Indianapolis: Liberty Fund, 1987), 77–103.

25. Kuyper, "Blurring of the Boundaries," 399–400; Bolt, *A Free Church, A Holy Nation*, 79; Kuyper, "Calvinism: Source and Stronghold of Our Constitutional Liberties," in *Abraham Kuyper: Centennial Reader*, 306–7; Kuyper, *Lectures on Calvinism*, 79.

26. George Harinck, "A Historian's Comment on the Use of Abraham Kuyper's Idea of Sphere Sovereignty," *Markets and Morality* 5 (Spring 2002): 277–84.

27. Kuyper, *Lectures on Calvinism*, 109; Kuyper, "Sphere Sovereignty," in *Abraham Kuyper: Centennial Reader*, 467, 480.

28. Henk E. S. Woldring, "Kuyper's Formal and Comprehensive Conceptions of Democracy," in *Kuyper Reconsidered: Aspects of His Life and Work*, ed. Cornelis van der Kooi and Jan de Bruijn (Amsterdam: VU Uitgeverij, 1999), 206–17 (quotation on 208); Kuyper, *Problem of Poverty*, 69; van Leeuwen, "Carrot and the Stick," 67.

29. Abraham Kuyper, *Ons Program*, 4th ed. (Amsterdam: Hoveker and Wormser, 1879), 208, 214, quoted in Bolt, *A Free Church, A Holy Nation*, 337, 396; Kuyper, "Sphere Sovereignty," 477.

30. Bolt, *A Free Church, A Holy Nation*, 285–86; James W. Skillen, "From Covenant of Grace to Equitable Public Pluralism: The Dutch Calvinist Contribution," *Calvin Theological Journal* 31 (1996): 84, 87.

31. Kuyper's commitment to Romanticism is a matter of some debate. Edward Ericson argued stringently against the notion ("Abraham Kuyper: Cultural Critic," *Calvin Theological Journal* 22 [1987]: 210–27). J. de Bruijn, James Bratt, and John Bolt, among others, argue for it: see J. de Bruijn, "Abraham Kuyper as Romantic," in *Kuyper Reconsidered*, 42–52; Bratt, "Abraham Kuyper: Puritan, Victorian, Modern," in *Religion, Pluralism, and Public Life*, 3–21; Bolt, *A Free Church, A Holy Nation*, 3–79.

32. Kuyper, "Calvinism: Source and Stronghold of Our Constitutional Liberties," 287; James D. Bratt, "Abraham Kuyper, American History, and the Tensions of Neo-Calvinism," in *Sharing the Reformed Tradition: The Dutch–North American Exchange, 1846–1996*, ed. G. Harinck and H. Krabbendam (Amsterdam: VU Uitgeverij, 1996), 100–106. Other interesting comparisons for Kuyper and American political figures might include Grover Cleveland (see James D. Bratt, "Abraham Kuyper's Public Career," *Reformed Journal* 37 [October 1987]: 12) and James Henley Thornwell, who was a Southern Whig (compare with Bozeman, "Science, Nature, and Society: A New Approach to James Henley Thornwell").

33. Peter S. Heslam, *Creating a Christian Worldview: Abraham Kuyper's Lectures on Calvinism* (Grand Rapids: Eerdmans, 1998), 258–61; Bolt, *A Free Church, A Holy Nation*, 443–64.

34. Heslam, *Creating a Christian Worldview*, 88–96; Bolt, *A Free Church, A Holy Nation*, 301, 308–9, 345; Dabney, "Monism," in *Discussions*, 3:523–35.

35. Kuyper, "Sphere Sovereignty," 488; Kuyper, *Lectures on Calvinism*, 30, 162–63; Kuyper, *Problem of Poverty*, 68; Heslam, *Creating a Christian Worldview*, 266–70; C. van der Kooi, "A Theology of Culture: A Critical Appraisal of Kuyper's Doctrine of Common Grace," in *Kuyper Reconsidered*, 98–99; Bolt, *A Free Church, A Holy Nation*, 227–55, 312–50 (quotation on 327); Harinck, "A Historian's Comment on the Use of Abraham Kuyper's Idea of Sphere Sovereignty," 279.

36. Dabney, "Anti-Biblical Theories of Rights," in *Discussions*, 3:521–22. Importantly, Kuyper's emphasis on common grace finds no parallel in Dabney.

37. James D. Bratt, *Dutch Calvinism in Modern America: A History of a Conservative Subculture* (Grand Rapids: Eerdmans, 1984), 204–21; Joel A. Carpenter, "The Perils of Prosperity: Neo-Calvinism and the Future of Religious Colleges," in *The Future of Religious Colleges*, ed. Paul J. Dovre (Grand Rapids: Eerdmans, 2002), 196–201.

38. Grant Wacker, "The Holy Spirit and the Spirit of the Age in American Protestantism, 1880–1910," *Journal of American History* 72 (1985): 45–62; Bratt, *Dutch Calvinism in Modern America*, 204–21.

39. Dabney, *A Defence of Virginia (And Through Her, of the South)* (1867; repr., Harrisonburg, Va.: Sprinkle, 1991), 104–10; Dabney, "Anti-Christian Theories of Rights," 503; Dabney, "The New South," in *Discussions*, 4:15–16; Dabney, "George W. Cable in the Century Magazine," *Southern Historical Society Papers* 13 (1885): 148–53. I owe the insights of the final lines of this paragraph to Carl Trueman.

40. H. Richard Niebuhr, *Christ and Culture* (New York: Harper, 1951); George Marsden, "Christianity and Cultures: Transforming Niebuhr's Categories," *Insights* 115 (Fall 1999): 11.

41. James Davison Hunter, *Culture Wars: The Struggle to Define America* (New York: Basic Books, 1991); D. G. Hart, *The Lost Soul of American Protestantism* (Lanham, Md.: Rowman and Littlefield, 2002).

42. Dabney, "The Uses and Results of Church History," in *Discussions*, 2:21. This paragraph draws from the final paragraph of J. Gresham Machen, *Christianity and Liberalism* (1923; repr., Grand Rapids: Eerdmans, 1994), 180.

Bibliographic Note

*D*abney's well-known prolixity served him well after his death; there is a wealth of Dabney documents still extant. The most important Dabney collections are housed at four institutions: the William Smith Morton Library at Union Theological Seminary (letters and sermons); the Alderman Library at the University of Virginia (letters and a manuscript autobiography); the Virginia Historical Society in Richmond, Virginia (letters); and the Southern Historical Collection at the University of North Carolina at Chapel Hill (letters). I also accessed collections at the following institutions: the Presbyterian Historical Society, Montreat, North Carolina (Dabney Collection, Charles Hodge Collection, Hoge Family Papers, W. M. McPheeters Papers, and C. R. Vaughan Collection), and the James P. Boyce Library at the Southern Baptist Theological Seminary (John A. Broadus Papers). Dabney was also well served by his first biographer. As is evident from the notes, I relied heavily on Thomas Cary Johnson's *Life and Letters of Robert Lewis Dabney* (1903; repr., Carlisle, Pa.: Banner of Truth, 1977). Johnson's compilation is the only source for some of Dabney's letters. Not only was Johnson a historian, but he was Dabney's contemporary and his confidante at the end of his life. As a result, Johnson's work can be read as both a primary and a secondary source. Dabney's sons also produced an excellent collection of reminiscences: *In Memoriam: Robert Lewis Dabney, 1820–1898,* ed. Charles W. Dabney et al. (Knoxville: University of Tennessee Press, 1899).

Dabney's dear friend C. R. Vaughan worked with Dabney to collect most of his important writings in four volumes. The *Discussions* (1890–97; repr., Harrisonburg, Va.: Sprinkle, 1982) are the single most important collection of Dabney documents. Yet they do not collect everything; Sprinkle Publications issued a fifth volume of *Discussions* in 1999, and a number of significant pieces authored by Dabney are still buried in Presbyterian newspapers. In addition, Sprinkle Publications has republished several Dabney books: *Christ Our Penal Substitute* (1898; repr., Sprinkle, 1985); *A Defence of Virginia (And Through Her, of the South) in Recent and Pending Contests Against the Sectional Party* (1867; repr., Sprinkle, 1991); *The Practical Philosophy: Being the Philosophy of the Feelings, of the Will, and of the Conscience, with the Ascertainment of Particular Rights and Duties* (1897; repr., Sprinkle, 1984); and *Life and Campaigns of Lieut.-Gen. Thomas J. Jackson* (1866; repr., Sprinkle, 1986). Banner of Truth has published its own version of the *Discussions* that combined volumes 3 and 4, as well as *Syllabus and Notes of the Course of Systematic and Polemic Theology*, 2d ed. (1878; repr. titled, *Systematic Theology*, Banner of Truth, 1985) and *Lectures on Sacred Rhetoric* (1870; repr. titled *Evangelical Eloquence*, Banner of Truth, 1999). Recently reprinted was *The Sensualistic Philosophy of the Nineteenth Century, Considered*, 2d ed. (1887; repr., Naphtali Press, 2003). Without these reprints, this book would have been much harder to complete.

Not only did this study rely on Dabney material, but it was also rooted in a significant amount of secondary literature, which, due to the study's format, is not listed in the notes. There have been several previous dissertations and theses on Dabney. By far the most useful was the biographical study written by David H. Overy, "Robert Lewis Dabney: Apostle of the Old South" (Ph.D. diss.: University of Wisconsin, Madison, 1967). The most thought-provoking thesis was Jonathan M. Young, "Psychology of the South: Robert Lewis Dabney, The Race God, and Sacramental Purity" (M.A. thesis: University of North Carolina, 1993); also challenging was the dissertation by Thomas E. Jenkins, "The Character of God in American Theology:

1800–1900" (Ph.D. diss.: Yale University, 1991), chapter 6 focusing on Dabney. Useful for setting Dabney's intellectual movements within the larger world of ideas was Merrill Matthews, "Robert Lewis Dabney and Conservative Thought in the Nineteenth Century South: A Study in the History of Ideas" (Ph.D. diss.: University of Texas at Dallas, 1989). Also worthy of mention for their vital importance for this book are E. T. Thompson, *Presbyterians in the South*, 3 vols. (Richmond, Va.: John Knox, 1963–73); Anne C. Loveland, *Southern Evangelicals and the Social Order, 1800–1860* (Baton Rouge: Louisiana State University Press, 1980); and Donald G. Mathews, *Religion in the Old South* (Chicago: University of Chicago Press, 1977).

Dabney's embrace of Southern ideals such as honor, gentility, and mastery can be gauged by comparing his views with those found in the following secondary literature: Bertram Wyatt-Brown's *Southern Honor: Ethics and Behavior in the Old South* (New York: Oxford University Press, 1980) as well as his *The Shaping of Southern Culture: Honor, Grace, and War, 1760s–1880s* (Chapel Hill, N.C.: University of North Carolina Press, 2001); Kenneth S. Greenberg, *Honor and Slavery* (Princeton, N.J.: Princeton University Press, 1996); Drew Gilpin Faust, *James Henry Hammond and the Old South: A Design for Mastery* (Baton Rouge: Louisiana State University Press, 1982); A. James Fuller, *Chaplain of the Confederacy: Basil Manly and Baptist Life in the Old South* (Baton Rouge: Louisiana State University Press, 2000); James O. Farmer, *The Metaphysical Confederacy: James Henley Thornwell and the Synthesis of Southern Values* (Macon, Ga.: Mercer University Press, 1986); and Erskine Clarke, *Wrestlin' Jacob: A Portrait of Religion in Antebellum Georgia and the Carolina Low Country* (1979; repr., Tuscaloosa, Ala.: University of Alabama Press, 2000).

Dabney's connection to the Southern tradition can be traced out with reference to Eugene D. Genovese, *The Southern Tradition: The Achievements and Limitations of an American Conservatism* (Cambridge: Harvard University Press, 1994); Richard M. Weaver, *The Southern Tradition at Bay: A History of Postbellum Thought* (New Rochelle, N.Y.: Arlington House, 1968); Weaver, "The Southern Tradition," in *The Southern Essays of Richard M. Weaver*, ed. G. M. Curtis III, and J. J. Thompson Jr. (Indianapolis: Liberty Fund, 1987), 209–29; M. E. Bradford, "Where We Were Born and Raised: On the Continuity of Southern Conservatism," *Southern Review* 25 (1989): 334–50; Paul V. Murphy, *The Rebuke of History: The Southern Agrarians and American Conservative Thought* (Chapel Hill, N.C.: University of North Carolina Press, 2001); and Twelve Southerners, *I'll Take My Stand: The South and the Agrarian Tradition* (1930; repr., Baton Rouge: Louisiana State University Press, 1977).

For a look at early denomination-building in Virginia, see Beth Barton Schweiger, *The Gospel Working Up: Progress and the Pulpit in Nineteenth-Century Virginia* (New York: Oxford University Press, 2000). Antebellum efforts at theological education are traced in Glenn T. Miller, *Piety and Intellect: The Aims and Purposes of Ante-Bellum Theological Education* (Atlanta: Scholars, 1990). On the 1837 Old School–New School split, see George M. Marsden, *The Evangelical Mind and the New School Presbyterian Experience: A Case Study of Thought and Theology in Nineteenth Century America* (New Haven: Yale University Press, 1970). The rising tide of professionalization in the nineteenth century is treated in Burton J. Bledstein, *The Culture of Professionalism: The Middle Class and the Development of Higher Education in America* (New York: Norton, 1976).

Several important works shaped my understanding of the role of ministers in the nineteenth-century South in general and Dabney's ministry in particular. For a historical treatment of the Southern Presbyterian view of ministry, see Robert N. Watkin, "The Forming of the Southern Presbyterian Minister: From Calvin to the American Civil War" (Ph.D. diss.: Vanderbilt University, 1969), 357–476. See also Donald M. Scott, *From Office to Profession: The New England Ministry, 1750–1850* (Philadelphia: University of Pennsylvania Press, 1978) and Erskine Clarke, *Our Southern Zion: A History of Calvinism in the South Carolina Low Country, 1690–1990* (Tuscaloosa, Ala.: University of Alabama Press, 1996). For an essay on Dabney as church constructor and designer, see Herbert Clarence Bradshaw, "The Preacher Who Designed Four Churches: Dr. Robert Lewis Dabney, Nineteenth Century Virginia's Outstanding Theologian," *Virginia Cavalcade* 8:2 (1958): 32–42. Dabney's ministry at Tinkling Spring is ably covered in Howard McKnight Wilson, *The Tinkling Spring, Head-water of Freedom: A Study of the Church and Her People, 1732–1952* (Fisherville, Va.: Tinkling Spring and Heritage Presbyterian Churches, 1954), 279–304.

Dabney's Scottish commonsense epistemology and Old School theological commitments can be set into context through consideration of a wide range of literature. Particularly helpful were Mark A. Noll, *America's God: From Jonathan Edwards to Abraham Lincoln* (New York: Oxford University Press, 2002); E. Brooks Holifield, *The Gentlemen Theologians: American Theology in Southern Culture, 1795–1860* (Durham, N.C.: Duke University Press, 1978); Holifield, *Theology in America: Christian Thought from the Age of the Puritans to the Civil War* (New Haven: Yale University Press, 2003); and Theodore Dwight Bozeman, *Protestants in an Age of Science: The Baconian Ideal and Antebellum American Religious Thought* (Chapel Hill, N.C.: University of North Carolina Press, 1977). Three dissertations and theses were useful in the section as well: Frank J. Smith, "The Philosophy of Science in Late Nineteenth Century Southern Presbyterianism" (Ph.D. diss.: City University of New York, 1992); David Kinney Garth, "The Influence of Scottish Common Sense Philosophy on the Theology of James Henley Thornwell and Robert Lewis Dabney" (Th.D. diss.: Union Theological Seminary in Virginia, 1979); and J. Ligon Duncan III, "Common Sense and American Presbyterianism: An Evaluation of the Impact of Scottish Realism on Princeton and the South" (M.A. thesis: Covenant Theological Seminary, 1987).

Specific studies of doctrines in Dabney's theological thought are generally nonexistent; one of the few is David F. Coffin Jr., "Reflections on the Life and Thought of Robert Lewis Dabney with Particular Reference to His Views on Divine Sovereignty and Human Free Agency" (Ph.D. diss.: Westminster Theological Seminary, 2003). Likewise, Southern Presbyterian theology has suffered neglect as a whole, with the exception of Thornwell's. One that begins the study is Morton H. Smith, *Studies in Southern Presbyterian Theology* (Phillipsburg, N.J.: P&R Publishing, 1987). A doctrine that has received some attention because of its social ramifications is the "spirituality of the church"; see Preston D. Graham Jr., *A Kingdom Not of This World*

(Macon, Ga.: Mercer University Press, 2002); D. G. Hart, "The Spirituality of the Church," in *Recovering Mother Kirk: The Case for Liturgy in the Reformed Tradition* (Grand Rapids: Baker, 2003), 51–65; Jack P. Maddex, "From Theocracy to Spirituality: The Southern Presbyterian Reversal on Church and State," *Journal of Presbyterian History* 54 (1976): 438–57; and Ernest Trice Thompson, *The Spirituality of the Church: A Distinctive Doctrine of the Presbyterian Church in the United States* (Richmond, Va.: John Knox, 1961).

Dabney's transition from moderate to Confederate secessionist is one of the most difficult questions to sort out. As noted already, several works have alerted me to the role of honor in Dabney's thought—Wyatt-Brown's *Southern Honor* and *The Shaping of Southern Culture* being the two most important. Also important for setting Dabney's context was *Religion and the American Civil War*, ed. Randall Miller, Harry S. Stout, and Charles Reagan Wilson (New York: Oxford University Press, 1998). Above all, the work of Eugene D. Genovese shaped my thought on Dabney during the war years as well as Dabney's proslavery beliefs. See especially *"Slavery Ordained of God": The Southern Slaveholders' View of Biblical History and Modern Politics* (Gettysburg, Pa.: Gettysburg College, 1985); *The World the Slaveholders Made: Two Essays in Interpretation* (1969; repr., Middletown, Conn.: Wesleyan University Press, 1988); *The Political Economy of Slavery: Studies in the Economy and Society of the Slave South* (1969; repr., Middletown, Conn.: Wesleyan University Press, 1989); *The Slaveholders' Dilemma: Freedom and Progress in Southern Conservative Thought, 1820–1860* (Columbia, S.C.: University of South Carolina Press, 1992); *The Southern Tradition*; and *A Consuming Fire: The Fall of the Confederacy in the Mind of the White Christian South* (Athens, Ga.: University of Georgia Press, 1999). Also important were three essays, the latter two authored with Elizabeth Fox-Genovese: " 'Our Family, White and Black': Family and Household in the Southern Slaveholders' World View," in *In Joy and In Sorrow: Women, Family, and Marriage in the Victorian South, 1830–1900*, ed. Carol Bleser (New York: Oxford University Press, 1991), 69–87; "The Religious Ideals of Southern Slave Society," in *The Evolution of Southern Culture*, ed. N. V. Bartley (Athens, Ga.: University of Georgia Press, 1988), 14–27;

and "The Divine Sanction of Social Order: Religious Foundations of the Southern Slaveholders' Worldview," *Journal of the American Academy of Religion* 60 (1987): 211–33. I found great profit as well in Elizabeth Fox-Genovese, *Within the Plantation Household: Black and White Women of the Old South* (Chapel Hill, N.C.: University of North Carolina Press, 1988).

For Dabney's thought on slavery, the following books provided context, in addition to the Genoveses' work: Larry Tise, *Proslavery: A History of the Defense of Slavery in America, 1701–1840* (Athens, Ga.: University of Georgia Press, 1987); Douglas Ambrose, "Of Stations and Relations: Proslavery Christianity in Early National Virginia," in *Religion and the Antebellum Debate over Slavery*, ed. John R. McKivigan and Mitchell Snay (Athens, Ga.: University of Georgia Press, 1998); Drew Gilpin Faust, "Evangelicalism and the Meaning of the Proslavery Argument," *Virginia Magazine of History and Biography* 85 (1977): 3–17; Faust, "A Southern Stewardship: The Intellectual and the Proslavery Argument," *American Quarterly* 31 (1979): 63–80; Faust, *James Henry Hammond and the Old South: A Design for Mastery* (Baton Rouge: Louisiana State University Press, 1982); Walter Johnson, *Soul by Soul: Life Inside the Antebellum Slave Market* (Cambridge: Harvard University Press, 1999); Jack P. Maddex, "Proslavery Millennialism: Social Eschatology in Antebellum Southern Calvinism," *American Quarterly* 31 (1979): 46–62; Maddex, "'The Southern Apostasy' Revisited: The Significance of Proslavery Christianity," *Marxist Perspectives* 2 (1979): 132–41; H. Shelton Smith, *In His Image, But . . . : Racism in Southern Religion, 1780–1910* (Durham, N.C.: Duke University Press, 1972); Mitchell Snay, *Gospel of Disunion: Religion and Separatism in the Antebellum South* (New York: Cambridge University Press, 1993; repr., Chapel Hill, N.C.: University of North Carolina Press, 1997).

The chapter on Dabney as a Presbyterian partisan relied mainly on primary sources. Several studies, however, guided my reading: Harold Parker's *The United Synod of the South: The Southern New School Presbyterian Church* (Westport, Conn.: Greenwood, 1988) was particularly helpful on the Southern Old School–New School reunion. Also useful was S. Donald Fortson, "Old School/New School Reunion in the South: The Theological Compromise of 1864," *Westminster Theological Journal* 66 (2004): 203–26. For a solid study of Protestant denominations during Reconstruction, see Daniel W. Stowell, *Rebuilding Zion: The Religious Reconstruction of the South, 1863–1877* (New York: Oxford University Press, 1998). Also useful for me here was Beth Barton Schweiger's study of Methodist and Baptist denomination-building in *The Gospel Working Up*. For information on E. O. Guerrant, see J. Gray McAllister and Grace Owings Guerrant, *Edward O. Guerrant: Apostle to the Southern Highlands* (Richmond, Va.: Richmond Press, 1950).

Dabney's public theology cannot be adequately grasped without several significant studies. I explored much of this terrain in greater detail in Sean Michael Lucas, " 'Hold Fast That Which Is Good': The Public Theology of Robert Lewis Dabney" (Ph.D. diss.: Westminster Theological Seminary, 2002). For the importance of positivism to contemporary theology, Charles Cashdollar's *The Transformation of Theology, 1830–1890* (Princeton, N.J.: Princeton University Press, 1989) was particularly insightful. On the connections between Dabney and antimodernism, the classic study is T. J. Jackson Lears, *No Place of Grace: Antimodernism and the Transformation of American Culture, 1880–1920* (Chicago: University of Chicago Press, 1981); also thought-provoking in this regard were Thomas A. Tweed, *The American Encounter with Buddhism, 1844–1912: Victorian Culture and the Limits of Dissent* (Bloomington, Ind.: Indiana University Press, 1992); D. G. Hart, *Defending the Faith: J. Gresham Machen and the Crisis of Conservative Protestantism in Modern America* (Baltimore: Johns Hopkins University Press, 1994); and Allen C. Guelzo, *For the Union of Evangelical Christendom: The Irony of Reformed Episcopalians* (University Park, Pa.: Pennsylvania State University Press, 1994). For the rise of modernism in the South, I am indebted to Daniel Joseph Singal, *The War Within: From Victorian to Modernist Thought in the South, 1919–1945* (Chapel Hill, N.C.: University of North Carolina Press, 1982); for the conflicts experienced by Victorian America, which had some bearing on Dabney's response, see *Victorian America*, ed. Daniel Walker Howe (Philadelphia: University of Pennsylvania Press, 1979); Ann Douglas, *The Feminization of American Culture* (New

York: Doubleday, 1977); and James Turner, *Without God, Without Creed: The Origins of Unbelief in America* (Baltimore: Johns Hopkins University Press, 1985). On Dabney's critique of industrial America, see David H. Overy, "When the Wicked Beareth Rule: A Southern Critique of Industrial America," *Journal of Presbyterian History* 48 (1970): 130–42, and Sean Michael Lucas, " 'Old Times There Are Not Forgotten': Robert Lewis Dabney's Public Theology for a Reconstructed South," *Journal of Presbyterian History* 81 (2003): 163–77.

On evolution, science, and the Woodrow affair, several books were helpful. My claim that Dabney bore similarities to the "Scriptural Geologists" was informed by Rodney L. Stiling, "Scriptural Geology in America," in *Evangelicals and Science in Historical Perspective*, ed. D. N. Livingstone, D. G. Hart, and M. A. Noll (New York: Oxford University Press, 1999), 177–92, and Milton Millhauser, "The Scriptural Geologists: An Episode in the History of Opinion," *Osiris* 11 (1954): 65–86. On Darwin, the rise of evolutionary thought, and religious response in England and America, see Adrian Desmond and James Moore, *Darwin: The Life of a Tormented Evolutionist* (New York: Warner, 1991); Frank M. Turner, *Between Science and Religion: The Reaction to Scientific Naturalism in Late Victorian England* (New Haven, Conn.: Yale University Press, 1974); Turner, "The Victorian Conflict between Science and Religion: A Professional Dimension," *Isis* 69 (1978): 356–76; Jon H. Roberts, *Darwinism and the Divine in America* (Madison: University of Wisconsin Press, 1988); and David N. Livingstone, *Darwin's Forgotten Defenders: The Encounter Between Evangelical Theology and Evolutionary Thought* (Grand Rapids: Eerdmans, 1987). The relationship between science and religion during the antebellum period is explored in Herbert Hovenkamp, *Science and Religion in America, 1800–1860* (Philadelphia: University of Pennsylvania Press, 1978); Walter H. Conser Jr., *God and the Natural World: Religion and Science in Antebellum America* (Columbia, S.C.: University of South Carolina Press, 1993); and Bozeman, *Protestants in an Age of Science*. For general essays on science and evangelical relation, two fine collections are *God and Nature: Historical Essays on the Encounter Between Christianity and Science*, ed. D. C. Lindberg and R. Numbers (Berkeley: University of California

Press, 1986), and *Evangelicals and Science in Historical Perspective*. A recent biography of James Woodrow is Robert K. Gustafson, *James Woodrow (1828–1907): Scientist, Theologian, Intellectual Leader* (Lewiston, N.Y.: Edwin Mellen, 1995).

For Dabney's debates with William H. Ruffner, see the following: Jack P. Maddex Jr., *The Virginia Conservatives, 1867–1879: A Study in Reconstruction Politics* (Chapel Hill, N.C.: University of North Carolina Press, 1970); William A. Link, *A Hard Country and a Lonely Place: Schooling, Society, and Reform in Rural Virginia, 1870–1920* (Chapel Hill, N.C.: University of North Carolina Press, 1986); Walter J. Fraser Jr., "William Henry Ruffner: A Liberal in the Old and New South" (Ph.D. diss.: University of Tennessee, 1970); Fraser Jr., "William Henry Ruffner and the Establishment of Virginia's Public School System, 1870–1874," *Virginia Magazine of History and Biography* 79 (1971): 259–79; and Thomas C. Hunt and Jennings L. Wagoner Jr., "Race, Religion, and Redemption: William Henry Ruffner and the Moral Foundations of Education in Virginia," *American Presbyterians* 66 (1988): 1–9.

Details of Dabney's final years at Union and Texas were pieced together by consulting primary sources, as well as Francis R. Flournoy, *Benjamin Mosby Smith, 1811–1893* (Richmond, Va.: Richmond Press, 1947) and Thomas White Currie Jr., "A History of Austin Presbyterian Theological Seminary, Austin, Texas, 1884–1943" (Th.D. diss.: Union Theological Seminary, 1958).

A range of sources served as the basis of comparisons with James Henley Thornwell and Abraham Kuyper in the final chapter. For Thornwell, I found the following useful: Bozeman, *Protestants in an Age of Science*; Garth, "The Influence of Scottish Common Sense Philosophy on the Theology of James Henley Thornwell and Robert Lewis Dabney"; Farmer, *The Metaphysical Confederacy*; John H. Leith, "James Henley Thornwell and the Shaping of the Reformed Tradition in the South," in *Probing the Reformed Tradition: Historical Studies in Honor of Edward A. Dowey, Jr.*, ed. Elsie Anne McKee and Brian G. Armstrong (Louisville: Westminster John Knox, 1989), 424–47; and Smith, *Studies in Southern Presbyterian Theology*.

For Kuyper, I used *Abraham Kuyper: A Centennial Reader*, ed. James D. Bratt (Grand Rapids: Eerdmans, 1998); Peter S. Heslam, *Creating a Christian Worldview: Abraham Kuyper's Lectures on Calvinism* (Grand Rapids: Eerdmans, 1998); *Kuyper Reconsidered: Aspects of His Life and Work*, ed. Cornelis van der Kooi and Jan de Bruijn (Amsterdam: VU Uitgeverij, 1999); *Religion, Pluralism, and Public Life: Abraham Kuyper's Legacy for the Twenty-first Century*, ed. Luis E. Lugo (Grand Rapids: Eerdmans, 2000); *Markets and Morality* 5:1 (Spring 2001); James E. McGoldrick, *Abraham Kuyper: God's Renaissance Man* (Darlington, England: Evangelical Press, 2000); John Bolt, *A Free Church, A Holy Nation: Abraham Kuyper's American Public Theology* (Grand Rapids: Eerdmans, 2001); Mary Stewart van Leeuwen, "Abraham Kuyper and the Cult of True Womanhood: An Analysis of *De Eerepositie Der Vrouw*," *Calvin Theological Journal* 31 (1996): 97–124; and van Leeuwen, "The Signs of Kuyper's Times, and of Ours," in Elizabeth Fox-Genovese, *Women and the Future of the Family* (Grand Rapids: Baker, 2000), 75–92.

For the comparison of Dabney with Southern fundamentalism, I profited from David O. Beale, *In Pursuit of Purity: American Fundamentalism Since 1850* (Greenville, S.C.: Unusual Publications, 1986); William R. Glass, *Strangers in Zion: Fundamentalists in the South, 1900–1950* (Macon, Ga.: Mercer University Press, 2001); Samuel S. Hill Jr., "Northern and Southern Varieties of American Evangelicalism in the Nineteenth Century," in *Evangelicalism: Comparative Studies of Popular Protestantism in North America, the British Isles, and Beyond, 1700–1990* (New York: Oxford University Press, 1994); Hill, *Southern Churches in Crisis Revisited* (Tuscaloosa, Ala.: University of Alabama Press, 1999); and Mark Taylor Dalhouse, *An Island in the Lake of Fire: Bob Jones University, Fundamentalism, and the Separatist Movement* (Athens, Ga.: University of Georgia Press, 1996). One whole dissertation attempted to connect Dabney to broader fundamentalism: see Jerry Robert Robbins, "R. L. Dabney, Old Princeton, and Fundamentalism" (Ph.D. diss.: Florida State University, 1991).

Index

abolition, abolitionism, 15, 95, 105, 106, 118, 119–20, 135, 155, 158, 166, 179–80
Adams, Henry, 166
Adams, John, 182
Adger, J. B., 137, 141, 142
adoption, 92
African-American Presbyterian Church, 149
African Americans, 135
  moral inferiority of, 127
  ordination of, 146–49
  sermons preached to, 252n22
  and suffrage, 223
Africans, 261n27
agnosticism, 167
agrarianism, 166, 187, 191
agriculture, 25, 187
Alexander, Archibald, 70, 255n30
Alexander, Henry, 197
Alexander, James W., 62
ambiguity, 34
American Constitution, 239
American Inland Mission, 161
American Revolution, 244
analogy, 84
Andover Seminary, 37

anger, 222
Anglo-Catholicism, 190
Anti-Revolutionary Party, 238, 239
antimodernism, 18, 190–91, 232, 239, 243, 263n2
antithesis, 241, 243–44
Antrium, George, 49
Arminians, Arminianism, 53, 88
Army Sermons, 258n31
Asheville, North Carolina, 214
assurance of faith, 57–58
atheism, 167, 170–71
Atkinson, J. M. P., 115, 144–45
atonement, 34, 91–92, 140–42
Augusta County, Virginia, 41, 252n31
Austin Presbyterian Theological Seminary, 267n23
Austin School of Theology, 18, 204–5, 207–8
authority, 181

Backus, J. C., 151
Bacon, Francis, 20, 81
Baconianism, 20, 84, 167–68, 174, 175
Baird, Samuel J., 144
Baptists, 73

Compromise of 1850, 101
Comte, Auguste, 85, 166, 168
concursus, 90
Confederacy, 24, 100, 110, 115, 229
congregationalism, 136
Congregationalists, 162
conservatism, 224
consumption, 189
contentment, 55–56
corporal punishment, 96
corporate capitalism, 18, 166, 187–89, 190
courage, 103, 129
Craig, J. M., 50
creation, 173–77
creation science, 178
cross-bearing, 56
Cullen, William, 49
culture-Protestantism, 243
culture wars, 244

Dabney, Betty (sister), 114–15
Dabney, Charles (father), 26, 34–35, 39
Dabney, Charles (son), 95–96, 200, 207, 214
Dabney, Charles William (brother), 37, 43, 44, 66, 111, 134, 251n10
Dabney, Colonel Charles (great-uncle), 25–26, 39
Dabney, Elizabeth Prince (mother), 28, 29, 31, 35, 36, 111, 249n6
Dabney, James (son), 46, 95
Dabney, Jane Meriwether (grand-mother), 26
Dabney, Lavinia (wife), 42–43, 96, 115
Dabney, Lewis (son), 96
Dabney, Robert Jr. (son), 45–46, 95
Dabney, Robert Lewis
  antimodernism of, 166–78
  appointment to Union Seminary, 65
  bitterness after war, 130–32
  blindness of, 207, 208

calling as a Presbyterian minister, 36
as chaplain, 115–17
correspondence of, 27–28
death of, 214–15
exile from Virginia, 136, 194, 201
fundraising for Union Seminary, 197
health problems of, 39, 40, 199–201, 206–7, 209
legacy of, 226–31, 243–45
love for the South, 23–24
moderation of, 18–19, 88, 105–6, 107–8, 109
moderator of General Assembly, 62, 151, 220
as patriarch, 96
piety of, 30
preaching of, 47–48, 50–62, 66
as Virginian, 130
Dabney, Samuel (grandfather), 26
Dabney, Samuel (son), 96, 210–11
Dabney, Thomas (son), 96
Danville Seminary, 63, 72, 95
Darwin, Charles, 167, 170, 171–72, 178, 233
Darwinism, 172
Davidson College, 213, 214
Davidson, Donald, 225
Davis, Jefferson, 114
Davis, John, 33
deacons, 72
deduction, 83
Defence of Virginia (Dabney), 117–28, 165, 221, 259n47
Democratic Party, 223, 240
denominational colleges, 203
denominations, 37–38, 71, 225
depravity, 52–54, 60, 91
determinism, 191
development, 189
discipline, 50
Discussions (Dabney), 205–6
dishonor, 109

reprobation, 88
resentment, 222
restitution, 33
retribution, 91, 222
revenge, 32, 33
revival, 47–48, 53, 66, 162
Rice, Mrs. John Holt, 27
Richardson, William, 40, 250n26
Richmond, Virginia, 211–12
Richmond *Enquirer*, 118
rights, 179–82, 232, 234
robber barons, 187
Robertson, J. I., Jr., 116
Robinson, Stuart, 27, 94, 148–49, 154
Roman Catholics, 185
Romanticism, 240, 243, 271n31
Ruffner, William Henry, 37, 166,
    183–84, 186, 194, 204
ruling elders, 72

Sabbath, 125–26
sacraments, 87
sacred-secular distinction, 104–5,
    241–42
Sampson, Francis, 16, 37, 69, 72, 214,
    255n29
Sampson, Thornton, 16
Say, Jean-Baptiste, 29, 30
Schweiger, Beth Barton, 225
science, 81–86, 87, 168–78, 227
    in theological curriculum, 76,
        254n12
    and theology, 76
Scott, Walter, 102
Scottish philosophy, 20, 81, 86, 87,
    167–69, 219
Scriptural Geologists, 178
secession, 99, 101, 106, 107, 112–14
secular and sacred callings, 111
segregation, 135, 183, 186, 230
seminaries. *See* theological education
Semmes, Joseph, 33

sensualistic philosophy, 18, 166–67,
    170, 175, 178
separatism, 230, 242
shame, 101
Shearer, J. B., 213
Sheridan, Philip H., 132
Sherman, William T., 132
sin, 52–53
sinfulness, human, 29
Skillen, James W., 239
slave marriages, 126
slave trade, 118–19
slavery, 24, 31–32, 46–47, 52, 93–94,
    105, 107–8, 117, 154, 218
    abuses of, 125–27
    biblical defense of, 120–21
    Dabney defense of, 17, 122–28, 129
    as race-based, 127–28
    and southern economy, 122
    Thornwell defense of, 218–19
"Sleepy Hollow," 46
Smith, Adam, 20
Smith, B. M., 42, 43–44, 62–63, 65,
    72–73, 94, 110, 154, 194–98,
    266n2
Smith, Hay Watson, 227
Smith, Henry Boynton, 150–51
Smith, J. Henry, 37
Smith, W. Robertson, 88–89
Smoot, Dan, 230
Smoot, R. K., 200, 204–5, 207
sociability, 28, 30
social contract, 179
social issues, 52
Socinians, 53
South, as "Yankeeized," 155, 189,
    195–96
South Africa, 235
South Carolina, 99, 106–7, 109
Southern Bourbons, 223, 226
"Southern civilization," 160
Southern education, 74, 97–98

Southern identity, 135
Southern Presbyterian Church, 25, 114,
117, 134–36, 222, 226
progressive designs within, 228–29
racial equality in, 148
reunion with Northern Presbyterians, 150–60, 229
Southern Presbyterian Journal, 228
Southern Presbyterian Review, 18, 21,
139, 151, 218
Southern slavery, 259n47
Southern tradition, 24–25, 224–25
Southern Zion, 134–36, 143, 163
Southwestern Presbyterian, 202, 213
specialization, 18, 76–77
Spencer, Herbert, 85, 166–67, 170–71,
178
sphere sovereignty, 237, 238, 241, 244
spiritualism, 191
Spring Resolutions, 135, 154, 157–58
state, 58–59, 93. *See also* federal government
states rights, 112
stewards, 189
Stewart, Dugald, 20, 81, 219
Stoicism, 32, 33, 103
Strickler, G. B., 27, 226
Stuart, Moses, 123
subordination, 181, 182
substitutionary atonement, 214
superiors, 185
supernaturalism, 82, 177
supralapsarianism, 88, 141
Swift Run Gap, 115
Swing, David, 159
syllogism, 84
Synod of North Carolina, 59
Synod of Texas, 210
Synod of Virginia, 59, 111–12, 145–48,
173, 195, 212, 252n21

Tabb Street Presbyterian Church, 129
Tate, Allen, 225

taxes, 183
teleological argument, 19, 21
teleology, 85
temperance, 52, 58, 252n31
Tenney, S. F., 16
Texas, 162, 200–211
theodicy, 92
theological education, 37–38, 63–64,
73–80, 196
theology, as science, 88
theonomy, 240–41
Thomas, John Newton, 227
Thompson, Ernest Trice, 15, 226
Thornwell, James Henley, 14, 50, 95,
105, 136, 137, 158, 226, 228,
229, 271n32
on common sense philosophy,
219–20
debate with Hodge, 70–71
on secession, 107, 114
on slavery, 218–19
Tinkling Spring Presbyterian Church,
24, 39–40, 41–42, 48–49, 53, 62,
66–67, 250n7, 251n16
transcendence, 190, 191–92
transformation of culture, 240–42, 244
Tucker, George, 29
Turretin, Francis, 70, 86–88, 220,
255n29
tyranny, 29, 113

uniformitarianism, 82, 177
Union, 98, 226
Union Theological Seminary, 15, 18,
24, 29, 36–38, 41, 62, 63–64, 79,
97–98, 111, 162, 213
Board of Trustees, 196–97, 200–201
Dabney burial plot, 214
Dabney Chair of Theology, 226
fundraising for, 69
progressive theology at, 227
recruiting sermons for, 253n33